D1190313

RJ 507 A77 F75 2007
Friedrich, William N.
Children with sexual behavior

AUG 09   JUL X X 2015

CUMBERLAND COUNTY COLLEGE LIBRARY
PO BOX 1500
VINELAND, NJ 08362-1500

WITHDRAWN

CHILDREN WITH SEXUAL
BEHAVIOR PROBLEMS

A Norton Professional Book

Children With Sexual Behavior Problems

Family-Based
Attachment-Focused
Therapy

William N. Friedrich

W. W. Norton & Company
New York • London

RJ
507
A77
F75
2007

Copyright © 2007 by The Estate of William N. Friedrich, Ph.D.
Foreword copyright © 2007 by W. W. Norton & Company, Inc.

All rights reserved
Printed in the United States of America
First Edition

For information about permission to reproduce selections from this book,
write to Permissions, W. W. Norton & Company, Inc.,
500 Fifth Avenue, New York, NY 10110

For information about special discounts for bulk purchases, please contact
W. W. Norton Special Sales at specialsales@wwnorton.com or 800-233-4830.

Manufacturing by Quebecor, Fairfield
Production manager: Devon Zahn

Library of Congress Cataloging-in-Publication Data

Friedrich, William N.
Children with sexual behavior problems : family-based, attachment-focused
therapy / William N. Friedrich.—1st ed.
p. ; cm.
"A Norton professional book"—P. facing t.p.
Includes bibliographical references and index.
ISBN 978-0-393-70498-3 (hardcover)
1. Attachment disorder in children. 2. Children—Sexual behavior.
3. Behavior disorders in children. 4. Family psychotherapy. I. Title. [DNLM:
1. Child Behavior Disorders—therapy. 2. Sexual Behavior—psychology.
3. Child Abuse, Sexual—psychology. 4. Child. 5. Family Therapy—
methods. 6. Object Attachment. WS 105.5.S4 F911c 2007]

RJ507.A77F75 2007
618.92'8914—dc22
2007011153

W. W. Norton & Company, Inc.
500 Fifth Avenue, New York, N.Y. 10110
www.wwnorton.com

W. W. Norton & Company Ltd.
Castle House, 75/76 Wells Street, W1T 3QT

1 3 5 7 9 0 8 6 4 2

CONTENTS

ACKNOWLEDGMENTS

A book that focuses on relationships could not be written without the very special relationships I have developed over the years with people who also persist in working with children with highly problematic behavior. I owe a huge debt of gratitude to Barbara Bonner, Lucy Berliner, and Eugene Walker for inviting me to be part of their National Center on Child Abuse and Neglect (NCCAN) project that examined treatment efficacy with children who had sexually problematic behavior. My continued involvement with them, and Lucy's specific encouragement to write this book, touches my heart. My connections with their Oklahoma-based colleagues, Mark Chaffin and Jane Silovsky, have been delightful and synergistic. In fact, my friendship with Mark has taken me to many Eastern European countries, and together we have imbibed strange food and drink, consumed large quantities of mystery meats, and advocated for children whose stories we recognize. Bill Pithers and Alison Gray invited me into their homes on two continents, and also as a consultant on their own similar NCCAN grant. I heard their perspectives on children with sexual behavior problems and was encouraged to further develop the Assessment and Treatment Manual, Part II of this book.

Numerous friends and colleagues in the American Professional Society on the Abuse of Children (APSAC) and the Association for the Treatment of Sexual Abusers (ATSA) have encouraged this process. One of those is David Burton, whose bravery under duress has been inspiring, and Paul Gerber, whose ribald take on clinical nuggets has often added the insight that I was searching for. I routinely turn to the writings of Judy Cohen and Tony Mannarino since they are not only relevant but carry with them the wisdom that comes from great clinicians and true mensches and friends. Bill Luecke deserves notice here as well, as he is a true friend who is also fascinated by these kids, and was the person with whom I was inspired to write the first article on the topic of sexual behavior problems in preteens. I have also greatly appreciated 2 years of conversations with Scott Schauss, another child psychologist and a dear friend who has helped me think in new ways about children with sexual behavior problems and parent-child interactive therapy.

Many of my colleagues here at Mayo have become both friends and inspiring conversationalists who have offered support in so many ways. My fellow child psychologists in particular are a rare and special group and deserve special mention. Recently, research and discussion with colleagues about self-injurious behavior has added to the way I think about this manifestation of rejection and how it is exacerbated by the accumulated stress and trauma in the lives of children with serious behavior problems. Countless postdocs, residents, and clinical trainees, as well as social work and psychiatry colleagues here at Mayo and around the country have asked to use the Assessment and Treatment Manual, done so, and offered comments. Some have sent copious notes on their process and other case experiences. This input has also added to the validity and utility of this approach. To all of you, I dedicate this book.

I also deeply appreciate the editing of Michael McGandy at W. W. Norton, who helped to focus and sharpen the message in this text. He has helped to make this a much better book.

Finally, I owe the largest debt to my family—wife Wanda, and children Hannah and Karl (Karl, an artist, created the monoprint on the jacket cover)—for encouraging and motivating me to write, knowing that this was what I needed to do even when ill, and standing by my side with abiding love and humor.

Wanda Friedrich and her children would also like to gratefully acknowledge the contributions of Barbara Bonner and Lucy Berliner, who generously gave their time to tie up all the loose ends of the book when Bill was not able to.

FOREWORD

I (BLB) remember the first time I saw Bill Friedrich. It was in a standing-room-only presentation at the American Psychological Association in 1986. I was a post-doctoral fellow at the time and ended up on the floor directly in front of the podium where Bill and others presented their research on child sexual abuse. I remember being particularly impressed with Bill's research, and then amazed to learn that he, too, was only a post-doctoral fellow. At the time, I guessed that he had a great career ahead of him, and I was certainly right.

Bill and I became colleagues and friends over the next 20 years. I stood, silently applauding and in amazement, as he set a clear direction in his research career and developed the scientific basis for his work step by step. We discussed problems, collaborated, thought through dilemmas, laughed together, and trained emerging professionals in Eastern Europe, and through it all, Bill led the thinking in the field of treating young children with sexual behavior problems. He was the one to turn to when major research, ethical, or clinical questions emerged. To resolve these problems, one always wanted Bill's perspective to be included.

Bill was one of those unique individuals that a person is lucky to encounter in a lifetime and to whom a field owes an immense debt of gratitude. As Bill himself often wryly noted, who would *plan* to become the world's leading expert on sexual behavior in children? But that he was. He came to the study of children's sexual behavior through his clinical experiences with children and the curiosity he brought to everything he did. He wanted to know what caused the behavior. How common was it? What should be done to help? Throughout his career he kept learning from the children and their parents, built on those experiences to formulate research questions, and then went out and tested them in a scientifically rigorous way. He was not one to look at human behavior through a single lens; he brought in theory and knowledge about a wide range of human experience to create a rich and multilayered perspective.

There are people who are very smart about scientific understanding of human behavior and there are people who intuitively know how to communicate and connect in the clinical setting. It is not common to find someone like Bill, who was amazingly adept at both. His clinical writings blend these two qualities in a way that leaves every reader with new knowledge about why children and their caregivers behave the way they do and with specific methods for transforming that knowledge into creative clinical strategies. Our clients will be so much the better for what he has taught us.

As it turned out, we were able to give a little something back to Bill. Our role in his book was to take over the sad task of addressing the copy editor's final queries, which became necessary because Bill died shortly after completing the manuscript but before he had time to polish the final product. He had suffered from cancer for many years and it finally caught up to him on September 26, 2005.

One of Bill's most amazing qualities was that he remained committed and involved in his life work up until the very end. He was literally still working on the book and his ideas about the treatment of children with sexual behavior problems during his last few days.

This book is wholly Bill's in both tone and content. In order to preserve his work and voice, we have made only minor editorial changes to clarify certain ideas and reorganize a few sections for smoother flow. Any weakness in organization or argument is due to our desire to avoid tampering with the text as much as possible. In every way we stayed true to Bill's vision, his conceptualizations, and his approaches to interventions. And of course, all of the case descriptions come directly from Bill's practice. We hope that our efforts have served to ensure that yet another of Bill's important contributions to the field be available to all who seek to understand children better and guide them and their families to healthier functioning.

As Mark Chaffin, PhD—a longtime colleague of Bill's at the University of Oklahoma Health Sciences Center—said when he read the manuscript, "It's like having a conversation with Bill." We agree, and we know that as you read the book, you will enjoy, learn, and work more effectively with children.

Barbara L. Bonner, PhD
Lucy Berliner, MSW

CHILDREN WITH SEXUAL BEHAVIOR PROBLEMS

INTRODUCTION

Child Sexuality Today and Therapeutic Possibilities

MY MOTIVATION TO write this book is grounded in two perspectives. The first is that far too many sexual behaviors that children exhibit are pathologized, while a small subset of children, usually older preteens, commits sexual behaviors that are not appreciated for the pathology they represent. The second perspective is that sexual behavior problems* are relational in nature and must be treated as such. This is even more the case with children and younger teens. However, treatment programs emphasize individual rather than relational variables.

One contribution of this book reflects the fact that I am both a clinician and a researcher. My current outpatient practice comprises children with sexual behavior problems and their parents. I have also done a considerable amount of research that provides me with a normative perspective on child sexual behavior (Friedrich, 1997; Friedrich, Fisher, Broughton, Houston, & Shafran, 1998; Friedrich et al., 1992, 2001). As a supervising clinician, I have had to make frequent decisions about allocating scarce clinical resources. Consequently, I have had to develop a method for identifying children whose parents simply need reassurance and support, children who need immediate treatment, and children to be concerned about, who require monitoring and some treatment. My plan is to bring clinical practice and the empirical research perspectives to bear in this book. In addition, everyone who works in this field needs to appreciate the huge developmental differences that exist between children with sexual behavior problems, adolescent sexual offenders, and adult sexual offenders. The therapy provided for each of these groups has to reflect these developmental differences.

---

* The term *sexual behavior problems* covers a broad range of behaviors by children. Specific definitions for these behaviors are provided on page 9.

When sexual behavior presents itself as an issue, professionals and parents have few places to turn for accurate perspectives. Regrettably, a few stereotypes then serve as reference points; the child is either a victim of sexual abuse or a future sex offender. Neither of these stereotypes is accurate for the majority of children who exhibit problematic sexual behavior. However, because of such stereotypes, children often face repercussions that do not correspond to their actions. For example, a child may be expelled from school as an overreaction to some behavior, such as using sexual language or exposing his or her buttocks on the playground, or because of inaccurate thinking, another child's obvious treatment needs may be ignored, even though he or she has exhibited a pattern of multiple victims along with increasing force and sophistication. Sexual abuse can be life altering not only for the victim; failure to address the misbehaving child's actions can pave the way for future inappropriate behavior.

A new set of perspectives is needed to understand children with sexual behavior problems. Paramount to this is a focus on attachment and relational issues in therapy. Sexually abused children are compelling, given their trauma, and command focus on the victimization experience and correcting the related impacts on affect and cognition. However, the larger attachment dynamics and family relations are often ignored, even though they are frequently the largest contributors to adjustment. Children with sexual behavior problems are similarly compelling, but they are more difficult to understand given the variety of pathways that can lead to intrusive behavior. Maltreatment, usually of more than one type, underlies the behavior that is most persistent and intrusive; furthermore, these children typically have severely problematic parent-child attachment. However, interventions with these children are typically individual in nature and focus on altering cognitions related to the child's sexual behavior.

My goal is to remind all of us of the centrality of relationships in both the etiology and treatment of children with sexual behavior problems. These children first learn to relate in a disturbed manner, and subsequently use this model of relationships in their interactions with other children. Altering the first model of relating can make a difference in how these children will relate to others, and I believe this is the most efficacious form of intervention.

A CONTINUUM OF SEXUAL BEHAVIOR

Few of us have any perspective on where our career might take us. I certainly had no idea during my graduate course work in the late 1970s that there would be a day when most of the children I saw were those with sexual behavior problems. Sexual development in children was never discussed in my graduate classes. In fact, the consensus in the fields of psychiatry and psychology was that there was a latency period, a now largely discredited holdover from Freudian thought that defined the large span of time between ages 6 and 12 as a period when children were not supposed to be interested in sexuality (Meyer-Bahlburg & Steel, 2003).

I now know that this is not true, and appreciate that sexual behavior can be quite common in children. If parents observed their children objectively, they could report numerous instances that suggest sexual behavior or thoughts. Because of my work, I have heard all of the following examples from parents, yet none expressed concern about their child's sexual behavior.

For example, a 5-year-old tells his mother to only use a certain 16-year-old babysitter since she is "so cute," and he hopes to "marry her." Or a 3-year-old, who is standing and beaming in front of a display of his favorite toys, tells his father, "I am so happy my penis is feeling wiggly." Or two 8-year-old female cousins who spend every waking moment with each other ask to bathe together several days in a row while the families are on vacation together. Or opposite-gendered 11- and 10-year-old stepsiblings are observed kissing and giggling 2 hours after seeing their parents do the same. In fact, in a study in which children were directly interviewed, more than half of the 8- to 9-year-olds said they were in love at the moment or had been in love before (Rademakers, Laan, & Straver, 2003).

I am referred several patients a week whose behavior is concerning to at least one, and typically more, adults. Listed below are actual questions from parents, physicians, nurse practitioners, or other professionals, which illustrate a broad range of concerns. I have had enough face-to-face contact with these children, and typically years of follow-up with them and their families, to have a high degree of certainty that my clinical conclusions were indeed correct.

My 5-year-old son seems to grab his penis more after he returns from weekend visits with his father. Is he being sexually abused?

Data from Friedrich (1997) found that 60.4% of 2- to 5-year-old boys in the normative sample exhibited this behavior at least once in the previous 6 months. I also obtained screening information from the mother. She reported no elevated behavior problems, including sexual behavior. In addition, other than the marital separation, stressful events were minimal in this child's life and he had many friends. The boy exhibited no personal boundary problems during a play interview with me. My conclusion was that he was a normal 5-year-old and there was no need for further investigation.

My sister-in-law thinks I am a pervert for letting my 4-year-old son and 2-year-old daughter bathe together.

Cobathing with siblings and parents is not associated with any type of behavior problem in the normative sample published in Friedrich (1997), in the absence of other risk factors. Neither parent had observed their children do anything but splash and play during this time and the home was stable. I concluded that cobathing was not problematic in this instance.

Should I be worried that my 8-year-old son sometimes sneaks a peek at his father's pornographic magazines?

Further interviewing of the mother found that the magazines were easily accessible. I obtained screening data that found no elevated generic or sexual behavior problems and minimal stress in the child's life. In addition, data from Friedrich (1997) found that 9.9% of 6- to 9-year-old boys in a normative sample were reported to do this occasionally. However, exposure to pornography is associated with increased sexual behavior, and I encouraged the mother to discuss with her husband how to keep these magazines out of the boy's reach. I concluded that no further intervention was necessary.

Why does my 5-year-old lick my neck sexually?

The parent's perspective is critical to the determination of whether or not the child has a problem. This single parent did interpret the behavior as sexually motivated and screening data found the boy to be elevated on social immaturity and inattentiveness, but not on other sexual behavior problems. His mother had a history of prior sexual abuse as a child and when queried, she indicated that her previous boyfriend had engaged in that behavior, and her son may have witnessed it. While it is true that random, unusual sexual behavior occurs in 3–4% of boys and girls this age, I concluded that a brief intervention was needed. I encouraged the mother to practice more privacy with her male friends, and she and I established a sexual rule for the boy and the mother in a joint meeting that addressed the behavior.

My 9-year-old mooned all the kids on his school bus and now has been kicked off for a month. Why did he do that?

This vignette captures the role of coexisting behavior problems in the emergence of what superficially appear to be problematic sexual behaviors. Upon interview, I found out the boy had attention deficit/hyperactivity disorder (ADHD), sometimes did not take his medication, and traveled for over 45 minutes on a bus with predominantly older children who had provoked him in the past. Screening information from the mother on the boy found elevations on inattentiveness and hyperactivity as well as learning problems. No significant sexual behaviors were reported. Similar findings were reported to me by the teacher. I concluded and reported to the mother that the behavior was a function of his ADHD and the social climate on the bus and not a sexual behavior per se. I encouraged more consistent use of his medication.

My 11-year-old was caught under the covers with his 7-year-old stepsister, who was visiting for the weekend. Both were giggling, and there did not seem to be any evidence that either was touching the other, but neither had any clothes on. Is my son a future sexual perpetrator?

The boy is a bit older than children who are observed to engage in "doctor play," although this behavior is fairly common (20–25%) in younger children (Larsson, Svedin, & Friedrich, 2000). In fact, 42% of college undergraduates reported that they had a childhood sexual encounter that typically involved hugging, kissing, or exposing themselves to another child (Haugaard & Tilly, 1988). All parties were interviewed and screening measures were obtained from parent figures and teachers. Both children denied having been sexually abused and also said that it had never happened before. The children's individual stories suggested that although the behavior was mutual, the idea most likely came from the 7-year-old, who reported that the idea for it came from her older sister, who reportedly slept with her boyfriend at her house. Her mother acknowledged that this was probably true. Both mother and teacher reported that the 7-year-old was immature, inattentive and impulsive, and moderately elevated on a sexual behavior measure, suggesting heightened sexual interest and knowledge. No elevations were noted on parent and teacher screening of the 11-year-old, who was profoundly embarrassed on interview but forthcoming to me. In a conference, I concluded that the younger child would benefit from increased supervision. Some rules about privacy were also set up for each home. No further incidents were reported over the next months of monitoring.

In each of these cases, the conclusions were that the children's sexual behaviors were relatively harmless. The examples clearly illustrate the role of modeling in child sexual behavior. But why did these cases come to me? Why didn't the involved adults feel they could appropriately interpret or respond to the child's actions? There are many reasons for this; the most benign, all-inclusive reason is that there is little easily accessible information on children's sexuality. Consequently, when we see a behavior of this type, we are confronted by something that truly feels out of our league. For many adults, the automatic response to childhood sexuality is that it is problematic and reflective of a sexually abusive experience. That explanation has seeped into our collective consciousness over the past 15 to 20 years, and while it is true in some cases, it only explains a small percentage of children's sexual behaviors. An option to our uncertainty is to step back, analyze whether our perspective is appropriate, and then create a sensitive response.

The above cases show a number of benign sexual behaviors by children, and explanations as to why I decided that therapy in longer-term interventions was not necessary. However, I want to balance these examples with one case that was highly disturbing not simply in terms of the child's behavior, but also in terms of the parental and child protective services responses.

The 9-year-old natural son of two parents told his parents that for the past 2 years, his 11-year-old adopted brother had been anally penetrating him on at least a weekly basis. He wanted to make sure his brother would not get into trouble but he was growing increasingly fearful of this activity and wanted it to stop. The parents sought me out and assured me their younger son was a good student and as far as they could see was not affected by his older brother's behavior. They had adopted the older boy when he was 4 and had little information about his background other than that he had been raised in a large Eastern European orphanage and had been a "dream child" for the first 2 years of his life with them. After age 6, he had become increasingly isolated but excelled in music and won awards.

I met both parents and each boy separately, and then spent another 3 hours with the 11-year-old. The older boy eventually admitted to one possible instance of having touched his brother. The younger boy, however, was tearful and shaking as he discussed the various incidents and his bother's use of coercion. I had earlier informed the parents that I could file an abuse report after my interviews, and that is what transpired. The abuse was investigated and substantiated, but over the next several months I had to work extremely hard to bring the child agency in charge to a perspective that protected the 9-year-old by removing the 11-year-old. The parents continued to reassure the agency that now that they knew the nature of the problem, they could protect both boys by adopting some of Dr. Friedrich's sexual safety rules. I had to argue in front of a family court judge that those rules would be insufficient and the older boy needed to be removed from the home. I had concluded that he was one of those uncommon preteens who was truly focused on disturbed sexuality and that other children in his life were vulnerable.

You are reading this book because you are a parent or professional interested in children's behavior generally and more specifically in one aspect of child behavior, sexuality. While insight and answers are provided in these pages, child sexuality is as much about child development, particularly social development, as it is about family and social context. Simple answers about the appropriateness of a single behavior should be avoided, since the behavior in question typically did not emerge fully articulated in the child's mind but required some combination of the child, the child's history, feelings at the time, opportunity, the social environment, behavioral repertoire, and the responses of adults. Thus, a question about the appropriateness of children occasionally touching their genitals could be answered easily just on the basis of frequency (yes, this is a common behavior in young children), but as you will see with the clinical cases presented throughout the book, there are often no simple answers.

Let's consider some of the variables. What if the child who is touching her genitals is an 11-year-old female? A child of this age certainly may touch her genitals for no pathological reason, but why hasn't she become more secretive the way the majority of 11-year-old children have? Is it a function of reduced social skills? Would only an extremely observant parent have noticed this behavior? What is the history of the adult's response to this behavior? Is it coercive in nature, thus fostering the persistence of the child's response? Or has it been reasonably sensitive and creative, but the behavior persists and is even more persistent, or is associated with recurrent urinary tract infections? Thus, simple questions often necessitate complex answers. However, some definitions of what constitutes problematic sexual behavior in children are in order, and that is the focus of the next section.

DEFINITIONS

The National Center on Sexual Behavior of Youth (NCSBY) defines children with sexual behavior problems as children "12 years and under who demonstrate developmentally inappropriate or aggressive sexual behavior. This definition includes self-focused sexual behavior, such as excessive masturbation, and aggressive sexual behavior towards others that may include coercion or force" (NCSBY, 2003, p. 1). Six additional qualifiers are provided to further understand what is meant by problematic: "(a) occurs at a high frequency; (b) interferes with child's social or cognitive development; (c) occurs with coercion, intimidation, or force; (d) is associated with emotional distress; (e) occurs between children of significantly different ages and or developmental abilities; or (f) repeatedly occurs in secrecy after intervention by caregivers" (p. 1).

This definition and the qualifiers are an excellent starting point, but the application of the definition still relies on the adults in the child's life. For example, what constitutes "excessive" and how is that decision made? In addition, developmental differences are an important consideration. Is there a difference between a 12-year-old who masturbates several times a week after he has gone to bed and a 5-year-old that masturbates a similar number of times per week and also at bedtime? A 12-year-old is close to adolescence, a period when masturbation is thought to be more common if not nearly universal (Gil & Johnson, 1993). Given the level of exposure to sexuality of children in our culture, most clinicians, in the absence of other information, would normalize the 12-year-old's behavior but want to investigate the reasons behind the 5-year-old's masturbation.

The definition also includes "aggressive sexual behavior," but many caregivers become concerned at behavior that overtly appears to be mutual and between similarly aged peers. What if the behavior appears to be mutual but there is an age difference of more than 2 to 3 years, such as an 8-year-old and a 4-year-old? The developmental and definitional issues are only two of many considerations that are examined in Chapter 1.

Caregivers and clinicians need help understanding what they should and should not be concerned about, and it is my hope that this book will identify those children about whom we need to be concerned. Chapter 4 offers information on screening and assessment that can assist in understanding what degree of importance to apply to single or multiple behaviors demonstrated by children ages 12 and younger.

In this book, the term *sexual behavior problems* is used to describe the spectrum of problematic sexual behaviors in children, from those that reflect overly sexualized behavior (e.g., excessive or public masturbation) to those that involve inappropriate or coercive sexual behavior with others. *Intrusive sexual behavior* refers to behavior that involves others, including animals, other children, or adults. *Aggressive sexual behavior* is reserved for those behaviors noted on the four additional items of the Child Sexual Behavior Inventory (CSBI; see Table 1.1). These behaviors are persisting in sexual behavior after being told not to, planning how to touch other children sexually, forcing other children to engage in sex acts, and inserting a finger or objects into another child's vagina or rectum.

The NCSBY (2003) provides a helpful fact sheet that examines common misperceptions about children with sexual behavior problems along with the most recent findings. For example, they report research that has found that short-term outpatient treatment is successful for the majority of children, and recommend that children live at home during treatment. Readers will find their Web page (www.ncsby.org) to be an important adjunct to this text.

ADULT PERCEPTIONS OF
CHILDREN'S SEXUAL BEHAVIOR

Therapists, teachers, caregivers, caseworkers, and juvenile court employees all have different vantage points on children's sexual behavior. For example, I often talk to school administrators about worrisome behaviors by students. I also speak to court officials about preteens who have been charged with sexual offenses. The desire for an effective intervention that addresses all behaviors in all settings and environments is huge. The thought is that a set of criteria would circumvent the emotionality that colors our thinking about children and sexuality.

For example, child protective service systems in every state struggle with how to manage children who enter foster care and then exhibit sexual behavior (Farmer & Pollock, 1998). When sexual contact occurs between two foster children, the foster placement is typically disrupted and the child is moved to a setting where no other children are present. Some foster children can be so sexually focused that their best hope is to be placed either in a residential facility or with a female foster parent so that no adult male is accused of sexual abuse. These children then may lose contact with siblings whom they were placed with initially. Their adoptability, in those cases where that is an option, is also reduced.

A real-life example of this exact process comes from a populous midwestern state that struggled with the management of these children who were in foster care. State officials established a process that superficially seemed humane but also reflected a clearly distorted view of child sexual behavior. The process included four components. The first identified foster children who exhibited sexually inappropriate behavior. These children were then labeled and moved to a new setting. The next step was for them to receive specialized treatment. Finally, the children would get back on track for adoption.

I had the privilege of reviewing this program with Dr. Barbara Bonner, the director of NCSBY. We found that the individuals who did the labeling often misinterpreted the behavior in a manner that reflected their own biases. For example, preschoolers were placed because it was reported that they touched the teacher's breasts, a behavior that has been determined to be relatively common (42–43% in the previous 6 months) in nonabused preschoolers (Friedrich, 1997). Once these children were placed in a new setting, they rarely received specialized treatment. Many of them were placed on multiple psychiatric medications, few with any proven efficacy with children. These children also missed out on adoptions. To the credit of the state, the program was finally stopped.

This specialized program was based on a belief that sexual behavior in children is always disturbed, will only get worse with time, and reflects severe problems in the child. However, there are no data to support these contentions. Too often, the emotions and biases of the adults involved drive the standard of care, and data are rarely turned to. If you practice in this field, you will receive referrals from a host of professionals, such as family physicians, pediatricians, parents, schools, and day care providers, as well as social service agencies; all of them will be confused about the most appropriate perspective with these children.

Disturbed sexuality is a topic that is controversial and affect laden. Adolescent sex offenders are considered as dangerous as adult offenders and the residential treatment of young sex offenders is a growth industry (Zimring, 2004). The same phenomenon is true for preteens with sexual behavior problems, and, as of 2002, there were 410 outpatient and residential treatment programs to treat these children (see Table IN.1). Their primary treatment foci are: offense responsibility, cognitive restructuring, intimacy and relationship skills, social skills training, victim awareness and empathy, relapse prevention, arousal control, and family support networks (Longo & Prescott, 2005). The individually based foci are very different than those that are argued to be primary in this book.

TABLE IN.1. Safer Society Nationwide Survey:
Number of Programs in Each Survey, 1986–2002

YEAR	ADULT	JUVENILE	CHILD	TOTAL
1986	297	346	N/A	643
1988	429	573	N/A	1,002
1990	541	626	N/A	1,167
1992	745	755	N/A	1,500
1994	710	684	390	1,784
1996	527	539	314	1,380
2000	461	291	66	818
2002	951	937	410	2,289

Source. From Longo and Prescott (2005).

CURRENT TREATMENT TRENDS AND THEIR IMPACT

At least two major issues interfere with children with sexual behavior problems receiving the most appropriate treatment. The first is that these children are typically being viewed in the same manner as adolescent sex offenders, who themselves have been assumed to be relatively similar to adult offenders, and consequently, adult treatment approaches are thought to be the treatment of choice. The second major issue is that the criminal justice system is sometimes involved in these children's lives. Neither of these solutions is appropriate.

I am not an apologist for sexual offending. In fact, I am in this field because of my long-standing commitment to victims. Sexual offending must be stopped. But the type of illogic that denies the enormous heterogeneity of adult and adolescent sex offenders has been translated into the child treatment field. The view is promulgated that all sexual offenders, regardless of age, are deeply disturbed and their offending is the product of distorted cognitions that reside deep inside the offender. This suggests that inpatient treatment and cognitive behavioral therapy are the best treatments. In fact, treatment guidelines published by the Association for the Treatment of Sexual Aggression (ATSA) make cognitive behavioral therapy the centerpiece of treatment (ATSA Professional Issues Committee, 2005).

While these recommendations serve some adult offenders and fewer adolescent offenders well, they are insensitively applied to children with sexual behavior problems. For example, consider the belief that cognitive restructuring is an important treatment focus for these children (Longo & Prescott, 2005). Many of these children grow up in families where they are never taught to think about their thinking. They never develop a lexicon for emotions because no parent is commenting on them and saying such things as, "I wonder if you are feeling sad" (Beeghly & Cicchetti, 1994; Bretherton, Fritz, Zahn-Waxler, & Ridgeway, 1986; Toth, Cicchetti, Macfie, & Emde, 1997). The type of hypothetical thinking required with cognitive therapy is outside the realm of possibility for these children. As a result, much of what they receive is psychoeducation. While this can make an excellent introduction to subsequent cognitive therapy, if there is to be any chance of success and safety for the young child, more needs to happen than psychoeducation. Children are embedded in their families and for treatment to be successful, the parents must change how they relate to the child. Only then can the child adopt a new, nonsexualized interpersonal model. Thus, outpatient treatment that involves the parent should be viewed as the treatment of choice.

A broader view that raises issues of attachment and developmental level is too often ignored in this treatment culture. Sexual offending is interpersonal and the interpersonal relationships and primary models of relating that shaped the offender must be addressed and new ones substituted. For example, Gilgun (1990, 1991) contrasted men who were molested as children and went on to commit sexual offenses with men who were similarly molested and did not sexually offend. Her findings strongly suggest that it is the presence of corrective relationships that is critical to interrupting the offending process.

However, many teen offenders are housed in remote facilities that make family therapy more difficult. This is despite the fact that family issues, such as modeling of coercion, overt sexuality, poor monitoring, and so on, are largely responsible for their behavior and subsequent placement. A paper by Walker and McCormick (2004) found that family therapy was relatively uncommon in residential facilities for juvenile sex offenders.

The same confused perspective on sexual offending has translated into the treatment of preteens who are sexually intrusive or aggressive with other children. Treatment programs for these children emphasize altering cognitions and improving empathy, often in individual or small group formats (Longo & Prescott, 2005). Family therapy is frequently secondary and when it does occur, therapists are often not sure what to do with these families.

The impact of the increased involvement of these children in criminal justice systems is also very troubling. We should also be deeply concerned by the fact that preteens are included in sex offender registries in a number of states (Zimring, 2004). This means they have been charged and convicted with a criminal offense that was first developed for adult offenders. This is an additional example of the developmental insensitivity that the mental health and criminal justice systems afford to preteens.

A motivator for residential treatment is the presumed reduction in risk. However, we do not know how to predict risk for violence very successfully with adults. Our skills at predicting future risk of sexual violence with preteens and teenagers are even weaker. There is reason to believe that future risk for sexual acts by teens and children with prior SBP is much lower than that of adults. Yet these younger offenders receive the same type and amount of treatment (Zimring, 2004).

However, there are voices of reason (Chaffin, LeTourneau, & Silovsky, 2002). Long-term outcome data with adolescent sexual offenders show only a modest effect of treatment (Worling & Curwen, 2000). Alexander (1999) calculated a reoffense rate for juvenile sex offenders for the short to moderate term of 7%. These teens are now better able to control their impulses and appreciate the consequences of their behavior.

Let's acknowledge that a significant percentage of children with sexual behavior problems act out impulsively and as a function of their experiences and environment. So let's make a commitment to changing that environment. The single best way is to make the parent-child system the cornerstone of the therapy process. The approach described in this book expects that as a therapist, you will spend as much time, if not more, with the parent as with the child. I expect parents to change their views of the child, adopting a more positive perspective. I also expect them to start interacting more positively and consistently. I do this since I want the child's internal working model (Bowlby, 1969), or map of relationships, to include positive and appropriate parent and child interaction. When that happens, I believe that any tendency toward behaving coercively and sexually with others will be extinguished from the child's repertoire.

OVERVIEW OF THE BOOK

The reader needs to know that Part II, Assessment and Treatment Manual, came first. Part I of this book, Theory and Therapeutic Strategies, serves as background, elaboration, and support for the Assessment and Treatment Manual and the stages and strategies that it outlines. Expect that you will go back and forth between Parts I and II as you read the book. The Assessment and Treatment Manual provides both a treatment guide and assessment and therapy measures and strategies.

I wrote a first draft of the Assessment and Treatment Manual after having seen several families of children with sexual behavior problems. I was aware that I reliably used several strategies with each family, including addressing parent-child attributions, increasing positive involvement between parent and child, establishing sexual rules, and increasing safety by reducing post-traumatic stress disorder (PTSD) triggers, interpersonal conflict, and addressing overt sexuality. In addition, my individual therapy with children also included some structured activities, such as helping children understand the origins of the behavior, expanding their vocabulary of emotions, addressing PTSD symptoms, and learning self-control strategies that were always shared with the parent figures. I had earlier developed a protocol for sexually abused children who masturbate (Friedrich, 1990) and was pleased with its efficacy; I had taught the protocol to many coworkers and supervisees. However, I had also learned that in order for it to be effective with all parents, I needed to spend some time repairing the parent-child relationship, or the child would not cooperate.

I also needed a vehicle through which to teach and supervise a postdoctoral trainee who was going to treat a child with sexual behavior problems. A few changes were made after this experience, and in fact, the Assessment and Treatment Manual has been an ever-evolving set of guidelines. It is designed to cover the issues that come up with the majority of the families that you will see. Some cases have been quite brief since the problematic behavior is developmental and the family context is positive. Others are long-standing and may involve child care. In these cases, I spend more time with the child than I wish and less time with the foster parent or other significant adults. Other families are textbook cases for parent-child interaction therapy since the behavior is largely oppositional and reflects an estranged parent-child relationship. Some of the cases require 10 to 12 parent-child sessions before the child is symptom free and the parent feels more empowered and connected.

I also appreciate that some families are very disturbed and treatment resistant, and may require a very creative approach if they remain in treatment. This book was written to address these difficult cases. Sexually aggressive children do exist and many are quite troubling, both in the moment and also with an eye toward their future potential risk. However, they need to be treated in the manner that is most respectful of their developmental level. Rather than relying on a purely cognitive therapy approach, I work to help children understand both verbally and visually the situation they are in. This type of languaging of the experience is both corrective and helps to inhibit future acting out (Bodiford-McNeil, Hembree-Kigin, & Eyberg, 1996; Cicchetti & Rogosch, 1997). The approach I suggest combines parent-child therapy with psychoeducation. It also provides a new type of support for both the parent and the child, in the context of an environment that fosters self-regulation and inhibition of inappropriate impulses. In addition, if the child has treatable symptoms (e.g., PTSD related to prior abuse, or ADHD), then those should also be addressed.

Parents and children also vary widely in the degree to which they are ready to work with you. The more severe the sexually intrusive behavior, the less likely the family of a preteen with sexual behavior problems will be to immediately jump in and tackle the problem. There may be some initial energy and distress, but too often it fades quickly. I see some parents for one to two sessions and then need to coordinate additional appointments only with the help of the caseworker, or occasionally a juvenile court worker. In fact, Hall, Mathews, and Pearce (2002) found that none of the families in their most severe group finished treatment. I have found the same to be true; it is extremely hard to treat families in which the child was not only sexual with other children but was also premeditative and coercive. This type of child almost always lives in or comes from a family that is very compromised and has antisocial aspects.

Rather than let that fact daunt me, I think about each of these families as located somewhere along the change continuum (Miller & Rollnick, 1991). The more therapy-naive, support-aversive the family, the more likely they have not even started to think about making any changes. This places them in the precontemplation stage of change. Rather than get upset and disheartened by this type of family, I assume the role of the interested and concerned educator.

I take on this role since there are data to support the fact that "these tough families" who are in the precontemplation stage are served best by education that provides "feedback in a sensitive empathic manner" (Miller & Rollnick, 1991, p. 192). I also try to make sure that even though the family is not ready for treatment, the community agencies involved with the family are aware that their child is very concerning and should not be overlooked.

I believe that there is evidence for the efficacy of a combined parent-child approach to these cases. Since single mothers are the majority of the parents I see, and since fathers are so remarkably absent from the developmental psychopathology research literature, it may seem that mothers are the only players in these children's lives based on the case examples provided and the literature reviewed. That is not the case, since these same mothers are the ones who change and create better lives and repair relationships. Please understand that my arguments hold for fathers and when they are present, their roles also need to change, and their relationships with their children must also be altered.

I also believe that practitioners should use evidence-based psychotherapies (Kazdin & Weisz, 2003), an increasing focus in the victim field (Chaffin & Friedrich, 2004; Saunders, Berliner, & Hanson, 2004). Nondirective, experiential play therapy is not proven to be effective with children who have externalizing problems and should not be the primary treatment with this group. The parent-training strategies and cognitive and goal-setting techniques have an empirical basis and form the foundation of the Assessment and Treatment Manual. Not only do I typically use empirically based techniques with these children and their parents, I have also attempted to validate the work that I do by obtaining pre- and postdata and some follow-up data on as many of the families treated with this Assessment and Treatment Manual as I can locate.

I invite you to read this book, study the Assessment and Treatment Manual, and then apply it to a preteen child that comes into your practice after having touched another child sexually or engaged in some other type of concerning and persistent sexual behavior. Learn to appreciate the individual nature of each of these children and their parents and make a decision to treat based on the data you systematically obtain. Work hard to engage the parents, help them see that the answer to their child's problem is a relational solution, and then reward them for their efforts by helping them learn how to enjoy their child again, or even for the first time. With this increase in mutual and positive interactions between parent and child, the child's internal map of relationships will begin to change, and ideally, the developmental course will be righted.

SPECIAL CONSIDERATIONS

A variety of special issues need to be considered in working with this population of children. These include child abuse reporting laws, parent-child confidentiality, and dual relationship issues. Parents need to be informed that abusive behavior is reportable and that you need to abide by the laws of your state. Children may reveal more acts or victims over the course of therapy and you and your local social services system need to have conversations ahead of time about the best way to handle these. Preferably, the only reports you will have to consider filing are those rare ones that constitute extreme abuse and include repetitive and coercive behavior, typically by an older preteen, often a sibling or half sibling of a child you are seeing. This is typically revealed by a child victim and not the older victimizing child. Protective services need to be brought into play that so that appropriate services can be provided.

I believe that frequent involvement with parents is needed and that much of this should be separate from the child. At the same time, children need to feel that they have you as an advocate. You will hear things parents do not know but need to be aware of since they are treatment issues, such as sexual thoughts you would like children to monitor but that they can only reliably keep track of with parental support, or children's belief that parents are overly critical and harsh, and so on. Children need to know that adults can talk to each other in ways that enable change to occur but do not result in blaming or implicating the child.

Many of these children are in school. At times the issue of the safety of their classmates is raised. I rarely believe that informing school personnel is necessary. I do have to work with schools if the incident that brought the child to me occurred in the school. However, if that is not the case, my suggestion is that there is little need to contact the school and risk further treatment issues due to the possibility that the school may respond insensitively to the situation. Few of the children I see are so dominated by their sexual thoughts that they are unable to inhibit their sexual actions subsequent to having been caught. That makes it much less likely that they will reoffend in the short term.

My typical therapy client is a child for whom I complete an extended evaluation for given concerns about undisclosed abuse. This combines the two roles of evaluator and therapist. Given my belief that you are doing both when evaluating properly, the roles are not divisible with children and families involving behavior that should not be viewed as criminal but as a derivative of trauma and parent-child issues. Protective services are the model to follow at this point, and service providers often wear multiple hats.

Another issue is definitional and involves what is meant by the word *abuse*. When I identify a child in this book as sexually abused, it is because he or she was confirmed as sexually abused by the appropriate authority in the state in which he or she lives. The same is true when I use the words *physical abuse*. However, I do believe that all readers need to be aware of the continuum of sexual abuse. For example, in one excellent study, you will read that sexual abuse could not be confirmed for the majority of preschoolers (Silovsky & Niec, 2002). However, many unidentified children with unconfirmed abuse may have been exposed to sexualizing environments, but I have never seen an investigative body identify this as sexually abusive. A few may perceive these environments as neglectful, but there may never be a treatment referral. Thus it is important to think about sexual abuse both broadly and more narrowly as you work with these families.

When working with children and families in which problematic sexual behavior has occurred, it is important to be aware of complications and how they can arise in these cases. Therapists should periodically review the ethical guidelines and standards of care of their professional organizations and seek consultation when questions arise in their practice. State licensing boards or professional organizations are good resources to use.

PART I

THEORY AND
THERAPEUTIC STRATEGIES

1

OVERVIEW OF RESEARCH ON CHILDREN WITH SEXUAL BEHAVIOR PROBLEMS

EARLY RESEARCH ON the sequelae of sexual abuse was atheoretical and focused on a diverse collection of acute symptoms. Behavioral regression (e.g., secondary enuresis) and problems with self-regulation (e.g., sleep problems) were once thought to be the key symptoms reflecting a child's distress following sexual abuse. That children became sexualized in response to sexual abuse, and that sexual abuse was associated with variable rates of PTSD, was not appreciated as the field started to develop (Kendall-Tackett, Williams, & Finkelhor, 1993). In the past 10 years, research has provided increasing information on the development of sexual behavior problems in children and effective treatment intervention for this group of children.

This chapter summarizes what we know about children with sexual behavior problems. The topics covered include the prevalence of prior sexual abuse, demographic and abuse features that predispose children to exhibit sexual problems, comorbid behavior problems, and factors that potentiate the likelihood of sexual behavior problems. Finally, I will suggest an integrative model that helps us understand the emergence of sexually problematic behaviors.

Several threads continue throughout the literature. The first is that sexual behavior problems exist along a continuum, with some more normative and others more problematic. A second thread is that children appear to exhibit concerning sexual behavior for a variety of reasons and come to it via many pathways. A final thread is that children with sexual behavior problems appear to come from more troubled families and have experienced more adversity than their peers. Their families have not provided the secure base so essential for healthy attachment and the development of respectful relationships.

RISK FACTORS

Children develop sexual behavior problems through a variety of pathways. Several risk factors have been associated with the development of sexual behavior problems, but no single factor has been found in all children who have these problems.

Five different variables that reflect the child sexual abuse experience were identified (see top portion of Table 1.1; Hall, Mathews, & Pearce, 1998). These include (1) the child becoming sexually aroused during the abuse; (2) experiencing sadistic abuse; (3) an active involvement of the child in the sexual activity; (4) the child acting in an "offender" role during sex acts with another child, usually orchestrated by the adult perpetrator; and (5) the child blaming himself or herself for the victimization, or feeling ambivalent about whom to blame for the sexual abuse. This ambivalence reflects persisting loyalty to the perpetrator as well as confusion about the nature of the act.

While sexual arousal and sadistic abuse seem to be superficially contradictory, both of these risk factors reflect the abuse being overwhelming and dysregulating for the child. Children who are sexually aroused will view subsequent sexual behavior more positively and disregard restrictions imposed by the caregiver on their pursuit of continued sexual activity. For example, research found that children who had only observed pornography were more focused on sexuality (as measured by Child Sexual Behavior Inventory scores) than were children with a history of sexual abuse (Elliott, Kim, & Mull, 1997).

Seven child features are included in Table 1.1. These children (1) were often unempathic; (2) had a restricted range of emotional expression; (3) voiced hopelessness and depression in response to their victimization; (4) did not know the difference between right and wrong; (5) blamed others for their behavior; (6) had other general boundary problems that were nonsexual in nature, including interest in behavior with adults, not respecting property rights, and so on; and (7) a subset of these children was also quite overtly sexualized and their frequent masturbatory behavior or sexual comments and gestures characterized this.

Included in the child's history were four additional risk factors, including (1) chaotic living experiences including multiple moves and disruptions; (2) physical abuse; (3) emotional abuse; and (4) for the males in the sample, the permanent loss of a father figure. Regrettably, boys with sexual behavior problems are typically being raised by a single parent with a long history of relational difficulties. This only increases the probability of attachment insecurity.

TABLE 1.1 Risk Factors for Sexual Aggression

Sexual abuse experience of the child
❑ Sexual arousal of the child during the abuse
❑ Sadistic abuse
❑ Active involvement of the child in the sexual activity
❑ Child acted in "offender" role during child-to-child sex acts ($p = .002$)
❑ Child blames self or is ambivalent about whom to blame for the sexual abuse

Child
❑ Lack of warmth/empathy
❑ Restricted range of affective expression
❑ Hopelessness/depression
❑ Poor internalization of right and wrong
❑ Blames others/denial of responsibility
❑ General boundary problems (nonsexual)
❑ Sexualized gestures or frequent or compulsive masturbation

Child's history
❑ Frequent moves
❑ Physical abuse
❑ Emotional abuse
❑ Permanent loss of father (males)

Parent-child relationship
❑ Intrusive or enmeshed mother-child relationship
❑ Sexualized interaction style within family
❑ Role reversal, inappropriate parent-child roles

Caregiver characteristics
❑ Mother shows PTSD symptoms
❑ Mother competes with child/high level of neediness
❑ Mother has history of childhood physical neglect
❑ Father observed family violence in own parents during his childhood
❑ Mother experienced childhood separation or loss of own parents
❑ Maternal boundary problems with child

Note. Check all that apply to this child's case.
Source. From Hall, Mathews, and Pearce (1998).

Attachment insecurity is reflected in the three risk factors pertaining to the parent-child relationship: (1) a mother-child relationship characterized by intrusive and enmeshed behavior reflecting a lack of attunement and sensitivity to the child; (2) parents interacting with their child in a sexualized manner; and (3) frequent role reversal that places the child in a parentified stance with the parent. As such, the child is forced to be a source of emotional support or may also be forced into a surrogate parent role with a younger sibling. If this parentified child sexualizes the caregiving of this sibling, the probability of additional victimization increases.

The final cluster of six risk factors pertains to features of the caregiver, typically the mother. These include (1) a history of physical neglect; (2) PTSD symptoms usually related to prior trauma; (3) childhood separation and loss permeating the parent's history; and (4) an inability to nurture the child since the parent has such a high level of need. Other factors include (5) domestic violence in the fathers in the sample and (6) boundary problems that the mother has with the child. (The risk factors in Table 1.1 are also presented in a tabular form for assessment purposes in the Assessment and Treatment Manual, Chapter 8, Form A.)

Each of these risk variables can be assessed and considered when planning treatment. Hall and her colleagues (2002) found that the more risk factors, the more difficulties the family had with the treatment process. Convergent validity for these risk factors comes from a study of sexually abused adolescents, some of whom were sexual offenders and the rest of whom were delinquents (Burton, Miller, & Shill, 2002). Although both groups had been sexually abused, the sexually offending teens had a closer relationship with their perpetrator, a greater chance of a male perpetrator, longer duration of abuse, and abuse that was both more forceful and involved penetration. Most of these map onto the risk factors listed under sexual abuse experience (Hall et al., 1998).

HISTORY OF SEXUAL ABUSE

The fact that sexually abused children differ from nonabused children primarily on the basis of sexual behavior was not established until the mid-1980s (Friedrich, Urquiza, & Beilke, 1986). Only two years later, several papers were published indicating that some sexually abused children engaged in sexually intrusive behavior with other children (Friedrich & Luecke, 1988; Johnson, 1988, 1989). In the Friedrich and Luecke study, the majority of children (N = 13 of 16) were sexually abused and one additional child was suspected of being sexually abused. However, prior sexual abuse varied considerably by age in the larger sample from Johnson (1988). She found that 72% of the 4- to 6-year-old children with sexual behavior problems had a history of being sexually abused, compared with 42% of the 7- to 10-year-olds, and 35% of the 11- and 12-year-olds. This early research suggested that girls who engaged in sexually intrusive behavior were more likely to have a history of sexual abuse than were boys who were sexually intrusive. For example, all of the girls in both the Friedrich and Luecke and the Johnson (1989) studies had a history of molestation. However, the total number of girls in these samples was small.

This early research with small samples of children was followed by studies using much larger samples that resulted in different findings, that is, that many children who act out sexually either have not experienced contact sexual abuse or have an uncertain sexual abuse status. For example, there have been two federally funded research studies of the treatment of children with sexual behavior problems. The Oklahoma-based study ($N = 201$; Bonner, Walker, & Berliner, 2000) found a rate of prior known sexual abuse to be 48%. However, abuse status was uncertain for another 36%, with 15% most likely not abused. (The ambiguous cases are a very common clinical issue.)

The Vermont-based study ($N = 127$) found a rate of prior sexual abuse of 84% (Gray, Busconi, Houchens, & Pithers, 1997), with the rates of prior abuse varying from 93% of females to 78% of males. However, these rates were provided by the mothers and did not represent only abuse that was substantiated by social services or the courts, as was the case with the Oklahoma group (Silovsky & Niec, 2002). This group also found that 56% of their sample had been victims of multiple forms of maltreatment, the most common combination being sexual and physical abuse.

Lower rates are reported for preschoolers. For example, Silovsky and Niec (2002) systematically investigated 37 children, ages 3 to 7 years, who were referred for treatment due to sexual behavior problems. They found that the majority (65%) of these children were female. Sexual abuse was only confirmed in 13 (38%) of these children, and an equal number of preschoolers (13, 38%) were suspected of being sexually abused, but it could not be substantiated. Many of these children had experienced physical abuse (47%) or witnessed domestic violence (58%). Only 4 (11%) of these children had no known history of sexual abuse, physical abuse, or witnessing domestic violence.

Letourneau, Schoenwald, and Sheidow (2004) also found lower than expected rates of sexual abuse in a large sample of 5- to 19-year-olds who exhibited noncriminal sexual behavior problems (SBP), such as excessive masturbation, sexual preoccupation, and gender issues. Three groups were created based on their level of sexual behavior: No-SBP, Low-SBP, and High-SBP. Combined sexual and physical abuse rates were highest in the High-SBP group (32.4%) and ranged downward to the Low-SBP (24.7%) and No-SBP groups (20.3%).

Finally, specifically sexually aggressive behaviors were studied in a large ($N = 575$) consecutive sample of outpatients (Friedrich, Tiegs, & Damon, 2003) whose parents completed an extended version of the 38-item CSBI (Friedrich, 1997), the CSBI-III (described in Friedrich, 1997). Slightly more than one in five of these children (20.7%) had a confirmed sexual abuse history. Four sexual aggression items were created and their endorsement frequency is reported below. The endorsement rates are quite low for all four items, ranging from 2.1% to 5.9%. However, three out of four of these items were reported more often by non–sexually abused (NSA) children. This is most likely related to the issue of base rates, a topic discussed later in the chapter.

1. Persists in touching other children after being told not to (endorsed for 5.9% of total sample, 64% of those by NSA).
2. Plans how to touch other children (endorsed for 2.5% of total sample, 64% by NSA).
3. Forces other children to engage in sex acts (endorsed for 2.1% of total sample, 42% by NSA).
4. Puts finger or object in other child's vagina or rectum (endorsed for 2.3% of total sample, 85% by NSA).

Another body of research has examined those sexually abused children who go on to exhibit sexual behavior problems and those who do not (Hall et al., 1998). The authors identified risk factors that were divided into the following categories: sexual abuse experiences of the child, child characteristics, child's history, parent-child relationship, and caregiver characteristics. These are presented as a checklist in Table 1.1. I believe many of these risk factors also apply to intrusive children without a clear history of sexual abuse. Consequently, with the exception of the factors related to the child sexual abuse experience, the remainder can be used as you assess the child in front of you and plan for treatment.

It seems very clear that prior sexual abuse is not a necessary condition for children to act out sexually or even intrusively. While it could be validly argued that the number of sexually abused preschoolers in the Silovsky and Niec (2002) sample is likely to be higher, given the problems inherent in identifying sexual abuse in preschoolers (Hewitt, 1999), the fact that sexual abuse has never been ubiquitous in the histories of children with sexual behavior problems cannot be ignored.

A key finding from Silovsky and Niec (2002) is that the majority of children in their sample had multiple risk factors in their lives, including observing adult sexuality. Their findings suggest that the sexual behavior problems noted in these young children were not only activated but also magnified by the dysregulating effect of living in chaotic homes and witnessing adult sexuality.

DEMOGRAPHIC FACTORS

Sexually intrusive behavior is associated with younger children (Friedrich, 1997, 2002; Letourneau et al., 2004). This is also supported by research with the CSBI-III, wherein the sum of the four sexual aggression items is also significantly associated with younger age (Friedrich et al., 2003). This same study found more sexually aggressive behavior when the child was living with a foster family and when sexual abuse was suspected but not confirmed. In fact, these four aggression items were not significantly correlated with a sexual abuse history (Friedrich et al., 2003).

Examining single demographic or child variables is not likely to be very productive in understanding the origins of sexual behavior problems. For example, the finding that younger children are more likely to exhibit sexually intrusive behaviors is in part due to the fact that younger children are more closely monitored by their parents than are older children, who may exhibit intrusive behaviors of which adults are unaware. A related finding—that these children are often placed in foster care because they are difficult to manage in their home—reflects parents' unwillingness to manage sexually intrusive children, as well as the family disruptions that are common in the lives of deeply troubled children.

COMORBID BEHAVIORS

Research does suggest that the presence of sexual behavior problems in children is associated with greater overall psychiatric pathology. For example, LeTourneau and colleagues (2004) found the highest rate of behavior problems in the High-SBP group relative to the Low- or No-SBP groups. A study that included a 1-year follow-up of 10- to 12-year-old children in care in New York State (Friedrich et al., 2005) found both more sexual behavior problems and more persistent sexual behavior problems in the group of children who were in residential treatment rather than in a foster care system. These children also had more problematic relationships with caregivers, who rated them more negatively than other children in their care (Friedrich et al., 2005). Poorer peer relations are also reported in children with intrusive sexual behavior (Friedrich et al., 2003).

Data suggest that cognitive delays are relatively common in this group of children (Friedrich & Luecke, 1988). In addition, receptive language capabilities fell into the low average range in a sample of preschoolers with sexually problematic behavior (Silovsky & Niec, 2002). However, school-age children with sexual behavior problems did not differ from a comparison sample on a brief IQ measure (Bonner et al., 2000).

In the CSBI-III study of specific sexually aggressive behavior, the total of the four items were correlated with subscales from the Child Behavior Checklist (Achenbach, 1991a) and factor scores from the CSBI (Friedrich, 1997) for three age groups, 2–5, 6–9, and 10–12. (These factor scores were derived with factor analysis and are similar across all three age groups. They include the following factors: sexual knowledge, sexual intrusiveness, personal boundaries, self-stimulating behavior, and gender-specific behaviors.)

The sexual aggressive items correlated significantly with the Delinquency subscale from the Child Behavior Checklist (Achenbach, 1991a) for all three age groups, and with the Total Score and Externalizing and Aggression scales for the 6- to 9-year-olds. This would suggest that sexually aggressive behavior is associated with a pattern of rule-violating behavior. Furthermore, sexual aggression seems to be inconsistently associated with most other subclassifications of sexual behaviors, as measured by the CSBI (Friedrich, 1997), throughout early development. A notable exception, however, is its consistent and strong relationship with sexual intrusiveness, a scale measuring interpersonal sexual behaviors, mostly involving touching others' private parts. Table 1.2 summarizes these correlations.

HOW SEXUAL BEHAVIOR PROBLEMS DEVELOP

The longer we have studied children with sexual behavior problems, the more it seems true that sexual abuse is an important but not necessary contributor to intrusive sexual behavior. Other factors include growing up in a dysregulating home environment and other forms of maltreatment. Witnessing adult sexuality could also be called abusive in some cases, but we know little about what makes this problematic since minimal research is available. It is true that the variable "witnessing adults have sex" from the brief Family Sexuality Index used in the first CSBI studies (Friedrich, Grambsch, Broughton, Kuiper, & Beilke, 1991) did correlate with overall sexual behavior, and the correlation size increased based on the overall number of risk factors in the child's life. Consequently, exposure to adult sexuality probably does have a potentiating effect, particularly since it is associated with other problems in the family.

However, the specific effects of sexual abuse on sexual behavior cannot be minimized. A longitudinal prospective study found that as young adults, sexually abused girls were more preoccupied with sex, younger at first voluntary intercourse, endorsed lower birth control efficacy, and were more likely to be

Table 1.2 Significant Correlations With Sexual Aggression Items and Other Rating Scale Data by Age Group

VARIABLE	r	p
Preschool (2–5 years)		
CBC delinquency	.22	.005
Fac. 1 sex knowledge	.18	.03
Fac. 2 sexual intrusiveness	.27	.001
Elementary Age (6–9 years)		
CBC total score	.20	.002
CBC externalizing score	.24	.000
CBC delinquency	.32	.000
CBC aggression	.26	.000
Fac. 1 sexual intrusiveness	.66	.000
Fac. 2 sex knowledge	.41	.000
Fac. 3 poor boundaries	.45	.000
Fac. 4 sexual intrusiveness with adults	.13	.03
Fac. 5 self-stimulation	.38	.000
Preteen (10–12 years)		
CBC delinquency	.22	.005
Fac. 4 sexual intrusiveness	.87	.000
Fac. 5 gender role	.32	.000

Note. CBC = Child Behavior Checklist (Achenbach, 1991a); Fac = Factors from the Child Sexual Behavior Inventory (Friedrich, 1997).

teen mothers than nonabused girls (Noll, Trickett, & Putnam, 2003). For this sample, sexual preoccupation was predicted by anxiety when younger; sexual aversion was predicted by childhood sexual behavior problems; and sexual ambivalence (simultaneous sexual preoccupation and sexual aversion) was predicted by pathological dissociation. Sexual abuse by the biological father was associated with greater sexual aversion and sexual ambivalence.

Diversity characterizes sexually abused children with sexual behavior problems. Some children are quickly reactive to their abuse, and act out immediately or within a few months of the abuse (Friedrich, 1990). Often this action results in corrective feedback and the behavior seems to stop. Other children act out over a year later, sometimes waiting even longer. Those children are more confusing to me. They appear to have been affected by their abuse, but what have they done with the experience in the meantime? Why did they wait so long? Is their activity more premeditated and less impulsive than for children who act out immediately?

The absence of contact sexual abuse does not mitigate the deleterious impact of adult sexuality that the child witnesses. However, simple exposure to adult sexuality is rarely a reason for a referral to protective services. If a child is subsequently interviewed about sexual abuse because of sexual behavior, it is unlikely that the child will be asked about witnessing adult sexuality. I would certainly think of this child as being precociously aware of sexuality, and I think this awareness characterizes more of the children we see than many of us realize. In fact, we do not have sufficient information to truly know how sexual behavior problems develop since overt and covert sexual exposure does not get studied.

REASONS FOR ACTING OUT

Children may exhibit intrusive sexual behavior for several reasons. I will list the five that seem most important, but the list is not inclusive. The first is that many children are interested in sexuality simply because they have pleasant feelings when they touch themselves (normative). They observe the caregivers around them interacting with hugs and kisses and they decide they want to try that as well (normative).

A second reason could be that the child has been exposed to overt and troubling sexual behavior and they are now exhibiting it. This could include actual sexual abuse. The same principle applies, that is, modeling (Bandura, 1986), but the behavior is not normative.

A third reason is that the child is used to interacting coercively with other children. As the child gets older, sexuality enters into the coercive equation (Patterson, Reid, & Dishion, 1992).

A fourth reason includes those subtle family dynamics that emerge relative to a parental sexual abuse history. For some children, this means that their behavior is shaped into being more intrusive and even more overtly sexualized.

A fifth reason is that the child has been left with no model for intimacy. Research has shown that indiscriminate affection seeking, for example, is manifested more often by neglected and institutionalized children (O'Connor & Rutter, 2000). The same is true for poor personal boundaries and increased self-stimulation and masturbation. Because neglected children are poorly monitored, any early, occasional behavior that is left uncorrected can then grow into something more serious.

Children will invariably exhibit behavior that adult observers label as sexual. The 5-year-old in my first normative study who impulsively kissed his infant sister on her labia most likely did so, according to his mother, because he was 5 and he was closer to her labia than her mouth as she lay on the changing table. The act was impulsive and the mother saw it simply as that when I spoke to her (as one of the 12 people I called subsequent to the study). However, because she checked the behavior on the questionnaire, it was labeled as sexual. Other normative children will exhibit more specific sexual behaviors, such as touching genitals; most likely they do this because it feels good. As they get older, the frequency often drops due to parental limit setting or the child finding other enjoyable activities to do.

The younger the child, the more likely he or she is to act out in response to a predisposing event. One constant in the study of child psychopathology is that children who act out more often than not have an overabundance of adversity in their life. Adversity can take many forms, including poverty, race, reduced educational opportunities, and family moves and disruptions (Evans, 2003). For example, cumulative stress has been implicated in research on those who manifest PTSD after a traumatic event and those who do not (Wolfe, Sas, & Wekerle, 1994). Individuals whose history is dominated by adversity are primed to develop PTSD, among other disorders.

While cumulative stress may set the stage for pathology, there are other factors that most likely operate in the life of a child who is sexually aggressive. One of these aspects goes back to the child features listed in Table 1.1. Children who are oppositional are more likely to act on their impulses than are children who are more inhibited in their symptoms, such as anxiety. If any event has resulted in a sexual focus, then those oppositional impulses may take on a sexual focus.

Case Example: An Aggressive Boy

S.S. was a very aggressive, non–sexually abused boy who came to my attention after what seemed to be an evolving aggressive pattern that had a sexual focus. His older half brother, who at the time of the referral was in juvenile detention for assault, routinely poked S.S. in the crotch and had also kicked him there. The principal of the school S.S. attended told me that in the year prior, S.S. had a habit of kicking other boys in the crotch. But this year, he had expanded his repertoire. Not only did S.S. kick other boys, he made sexual insults to girls in his class. He was suspended after pinching a fellow fifth grader on her nipple and was referred to me for an evaluation.

The boy was guarded about himself, so I adopted the strategy of getting him to talk about other people, particularly his brother. I asked him if his brother had ever pinched another girl's breasts. S.S. gave me his first smile of the interview and proceeded to tell me about the numerous antics of his brother. His brother's behavior apparently had assumed a special role in this boy's ideas about how to relate to girls. By the end of the evaluation, I was fairly certain that social learning was an operative explanation (Bandura,

1986). S.S. was primarily imitating his older brother, and his coercive behavior with girls was an elaboration of his coercive relationship with his mother. The subsequent treatment was made very difficult by the fact that his single parent was more interested in blaming the school for her son's problems than accepting that both she and her son needed to make some changes.

Domestic violence and child maltreatment are excellent teachers of coercive behavior. Children exposed to each of these are more likely to think about relationships in terms of anger and coercion. As young children do not discriminate one arousal from another, some domestic violence may activate the same circuits that are occupied by both sexuality and aggression (Siegel, 1999).

This introduces a neurobiological perspective, which is very useful to keep in mind as you consider the child in front of you. Neurons are selectively pruned in the young child dependent on use. Fewer neurons in some neural paths and tracts lead to greater problems with affect regulation and relational capacity (Nichols, Gergely, & Fonagy, 2001). This is considered to be one reason why chronically overwhelming experiences in the early years can make children struggle to keep in control of their behavior as they grow older. This perspective also helps to explain why children who are older at adoption struggle more to form and maintain secure attachments with caregivers.

But what about the sexual aspect? We could start with oppositionality as one vehicle. Oppositional children are more likely to swear and use sexual words, which may set the stage for provocative sexual behavior, such as exposing oneself on the bus. Children with impulse control problems are also more likely to act on their impulses, or imitate the behavior that a parent has modeled, such as kissing or grabbing.

Another avenue can be the modeling of sexual behavior in the home. The parent's history of sensitivity to the child's well-being is related to whether a child is exposed to overt sexual behavior. A reduced level of sensitivity may be due in large part to a history of abuse, particularly sexual abuse. How parental history of sexual abuse manifests itself is discussed in more detail in Chapter 3, since that is an important aspect of family sexuality (Friedrich & Sim, 2005). However, parents' unresolved sexual abuse can predispose them to be more reactive to normal manifestations of child sexuality. Children quickly learn that they receive reinforcement from a parent if they touch their genitals or talk dirty. Some mothers with a history of sexual abuse find that the intimacy of child rearing is too much to manage and purposely withdraw from their children and spend less time with them (Denov, 2004). This opens children up to managing their intimacy needs in less healthy ways, such as masturbation or vulnerability to perpetrators.

TYPOLOGIES

Children with sexual behavior problems are a diverse group. Their behaviors, including their relative frequency, will vary from one child to the next. Some are more immediate to their abuse than others. A child who acts out right after being abused and never again is different than a child who acts out much later and persists in acting out. Some children are more self-focused (e.g., they masturbate) and another smaller percentage exhibit sexualized behavior that seems similar to that of older offenders.

Several efforts have been made to cluster these children into categories. The first attempts were clinically driven and not derived in an empirical manner. For example, Gil and Johnson (1993) described three groups. These are sexually reactive children, children who engage in extensive mutual sexual behavior, and children who molest other children. These authors believed that children in the sexually reactive group reflect one or more maltreatment types or exposure to adult sexuality that overwhelmed them. For reasons that will vary with each child (e.g., because they are overwhelmed and fragmented or sexualized), reactive children act out their experience. The children who engage in extensive and apparently mutual sexual behavior with other children lack close relationships with adults and turn to other children for connection. They find other children like themselves and coercion is not used. However, their relational view is dominated by their sexual focus.

Another clinical approach is reflected in the next model. A simple but useful schema for sexually abused children who later develop sexually intrusive behavior was developed by Downs (1993). It helps to explain a wide range of behavior in sexually abused children, from those who are avoidant of sexuality to those who are hypersexual and unusually focused. Presumably, the latter group would exhibit more sexual behavior problems, but I would expect that younger sexually abused children, before they have become more clearly differentiated, would exhibit avoidance at times and preoccupation at other times. They settle into more consistent patterns only as they get older.

Although Downs's (1993) dichotomy has not been the subject of research in children, Merrill's research supports this dichotomy in severely sexually abused females (Merrill, Guimond, Thomsen, & Milner, 2003). Over the years, my clinical impression is that teens in the first group seem to have a history of avoidant attachment prior to their sexual abuse, and teens in the second group have a resistant or coercive attachment history.

Two federally funded research studies, designed to evaluate treatment modalities with children exhibiting sexual behavior problems, have been completed (Bonner et al., 2000; Pithers, Gray, Busconi, & Houchens, 1998). Both studies found a diverse group of children, and both utilized cluster analytic techniques to sort them into groups.

The Vermont-based group studied 127 children, and five groups were identified and labeled as follows: nondisordered, sexually aggressive, highly traumatized, rule breakers, and abuse reactive (Pithers et al., 1998). The children in the nondisordered group were overrepresented by females, appeared to have no true psychopathology, and had typically committed the least severe offenses. However, they had sexually touched another child or exhibited sexual behavior that was deemed excessive. They generally had low levels of other behavior problems.

Sexually aggressive children were more often male, had the highest percentage of conduct disorder (CD) diagnoses, had the highest average number of penetrative acts, and seldom acknowledged their own maltreatment. The highly traumatized group had the highest number of psychiatric and PTSD diagnoses. They typically had an extensive history of child maltreatment, including multiple perpetrators of both physical and sexual abuse. Rule breakers were overrepresented by females and typically had psychiatric diagnoses related to oppositional-defiant disorder (ODD), CD, or ADHD. Finally, the abuse reactive group had the shortest latency from their own abuse to problematic sexual behavior, and were overrepresented in the ODD diagnostic category. The clusters seemed to be derived from two axes of variables, one based on the severity of the sexual act committed by the child, and the other on the degree of disturbance of the child, with ODD and CD children overrepresented.

Despite several efforts, the Oklahoma-Seattle group failed to identify consistent subgroups of sexually aggressive children with cluster analysis (Bonner et al., 2000). The researchers categorized the children into three groups on the basis of the severity and coercive aspects of their sexual behavior. An interesting finding was that the most severe group, Group 3, did not differ from Group 2 in terms of overall sexual behavior as measured by the CSBI. Mothers of the most sexually aggressive children did not necessarily report an inordinate amount of sexual behavior, nor had these children been consistently sexually abused. Recidivism rates of another sexual behavior for these children after two-year follow-up was 15%.

A combination of sorting techniques led to the five-group typology developed with 100 3- to 7-year-old sexually abused children from two Canadian provinces (Hall et al., 2002). All of the children in groups 2 through 5 exhibited some level of problematic sexual behavior. The five distinct groups, arranged in order of severity, were (1) developmentally expected; (2) interpersonal, unplanned; (3) self-focused; (4) interpersonal, planned; and (5) inter-personal, coercive.

As the majority of children that I see generally fall into one of these groups, I have found this typology to be the most useful clinically. It is the typology used to describe the children treated with the Assessment and Treatment Manual in Part II.

Early efforts at classifying children with sexual behavior problems indicate quite clearly that this is a diverse group. In the same way that there is no single and certain profile for an adolescent or adult sex offender, there is no profile for a child who is sexually intrusive. However, children who are either pre-meditative or coercive immediately raise concerns about problematic parental management, coercion in the home, and how to engage a family that typically starts therapy resistant to your efforts.

INTEGRATIVE MODEL FOR UNDERSTANDING CHILDREN'S SEXUAL BEHAVIOR PROBLEMS

Understanding why children develop persistent behavior problems has been the focus of considerable previous research. Mark Greenberg and his colleagues proposed a model derived from developmental psychopathological principles to explain why some preschoolers persist in extreme externalizing behaviors and others do not (Greenberg, Speltz, & DeKlyen, 1993). The model also suggests strategies for sensitive intervention.

Greenberg's model focuses on the interactions between four domains of risk commonly identified as antecedents of problem behaviors. Their model has been validated and includes child biological characteristics, parental management and socialization practices, family ecology, and the quality of early attachment relations. Results from one study suggest that preschool boys with insecure-avoidant attachment and high levels of emotional negativity are at greatest risk for future severe and persistent aggressive behavior (Keller, Spieker, & Gilchrist, 2005).

I borrowed from this framework to create four factors that appear to comprise a reasonable, developmentally sensitive model for how children develop sexual behavior problems. These four variables and how they correspond to Greenberg and colleagues' (1993) components are cumulative stress (family ecology), modeling of coercion (attachment, parental management), tendency toward externalizing behavior (biological features, attachment), and finally, disturbed sexual relating (parental management, attachment; Friedrich, Davies, Fehrer, Trentham, & Wright, 2003). This particular model has been tested with an independent sample (Friedrich et al., 2003), and each of the variables contributes a significant amount of variance to the final equation.

Let's examine each of these variables in turn. Cumulative stress is a summary of the adverse circumstances in a child's life. Evans (2003) suggested that it is the total stress load, and not the individual stressors, that are most closely related to childhood disturbance. Children can tolerate a certain level of adversity, if spread out over their lifetime (Garbarino, 1999). However, children who face parental divorce, poverty, and disrupted parenting all in the first few years of their life are less able to manage their behaviors and emotions, thus leaving them less capable of self-regulation. In fact, a child who has had this level of early stress is more impulsive (Ford et al., 2000), more likely to exhibit symptoms of ADHD (Carlson, Jacobvitz, & Sroufe, 1995), and more likely to be victimized and maltreated (Friedrich, 2002). They are also more likely to be labeled as having bipolar disorder, a diagnosis currently the subject of controversy in children (Garno, Goldberg, Ramirez, & Ritzler, 2005).

However, the model suggests that while cumulative stress creates a vulnerable child, it is not sufficient. Such children need to interact coercively with other children in order to persist in intrusive sexual behavior. This variable is related to the quality of early attachment and the modeling of respectful boundaries that securely attached parents do so well (Crittenden, 1995). Intrusive and coercive styles with others are developed via repeated experiences with either abuse or observing adults abuse each other. These children are then more prone to have externalizing problems, often bullying and treating others cruelly (Troy & Sroufe, 1987).

The last variable in the model is disturbed sexual relating. This may be related to the child's experiences of sexual abuse, living in a home environment with elevated and inappropriate sexual behavior in adults, or exposure to pornography. Families with high rates of violence are also more likely to exhibit sexually deviant behavior in the home setting (Kobayashi, Sales, Becker, Figueredo, & Kaplan, 1995). Children may then learn to relate in a sexually intrusive manner with others, or they may direct their sexual focus at themselves, for example, via masturbation.

Insecure early attachment is also associated with disturbed sexual relating. For example, children with impaired attachment also often have persisting problems with personal boundaries and self-stimulation (O'Connor & Rutter, 2000; Zeanah, Smyke, & Dumitrescu, 2002). While these behaviors may start off as self-soothing, over time they can assume a sexual meaning. Children can incorporate these behaviors into their relational maps (Zeanah, 2000), which may explain why caregivers view children with sexual behavior problems so negatively (Friedrich et al., 2005). Securely attached children can certainly have behavior problems, but they typically are not intrusive, are less clingy, and are more easily satisfied with reassuring pats on the head or the exchange of glances. It does seem that children who are typically intrusive of boundaries are more likely to eventually touch another child or adult in a sexual manner.

MANAGEMENT OF CHILDREN WITH SEXUAL BEHAVIOR PROBLEMS

Since the late 1980s, clinicians and parents have struggled to manage the behaviors of what seems to be a never-ending stream of children with sexual behavior problems. However, I believe there are at least four factors that interfere with our sensitive and informed management of these children.

The first factor is that children do not bring themselves to therapy. A concerned adult brings them. Consequently, it is the adult who has made the decision that the child has a sexual behavior problem. Parental decision making is subject to parental biases and misperceptions, which are exacerbated given the lack of systematic research on sexual behavior in children. These misperceptions can include a distorted perspective about a particular child in their care; for example, behavior may be seen differently if it comes from a boy rather than a girl. Consequently, the clinician owes it to all parties to sort through the operative biases, including their own.

A second factor is that many clinicians still automatically correlate intrusive behavior with a history of sexual abuse. They fail to appreciate the numerous pathways that can lead to sexual behavior, including impulsivity, a common feature of young children. The nonabused children who see these therapists sometimes endure repeated questioning about possible sexual abuse. The net effect is that the therapeutic relationship cannot move forward.

A third factor is that parents and clinicians fail to appreciate that some intrusive behaviors are relatively benign and surprisingly common. For example, the parents of roughly 25% of children between the ages of 4 and 7 report that their child has played doctor with a similarly aged child (Larsson et al., 2000). This frequency is likely to be an underestimate for several reasons. First, parents are unable to observe the entirety of their child's behavior. Second, Lamb and Coakley (1993) found that 80% of college undergraduate females reported sex play with peers prior to the age of 12 years. A behavior this frequent is very difficult to pathologize.

The fourth factor is that the therapies provided to children with sexually intrusive behavior are typically downward extensions of adult and adolescent sex offender therapies. These treatment approaches are largely informed by cognitive therapeutic approaches (Bonner et al., 2000) along with relapse prevention activities (Cunningham & MacFarlane, 1991). There are many reasons to question the validity of these approaches with children.

The primary reason is that important relational factors get ignored. As you will see, children with sexual behavior problems have extremely high levels of insecure attachment. They typically grow up in multiproblem families characterized by parent-child relational strain (Friedrich et al., 2003; Hall et al., 1998; New, Stevenson, & Skuse, 1999). By encouraging the parent to behave less intrusively and with more sensitivity, the child's relational problems will have a greater probability of improving as well.

Another reason is developmental. Cognitive therapy requires mature cognitive capacities, and therefore cognitive therapy with preteen children is typically more rudimentary and ends up being predominantly psychoeducational. This may represent an adequate initial effort, but it is not going to correct cognitions. The behavior of sexually intrusive children is also less likely to be cognitively driven. Finally, cognitive interventions for externalizing children work best when combined with parental behavior change (Brestan & Eyberg, 1998).

A third reason why cognitive therapeutic approaches may be inappropriate for children is that most adolescent sex offenders never reoffend sexually. Rasmussen (1999) found that only 7.6% of her sample of first-time juvenile sex offenders, followed over a 5-year period, committed another sexual offense. Barbaree, Marshall, and Hudson (1999) found that only 10% of adolescents who have been charged with a sexual offense reoffend sexually. Recidivism rates for treated and nontreated adolescent offenders ranged from 5.2% for the treated group to 17.8% for the nontreated group (Worling & Curwen, 2000).

Other research with larger samples has found that recidivism varies with the personality type of the teenage offender. For example, Worling (2001) identified four clusters in teenage offenders: antisocial/impulsive, unusual/isolated, overcontrolled/reserved, and confident/aggressive. He found that teenagers in the antisocial/impulsive and the unusual/isolated clusters were more likely to reoffend either sexually or nonsexually than the less severe personality types of overcontrolled/reserved and confident/aggressive.

These studies clearly indicate that sexual reoffending occurs in a minority of adolescents. Most likely the small group differences between treatment or no treatment conditions are due to the fact that adolescents who touch other children are a diverse group. Few teens persist in this pattern once they have access to same-age sexual partners. Their reoffense rates are considerably lower than the reoffense rates for adult sex offenders (Barbaree et al., 1999; Hall, 1995).

Consequently, the relative absence of treatment versus no treatment differences is not necessarily due to the efficacy or lack thereof of cognitive-behavioral therapy with this group of teenagers. The lack of differences reflects the fact that few reoffend once their hand is slapped. However, this knowledge has not translated into policy changes. Rather, it appears that policy setters are even more determined to punish juvenile sex offenders and in a similar manner pathologize the sexual behavior of preteen children. Zimring (2004) noted that the number of treatment programs for juvenile sexual offenders has grown dramatically since 1980 (see also the data from Longo & Prescott, 2005, cited in Table IN.1).

INITIAL IDENTIFICATION: DISTINGUISHING NORMATIVE FROM PROBLEMATIC SEXUAL BEHAVIOR

Let's reexamine the relatively common childhood behavior of playing doctor. It is a behavior that involves the elements of inappropriate sexual behavior. There are at least two children who expose their genitalia and maybe even touch each other. So what is it that moves playing doctor into the realm of something that warrants intervention?

Eliana Gil and Toni Johnson (1993) developed very useful guidelines and suggested that such features as similar age, size, and developmental status characterize natural and healthy sexual behaviors between children. In addition, the child's participation is voluntary, the behavior seems mutually enjoyable, and the children are friends or acquaintances. Playing doctor is not primary since the child has a balanced social life and the behavior stops when the children are instructed not to act in this manner.

PERSPECTIVE

Even if playing doctor is benign, an adult makes the decision about whether or not the child needs help. The individual sexual behavior that the child exhibits can be very concerning, but the key variable is the parent's perspective about the behavior in question. Do parents think that these things happen, the behavior is a rare occurrence, and the child is normal? Or do they pathologize the behavior, impose their adult perspective onto the behavior, and label it sexual, rather than something many children do?

I learned a great deal about perspective in my research with the first version of the CSBI. After running the analyses on the first normative sample (N = 880; Friedrich et al., 1991), I was truly amazed that each item had been endorsed by at least some parents. All of these were parents who had assured me that their child had not been sexually abused. I became convinced that some of the parents had misread the questionnaire and asked my IRB (Institutional Review Board) for permission to contact a few of them and double-check that they meant to endorse such items as "Puts objects in vagina or rectum" and "Puts mouth on another child's sexual parts."

I contacted a total of 12 parents from this large sample and each one reassured me that they had observed the behavior and their report was accurate. All but one of these parents had a benign interpretation of their child's behavior (e.g., "Boys will be boys"). While each of their children exhibited an overtly sexual behavior, it was not a persistent, genitally focused behavior of the type that characterizes the sexual behavior of adolescents and adults. In addition, the focus did not seem to be arousal, but a combination of exploration, happenstance, impulsivity, and curiosity.

One of these mothers endorsed the item "Puts objects in vagina or rectum" for her 4-year-old daughter. When I called her, she reported that she had seen this behavior only once. She was helping her daughter undress for a bath and a small doll fell out of her child's panties. She asked her why she had a doll in her panties. The mother reported that her child got very excited and said, "I got a little pocket between my legs and it fits in there so nice." The little 4-year-old then tried to demonstrate this to her mom, who told me, "I had to work hard to keep a straight face when she did this." The mother recalled telling the girl that she should probably not be doing that and said that she had seen no further instances. She also agreed that the daughter did not put the doll into the vaginal introitus but only between the labia. Technically, this was not insertion into the vagina, a behavior that has been accurately reported by parents. When present, insertion is much more serious and concerning, as the act can be painful and represents an unusual developmental knowledge of anatomy (Hewitt, 1999).

Another example comes from parents who express concern, in the case of two same age–same sex children playing doctor, that the children's actions are a sign of future homosexuality. If a parent has a pathological perspective on the young child showing his or her genitals to another same-sex child, I believe the parent signals the importance of this behavior to the child via some action. For example, the parental response is often rejecting. They may get overly angry, insult the child, or refuse to look at the child for some time. The child will think, "Oh, I did something wrong." If the history of the parent-child relationship is generally positive, the two move on and there will be little likelihood of reoccurrence. But reoccurrence is more likely when the relationship is strained or characterized by coercion, and the parent's negative reinforcement often activates an escalation in behavior by the child (Patterson et al., 1992).

Case Example: Two Cousins

A few years ago I had the privilege of conducting a clinical "experiment" that illustrates this point perfectly. Over a 6-month period, I met with two 8-year-old female cousins and their mothers, who were sisters. When they were 7, these girls had shown each other their genitals at a family get-together. Neither mentioned anything to their parents at the time. One year later, they saw each other at another family get-together. The next day, one cousin told her mother that she and her cousin had "kissed each other down there." The sisters spoke and each agreed to pursue professional input in their hometowns.

I met the first cousin, a highly embarrassed girl who was also quite angry with her mother (who had informed her daughter that all future sleepovers with friends were off until they could meet with me). The mother was laudatory of her daughter and expressed surprise at the recent behavior, but also said she was aware that sometimes this was just something that kids do. She did not believe her daughter had been sexually abused. The family had no pornography in the home, and the girl had no access to the Internet. She reported that she was in a good marriage, had no history of victimization, and that her daughter was doing well in school both academically and socially. A review of safety (see Safety Checklist, Form B, in Chapter 8) found no areas of concern.

When I met separately with the girl, she shared with me the earlier play at 7 years of age. She also elaborated on the kissing to state that it involved kissing each other on the lips and nipples as well as some dancing with their clothes off. She was not able to identify any prior abuse, or why these ideas had come to her. On screening measures (described in Chapter 4), risk issues were very low and no other behavior problems were reported. In addition, no boundary problems were noted (see Therapist's Rating Scale, Form D, in Chapter 8).

I made a decision to provide reassurance to the mother and father, and extended an invitation to check in monthly as to any other behaviors that occurred. I suggested to the entire family that these things sometimes come into children's heads and that if they sent positive reports for several months in a row, then the parents could decide if sleepovers were back on the agenda.

The second cousin went to see a therapist who immediately initiated weekly play therapy. Her parents initially supported this action, but after the cousin exhibited some serious behavioral regression (angry outbursts and sleep problems), her mother asked her sister to set up an appointment with me.

I performed a similar assessment and noted primarily strengths in the family and the girl. Both parents spoke of their daughter as having many positive characteristics. They had been confused by what to think about these two instances of playing doctor, but each could see that this was something that kids do. The child denied sexual abuse to me and reported a similar playing doctor situation as had her cousin. I also learned from her that her therapist thought her cousin had sexually abused her. One of her tasks was to write a letter to her cousin to tell her how upset she was.

Once again, I chose to normalize the behavior. When I met with the girl and her parents, I reiterated many of the same things I had said earlier to the first family. We agreed to have monthly phone check-ins and I sent a letter to the therapist explaining my thinking. This girl stopped therapy and quickly returned to normal. The family was grateful, and no signs have emerged in several years to suggest that my conclusions were in error.

This case illustrates the role of perspective as well as the speed with which we pathologize sexual behavior between children. The parents of the second child were less sure how to perceive this behavior. As a result, they initially adopted the therapist's stance that it was deviant and required therapy. The second child reacted with distress to this new perspective, finally exhibiting it at a level that warranted a second opinion.

However, before any of us can assume that it is only the parents' perspective, remember that each child's qualitative experiences of the same sexual interaction may be very different. I have seen several situations where one child seemed more resilient and the other child was actually less so, after what appeared to be a relatively benign, noncoercive interaction. Typically there are comorbid factors that are operative in the symptomatic child and these can be identified with careful assessment.

ASSESSMENT FRAMEWORK

Prior to forming a conclusion that a child's sexual behavior is problematic and developing a management plan, it is necessary to conduct an assessment. The following section discusses important aspects of an assessment including protective and potentiating factors, history of sexual abuse, nature of the sexual behavior, family features, and the child's characteristics.

PROTECTIVE AND POTENTIATING FACTORS

The seriousness of child-child sexual behavior acts should be considered in the context in which they occurred. For example, a 7-year-old boy was observed yelling obscenities from the school bus window. He was already well known to the principal, who called the parents to express her concern. His story was that an eighth grader gave him candy to do this. I asked myself if this was a sexual behavior or an impulsive behavior activated by peer pressure. This is an example of the role of context. Other contextual factors include the child's family history, other comorbid behaviors, and the child's developmental level.

Based on the research described earlier in this chapter, I have compiled a list of factors that appear to protect, or reduce the severity of a child's sexual behavior versus potentiating, or increasing the seriousness of this behavior. Table 1.3 illustrates a framework that describes both protective and potentiating factors. The variable clusters included are sexual abuse history, the nature of the act, family features, and child features.

So how do you use the information in Table 1.3 to guide your assessment? The more potentiating factors checked relative to protective factors, the more likely the behavior warrants clinical attention and ongoing monitoring of the child via therapy. The critical variables are the family variables. For example, I opted to make a case to simply monitor two older boys, ages 11 and 12, whose sexual behavior with younger children was quite adultlike, because of the complete absence of family risk factors. This allowed them to remain free of the criminal justice system, where they were headed if the judge had not agreed with my conclusions. After several years of follow-up, no other behaviors emerged and I had to conclude that these were random, impulsive acts and were unlikely to ever reappear.

However, the accuracy of the information a clinician receives depends largely on the parent and child. Both may be poor reporters because of defensiveness, lack of awareness, avoidance of painful topics, or reduced expressive language. When the source of information is doubtful, plan for closer monitoring in the context of regular therapy.

SEXUAL ABUSE HISTORY

Table 1.3 Decision-Making Criteria for
Children With Sexual Behavior Problems

VARIABLE		PROTECTIVE FACTOR	POTENTIATING FACTOR
Sexual abuse	1.	No history of sexual abuse	History of sexual abuse
Sexual behavior	2.	Self-focused	Other-focused
	3.	Mutual	Coercive
	4.	Spontaneous	Premeditative
	5.	No contact	Penetration
	6.	No age difference	Age difference
	7.	Single victim	Multiple victims
	8.	No status difference	Status difference
	9.	Single act and type of act	Multiple acts and types
	10.	Not focused on arousal	Arousal and genital foci
Family features	11.	No other maltreatment	Other maltreatment
	12.	Secure attachment	Insecure attachment
	13.	No parental history of sexual abuse	Parental history of sexual abuse
	14.	No domestic violence	Domestic violence
	15.	Family stability	Family instability
Child features	16.	Internalizing problems	Oppositional defiant disorder/ conduct disorder
	17.	Positive peer relations	No positive peer relations

The research review at the beginning of this chapter found variable rates of prior sexual abuse, dependent on the age, gender, and composition of the sample. A history of sexual abuse is a potentiating factor for several reasons. First, a history of any form of maltreatment predisposes the child to insecure attachment (Cicchetti & Toth, 1995) and behavior problems (Erickson & Egeland, 1987). If children respond to sexual abuse by acting out sexually, does this mean that their experience is more salient? Did it shape their view of relationships so much that they are now acting on it? With younger children, the mimicry between their sexual abuse experiences and their subsequent behavior is often startling. Some children will repeat the same acts and use the exact words or implements with one or more children that had been used with them (Friedrich & Luecke, 1988). The degree to which children act out their prior abuse also sets them up to develop a learned pattern of sexualized responses to other children—neurons that fire together wire together (Siegel, 1999).

Nature of the Sexual Behavior

A total of nine features of the sexual act are considered in the category of the nature of sexual behavior. My clinical impression, and that of Hall and her colleagues (2002) is that self-focused sexual behavior problems such as masturbation are less worrisome than other-focused behaviors. However, that is not a universal rule. For example, in my experience, very young children who become skilled at masturbation have often been taught the technique as part of either sexual abuse or the grooming that precedes abuse. I think that this subgroup of children who have a more developmentally advanced approach to masturbation are quite concerning, since the children often have other, more intrusive sexual behaviors in their repertoire.

How children masturbate also seems to be related to how they learned to masturbate. Using the treatment manual described in Chapter 8, I have treated 13 children whose primary sexual problem was high levels of masturbatory behavior. Eight of these were girls who fell into two categories based on how they masturbated. Those girls who used their hand and were more directly stimulating were more likely to report having been sexually touched on their genitals. The group who masturbated by moving against a stuffed animal, clenching their legs or contorting their body in some fashion were typically unable to report whether they had been molested, although the suspicion was elevated for all but one of them.

These cases present several levels of difficulty based on their history. For example, one 8-year-old girl was in foster care and generally adapting well, other than the fact that she masturbated most nights by rocking against a stuffed animal. The fact that she was so overt—she panted and perspired heavily—seemed to concern her caregivers the most. I treated her by rationalizing that by her age, she should learn to be more discreet. In addition, she had problems with personal boundaries when I met her. Prior sexual abuse seemed likely after I spoke to the caseworker, which I justified as another treatment issue. By the end of therapy, her foster mother liked her more since the behavior had diminished, and that also seemed to be helpful to her adjustment.

In general, children quickly learn to hide their masturbatory behavior. Consequently, I am left with some questions when foster parents report that a preteen masturbates every night as part of falling asleep. First, is it truly masturbation? Is it a comforting, learned response that is not masturbatory? What is the child thinking during this activity? Preteens that I meet are usually not very forthcoming about their thoughts or fantasies at these times. My suggestions to parents include finding ways for children to tire themselves out before bed by doing a calming, soothing activity, and teaching parent and child other means of falling asleep (e.g., via imagery, etc.). However, if the stimulation alienates peers or is injurious, it would move the child into a higher risk category.

A factor to consider when another child is involved in the sexual behavior is whether the act was mutual or if any coercion was involved. You will want to ask whether the child or children involved exhibited planning and forethought, rather than impulsivity, with the former implying more reason for concern. Children are very concerning when they are preoccupied with pornography, fail to respond to limit setting, and their sexual behavior interferes with peer activities.

Another factor pertaining to the nature of the sexual act includes frequency, as well as persistence, particularly after limit setting by a caregiver. Sexual behavior that is more adultlike usually indicates that the child has a connection between the behavior and arousal, which serves as further reinforcement of the behavior. I have learned not to be surprised when I hear that the parents of children with sexual behavior problems have never set consistently clear limits with the child. Once limits are established, milder cases are quickly corrected.

Finally, the more genitally focused the behavior where arousal is the goal, the higher the probability that the child has been eroticized. The child has precociously learned that sexuality can be a primary emphasis since it is pleasurable. Genitally focused behavior reflects more of a preoccupation, particularly in older children, and is less related to impulsivity.

A companion set of descriptors of the sexual behavior comes from Hall and her colleagues (1998). These are: (1) nonmutuality; (2) harm or discomfort caused in others or self; (3) complaints by others; (4) differential power, behavior/not between peers; (5) persistence despite limit setting by others; (6) coercion or bribery; (7) force or threat of force; (8) premeditation or planning; and (9) extensive adult-type sexual behavior. Some of these overlap with Table 1.3 and can serve to refine your assessment of the severity of the child's intrusive behavior, separate from contextual features.

Another act-related factor is the age difference of the children involved. It seems more likely that no age difference would be a protective factor. The same would be the case for status differences. Playing doctor between two peers by itself is likely to be more benign than if there is a power imbalance and one of the children has a history of bullying the other. In fact, Lamb and Coakley (1993) wrote that age and status differences were associated with a less positive perspective by female undergraduates who were reporting about their child sexual play experiences.

FAMILY FEATURES

Characteristics of the family have the greatest potential to protect the child and over time shape the child's behavior so that it is more appropriate. A key aspect is the absence of other maltreatment. This is most likely in the context of secure attachment, a critical protective factor. The clinical presentation of a securely attached parent and child are described in some of my earlier writing (Friedrich, 1995, 2002). These parents' interactions with their children are typically sensitive and not overwhelming. When a referred child is actually better behaved with you in the absence of the parent, you have reason to believe that the parent does not represent safety or security to the child and, hence, is not a positive model of nurturing and respectful interaction.

Families that are characterized by domestic violence and a parental history of sexual abuse potentiate the intrusive sexual behavior because they are accompanied by less consistent models of adult self-control (Friedrich, 2002). Stable families characterized by intact marriages are also protective. All of the protective factors in this domain prevent the child from feeling overwhelmed and out of control, or dysregulated (Friedrich, 1995). A central contribution of secure attachment is that the child is able to manage overwhelming thoughts and feelings and remain resilient in the face of stress (Siegel, 1999). The child has internalized a sense of security and safety.

CHILD FEATURES

A careful assessment of the child's predisposition to acting out or behaving provocatively will help you place the behavior into a more understandable context. This means that it is critical to examine for any history of defiant or disruptive behavior, which could range from ADHD to conduct disorder. In addition, the more socialized children are, as manifested in good peer relations, the more likely they are to have a positive manner of relating to other children. Interacting sexually is just not as salient to well-socialized children whose history of social interaction involves sharing and mutuality. Their motivation is to make friends, not drive them away.

DEVELOPMENTAL DIFFERENCES IN ASSESSMENT AND TREATMENT

It is essential to look at sexual behavior in children, including intrusive behavior, with a developmental perspective. It is inappropriate to use adolescent or adult perspectives with these children. For example, it is inappropriate to view these children as having a paraphilia, or to assume that their arousal patterns are fixed and that recidivism is likely (Chaffin et al., 2002). We also must appreciate that their family relationships are critical. However, it is appropriate to think that children may reflect a different compilation of etiological factors than do adolescents, and that adolescent offenders differ from both adult offenders and children with sexually intrusive behavior.

What do we truly know about the long-term behavior of a child who exhibits intrusive sexual behavior? What percentage goes on to either reoffend or become an adult that sexually offends? There are no consistent, irrefutable sources of data for us to turn to for answers.

One study that helps to begin answering this question comes from David Burton (2000). He examined three groups of incarcerated teens ($N = 263$). One group had a history of sexual aggression only before the age of 12; another had a history after the age of 12; and a third exhibited a pattern of offending before and after the age of 12. This group was labeled continuous offenders. More than 46% of the sexually aggressive teens began their offending behaviors before the age of 12, and level and complexity of the perpetration acts were more severe for the continuous offenders than for the other two groups. The earlier and more continuous the pattern of offending, the more likely the preteen is to go on to more severe activities.

This finding echoes what is known for conduct-disordered youth who are labeled either life course persistent or adolescent limited (Moffitt, 1993). The life-course-persistent offenders typically exhibited interpersonal aggression by kindergarten and were three to four times more likely to be involved in the criminal justice system as adults than the subgroup who first offended as teenagers. We do not have the longitudinal research to help us understand what percentage of sexually intrusive children might truly fall into a life-course-persistent category.

While these data need to be considered when assessing a child with sexual behavior problems, there are no data to indicate that preteens with sexual behavior problems are budding juvenile sex offenders. Courts that routinely order these preteens into a sex offender treatment program, without appreciating their diversity, are acting in error. While I have evaluated many sexually aggressive preteens about whose future I am very pessimistic, I have evaluated vastly more for whom I am optimistic, and subsequent follow-up supports my initial optimism.

Consequently, developmentally sensitive alternatives to the treatment of these children are still warranted. We must be aware of our "adultcentric" perspectives on sexuality and separate those from developmentally more appropriate perspectives. Rather than criminalize these children, we must argue for sensitive responses (Chaffin & Bonner, 1998).

An example comes from two boys, a 9-year-old and a 4-year-old, who put their mouths on each other's penises. When their mother found them upstairs, they were very embarrassed, but eventually she heard from them, "I licked his since it looked like a popsicle and I wanted to see what it tasted like." An evaluation of the 9-year-old found him to be moderately delayed, and the developmental difference between the two boys was minimal. It was determined that these were two impulsive, nonabused boys who engaged in this behavior because to them, penises did look like popsicles. This was a far cry from the sexual motives that the older boy was first impugned with.

There are other developmental considerations in childhood sexual behavior. One of these relates to age trends in overt behavior. While it is true that some of the dropoff in reported sexual behavior is due to children becoming increasingly discreet and hiding from their parents, school-aged children are less overt about sexual behavior. Latency-aged children who are more overt are outliers and come to our attention, sometimes because they have been abused but other times because they are not as socially skilled.

Another critical assessment dimension is the context of the sexually aggressive behavior. A behavior tells us little without consideration of the behavioral context. For example, what happens if you take the behavior, "Touches another child's sex parts" (CSBI Item 9) reported by the mother of an 11-year-old boy, and examine it more closely? The behavior in question was directed at the boy's 8-year-old stepsister, who just prior to the event had insulted him; he retaliated by grabbing the front of her T-shirt and pinching her chest in the process. The context variables described above, particularly if this was a one-time incident, would minimize the sexual severity of this behavior and more precisely capture it as peer retaliation.

Earlier in this chapter, I mentioned the dearth of studies of teens with a history of sexual abuse. Research on adolescents can also indirectly inform us about the persistence of sexual behavior problems in victims. For example, 38% of sexually abused adolescents, in two of three studies reviewed in Kendall-Tackett and colleagues (1993), displayed promiscuity. Since that review, several other studies have been published. Sexually abused adolescent males who were psychiatric inpatients had significantly more sexual concerns (Hussey, Strom, & Singer, 1992). A more recent longitudinal study found that sexually abused teenagers were significantly more likely to have become pregnant than their nonabused counterparts after 5 years had elapsed (Swanston, Tebbutt, O'Toole, & Oates, 1997). Research with the Adolescent Clinical Sexual

Behavior Inventory has found that both parents and teens report more risky and self-destructive sexual behavior and a greater number of sexual partners in teenagers with a sexual abuse history compared to those without that history (Friedrich, Lysne, Sim, & Shamos, 2004). All of these studies indicate that, at least for a subset of teenagers, sexual behavior problems can persist for years.

FREQUENCY OF INTRUSIVE BEHAVIOR IN NONCLINICAL CHILDREN

In addition to the qualitative and diagnostic features described above, data now exist on the frequency of intrusive and self-stimulating behavior in preteen children. This information, which is derived from research with the CSBI (available from www.parinc.com; Friedrich, 1997), can be useful in gaining an appreciation for the relative frequency of intrusive behavior in a normative sample of children (N = 1,114) screened for the absence of sexual abuse and developmental delay. For example, while you may never have met an 8-year-old boy who has flashed another child, it can be very helpful for you to appreciate that 4.7% of the 6- to 9-year-old boys in the normative sample have done this at least once in the last 6 months. This information can temper your understanding of such a boy who may now be sitting in your office. For example, you may think about alternate explanations, such as ADHD, for the behavior. It is also helpful to know that the frequency of this behavior goes up in children with behavior problems (Friedrich et al., 2001). Table 1.4 describes the most relevant frequencies.

A consistent feature of the sexual behaviors listed in Table 1.4 is a reduction in frequency as the child gets older. While one can make a good argument that this reduction is in part a function of fewer opportunities for parents to observe peer activities at the older ages, there are two other, reasonably compelling reasons. The first is that the majority of children find their time occupied by more normative peer and academic activities as they move through elementary school. The second is that children of this age know the rules of social interaction, regulate their emotions, and, in fact, typically behave in quite conventional ways (Cole, Martin, & Dennis, 2004). For example, CSBI Item 27 (kisses other children) is endorsed by 8.1% of parents for 2- to 5-year-old boys and 7.1% for 2- to 5-year-old girls. This drops to 1.0% and 1.2% respectively for the 6- to 9-year-old boys and girls (Friedrich, 1997).

Another feature is that while intrusive behaviors are of low frequency overall, they are still present to some degree, particularly in younger children. However, as noted in Table 1.4, very small percentages of 10- to 12-year-olds

Table 1.4 Percentages of Sexually Intrusive Behaviors by
Boys and Girls Across Three Age Groups

	BOYS/GIRLS 2–5	BOYS/GIRLS 6–9	BOYS/GIRLS 10–12
7. Touches mother's breasts	42.7 / 43.7	14.1 / 15.9	1.2 / 1.0
9. Touches other child's sex parts	4.5 / 8.8	7.9 / 1.2	1.2 / 1.0
10. Tries to have intercourse	0.3 / 1.1	0.0 / 0.0	0.0 / 0.0
11. Puts mouth on sex parts	0.7 / 0.0	0.0 / 0.0	0.0 / 0.0
13. Touches adult's sex parts	7.7 / 4.2	1.6 / 1.2	0.0 / 0.0
14. Touches animal's sex parts	2.8 / 2.5	0.5 / 0.6	0.0 / 0.0
16. Asks others to do sex acts	0.4 / 0.4	0.5 / 0.0	0.0 / 0.0
24. Kisses adults not known well	7.8 / 6.0	1.0 / 2.4	3.7 / 1.1
27. Kisses other children	8.1 / 7.1	1.0 / 1.2	0.0 / 1.1
29. Undresses other children	1.4 / 2.1	1.0 / 0.0	0.0 / 0.0
33. Shows sex parts to children	9.2 / 6.4	4.7 / 2.4	0.0 / 1.1
34. Undresses adults against their will	4.2 / 2.1	0.5 / 1.2	0.0 / 0.0

Source. From Friedrich (1997).

are reported to exhibit a few of the intrusive behaviors; for example, Items 7
(2.2%), 9 (2.2%), 24 (4.8%), 27 (1.1%), and 33 (1.1%), and these percentages
are derived from children without a history of sexual abuse. A nonpatholo-
gizing perspective, which is appropriate for many children, would be that,
though these behaviors do exist, they are rarely observed and may not have
any deep, pathological impact on either child involved.

So what do you do when you meet a child who has touched another child's
sexual parts (CSBI Item 9)? Begin the process by first appreciating that this is
not that uncommon, particularly for younger children. Do not initiate interventions without gathering other information. Evaluate other behaviors the
child exhibits, and the context in which the behavior occurred. In addition,
determine how their primary caregiver interprets the behavior. If the parent
is willing to hear that this has happened, is not immediately defensive, and
does not deny the behavior or blame the other child, these are additional
protective factors. The tipping points that move you from no intervention to
monitoring plus some intervention to weekly therapy appointments, or some
point in between, are not easily quantified, but they will become clearer with
each child you see.

BASE RATES

The fact that intrusive sexual behavior does occur in a nonclinical sample
leads directly into a discussion of base rates, a concept that is very important

to understand (Wood, 1996). Base rates are the frequency at which a behavior is present in the environment for various groups of individuals. While intrusive sexual behavior is more common in sexually abused children, the total number of sexually abused children is still smaller than the total number of nonabused children.

An example illustrates these different frequencies for a town with 27,000 preteens. I have established the arbitrary rate that one in nine of the children has been sexually abused. The intrusive behavior in question is "touches another child's sex parts." This behavior is reported in 4.1% of the non–sexually abused group. This frequency is then contrasted with the frequency of 24.95% for sexually abused children. (The rates for the two groups were calculated by adding the frequencies for the six age and gender groups and then dividing by six.)

Sexually Abused	Non–Sexually Abused
3,000	24,000
$\times .2495$	$\times .041$
748	984

Even if sexually abused children are six (.2495 vs. .041) times more likely than nonabused children to "touch another child's sexual parts," non–sexually abused children are 1.3 (984 vs. 748) times more likely to be identified as sexually intrusive. This is due to differences in base rates and percentage of the sample that is affected by the problem (touching another child's sex parts).

There is a big difference between 4.1% and 24.95%. And if you ignore base rates, you could say that this behavior is six times more likely to occur in sexually abused children. You could then operate on the erroneous assumption that the majority of children who touch another child's sexual parts have been sexually abused.

When these frequencies are plugged into the example above, one can see that more nonabused children exhibit this behavior than do abused children, despite the higher frequency in the sexual abuse sample. This fact does not remove this behavior as potentially indicative of sexual abuse, but it does necessitate that you examine the behavior more closely and consider alternate explanations. For example, it is possible that a sexually abused child will exhibit this behavior at a higher intensity, for example, touching another child four times rather than once. Intensity of the sexual behavior, over and above absolute frequency (yes or no) may distinguish a child who does this once from a child who is persistent. However, knowledge derived from base rates should also lead us to wonder what other pathways exist. A nonabused child might exhibit this behavior or, for that matter, a sexually abused child may not exhibit this behavior.

CONCLUSION

Children with sexual behavior problems come to your office via a number of pathways. The severity of their problems will vary from mild and transient to severe and longstanding. The typologies presented above underscore how varied they can be. Until we have more long-term follow-up information, it will be impossible to determine which of these children do become adolescent and even adult perpetrators. I expect that even a child with a history of acting out in a relatively coercive manner will be affected by the same relational factors Gilgun (1990, 1991) identified in her studies of adults who had a history of sexual abuse but did not go on to offend as adults.

Consequently, careful assessment and developmentally sensitive interventions are necessary. If our field were to pathologize and criminalize preteens with sexual behavior problems as a group, then we would be simply adopting the same inappropriate adult offender perspective that has been applied indiscriminately to many adolescents. However, beginning to act sexually is part of teenage behavior, and it is not part of the preteen's repertoire in our culture. Consequently, it may be that a somewhat larger percentage of preteens who act out sexually have internalized elements of disturbed intimacy seeking or distorted sexual views, compared to adolescents who act out intrusively. These problems are derived via relationships. Given the high percentage of one or more types of maltreatment in the lives of preteens with sexual behavior problems, it is extremely likely that they have insecure attachment and associated problems with interpersonal intrusiveness and reduced empathy and self-regulation skills. I certainly have found this group of children to be uniformly more compromised than their sexual abuse victim counterparts.

Because of this history of early impaired relationships, it is very appropriate that primary treatment is also relationship based. In addition, developmental issues also support treating the child in his or her family and tailoring individual treatment to the child's developmental level. The practicalities of doing this are discussed in Chapters 5 and 6.

2

THE ESSENTIAL ROLE OF ATTACHMENT-BASED FAMILY TREATMENT

FAMILY-BASED TREATMENT for children with sexual behavior problems is a critical component of therapy for these children. Support for this position comes from research on the treatment of oppositional-defiant children, an externalizing disorder. Many of the children who exhibit sexual behavior problems also have a comorbid diagnosis of an emerging or existing externalizing disorder (Hall et al., 2002; Pithers et al., 1998). In addition, intrusive sexual behavior correlates more strongly with the externalizing factor on the Child Behavior Checklist than the internalizing factor (Friedrich et al., 2003). According to the treatment outcome literature, parents are essential to the successful treatment of oppositional children (Brestan & Eyberg, 1998; Kazdin, 2003).

A second reason for a family-based approach is the contribution of family sexuality to the emergence of sexual behavior problems, which is explained in Chapter 3. To lessen the impact of family sexuality, the parents who contribute to it must be involved.

A third reason comes from research on adult romantic relationships, which has implications for how sexual behavior and attachment are interconnected. Data now exist to suggest that adult romantic relationships correspond to the history of attachment security for each individual in the dyad (Hazan & Shaver, 1987). The fact that adult romantic relationships are associated with early attachment history is one more reason to believe that sexual behavior is also related to one's attachment history.

A broader rationale for this book, and much of its theoretical underpinnings, lies in attachment theory. Traumatized children must be considered as part of a relationship. Although the parent figures they live with are often very troubled and bring their own relational and trauma history to the parenting equation, the family remains the arena in which improvements in safety and monitoring occur. A child's attachment insecurity is also related to the emergence of all types of problematic sexual behavior (Zeanah & Zeanah, 1989). In this chapter, I present evidence for each of these points.

Additionally, I outline an attachment perspective to explain how children who have been maltreated and have impaired attachment are at special risk of experiencing subsequent problems, particularly with regard to child sexual behavior. A brief overview of attachment theory is provided along with a review of a model of attachment that explains how cognition and affect become integrated. Next, the research on attachment and sexual abuse is described, as well as the research on attachment and child outcome. Potential family and relational treatment issues will be identified. The malleability of the attachment relationship is also discussed so that therapists have a clearer sense of what can actually change for the better in an initially disturbed parent-child relationship. Finally, a case study is presented that illustrates the dynamic relationship between maternal sexual abuse and child sexual behavior.

OVERVIEW OF ATTACHMENT THEORY

Attachment is a central component of research in the field of developmental psychopathology. One reason for its primacy is that maladaptive functioning is best studied in the context of development and relationships (Sroufe, 1989). Attachment is an instinctual process that guarantees most children a felt security and sets the stage for emotional regulation. Attachment security is enhanced when parents are committed to their children, act in a sensitive and attuned manner, and make efforts to repair ruptures in felt security on the part of children. Attuned and sensitive responding by the parent is essential. An attuned parent's actions will validate the child's feelings on a very basic level, for example, "I am worthy of being noticed," thus enhancing the child's feelings of support and contributing to the child's increasing autonomy with age.

The immature child "borrows' from the parent's mature mind to incorporate answers to such critical questions as "Should I be worried?", "Is she there for me?", and "What should I do next?" (Siegel, 1999). Over time, the attachment dynamics become internalized and aid the child in behaving in a more automatic and efficient manner. The child does not have to reinvent how to behave with each new relationship. This process results in an internal working model, in which both the cognitive and affective components of attachment relationships are encoded (Crittenden, 1995).

The attachment relationship primarily reflects the affective qualities of the parent-child relationship in the first months of an infant's life. However, the infant is also beginning to cognitively appreciate behavioral sequences. He or she is developing a rudimentary but cognitive understanding of the nature of relationships. In most situations, negative emotions will not become too overwhelming for the child because the parent will try to modulate the intensity of the affect. Positive affect is maximized, but it too is modulated. Because of this parental regulation in the attachment relationship, the child will ultimately learn an essential skill: self-regulation.

The development of attachment constitutes an increasingly sophisticated integration of cognition with affect (Crittenden, 1995). For example, the infant begins to recognize a relationship between maternal behavior and how he is feeling. The infant also starts to appreciate the communicative or predictive effect of his affective signals on parental behavior. As the child matures, he will become more capable of integrating these affective signals with his own cognitions about himself and his parents. Interaction with attachment figures influences infants to preferentially attribute meaning to some types of information as opposed to others.

The nature and frequency of these critical early interactions are shaped by parental factors such as depression, problems with intimacy, and having a fragmented perspective about themselves and relationships. For example, depressed parents interact less frequently with their infant (Dodge, 1990; Dozier, Stovall, & Albus, 1999), and the interactions are more negative. Parents who have problems with intimacy and who lack resilience will also have less interaction than is ideal. The fragmented, multiply traumatized parent will add to a lower level of interaction by behaving in ways that are less likely to be felt as safe by the child. A geneticist might say that a depressed parent gives rise to a depressed child via a genetic pathway, whereas I would suggest that the most important early pathway is interactive, and reflects dozens and dozens of interactions per day. When there are problems in parent-child interaction, the child is more prone to subsequent interactional difficulties with other adults, siblings, and peers. Support for the importance of this early attachment security comes from research that has found that traumatized parents who have a history of secure attachment are much more likely to have a securely attached child than are similarly traumatized parents with a history of insecure attachment (Siegel, 1999).

Although the majority of children have secure attachments to their caregivers (typically 60–65% in nonclinical settings), nearly one third of children in nonclinical settings have insecure attachment styles (Ainsworth, Blehar, Waters, & Wall, 1978; Crittenden, 1995). There are three common forms of failure in the parent-child relationship that lead to insecure attachment (Fonagy et al., 1995). First, the parent may not recognize negative affective signals (failure of attunement). Second, the parent may locate the source of the distress but fail to attend to the quality of the distressing affect, and then fail to reflect a combination of congruent affect and mastery in response to the child. Third, the parent may fail to respond empathically to the infant's early manifestations of individuation and intentionality.

Based on this faulty caregiving, insecure attachment styles take three forms: (1) insecure-avoidant, (2) insecure-resistant, and a more recent designation, (3) insecure-disorganized (Ainsworth et al., 1978; Lyons-Ruth & Jacobvitz, 1999). The Strange Situation is a laboratory-based paradigm that was used to formulate the various types of insecure attachment. It is typically reserved for children 36 months and younger, and allows the observer to examine how infants react to separations and reunions both with their parent and with a stranger.

In the Strange Situation assessment paradigm (Ainsworth et al., 1978), avoidant children keep their distance from the parent upon reunion because they have learned that the parent will not meet their needs. In addition, the parent is not necessarily a consistent answer to their distress. This results in the inhibition of affect and teaches infants that the expression of affect is counterproductive. Since the mothers of avoidant infants use affective signals in confusing ways, this is further reason why avoidant children discount affect. Avoidant children are less likely to display distress and consequently their affect is often thought to be false, although their cognitions—for example, about the meaning of parental behavioral sequences—are generally accurate.

The resistant child has typically had an inconsistently reinforcing caregiver, sometimes quite capable and other times deeply frustrating. The mother's affective signals may be clearer than those of the mother of the avoidantly attached child, but she is inconsistently responsive to her infant's signals. In the Strange Situation paradigm, the child responds with frustration upon the caregiver's return, alternately seeking and rejecting the parent's offers of support (Ainsworth et al., 1978). When infants cannot predict the parental response, they become anxious and angry, which has been aptly described as ambivalently attached. For example, physically abused children in day care responded to distress by turning to a caregiver, but the child's approach was characterized by ambivalence (George & Main, 1979). For example, they would turn their back as they approached the caregiver or strike this person as soon as they were close. Ambivalent infants end up reinforced for affective behavior (e.g., whining), but as they become toddlers, they will not have learned cognitive organization (e.g., the predictability of parental behavior). As such, they tend to display very genuine affect when distressed, but differ from the avoidantly attached child in that their cognitions about the parent-child relationship are less accurate.

For many children with sexual behavior problems, the disorganized attachment style seems to have the most relevance for understanding them. A relatively recent discovery, this type of insecure attachment is associated with parents who have a history of unresolved trauma or maltreatment, prolonged absences from their child, substance abuse, maltreatment of their child, or major psychiatric problems (Lyons-Ruth & Jacobvitz, 1999). Caregivers with this type of history will be frightening to the child, and the intimacy of the parent-child relationship may also frighten the parent. The infant's instinctual need for security will result in an insoluble dilemma in which the parent is not the child's source of safety. This contradiction between desire for the parent and fear of the parent is too much for children to integrate into a coherent working model at this early stage of life. Consequently, their behavior in infancy and toddlerhood often is paradoxical and disorganized. Their behavior in the Strange Situation may contain some elements suggestive of secure attachment but other behaviors that are confusing, such as wandering aimlessly when the caregiver returns (Main & Solomon, 1990).

By school age, children with disorganized attachment more consistently fall into one of two categories: controlling-punitive and controlling-caregiving (Lyons-Ruth & Jacobvitz, 1999). Children are classified as controlling if they "seem to actively attempt to control or direct the parent's attention and behavior and assume a role which is usually considered more appropriate for a parent with reference to a child" (Main & Cassidy, 1988, p. 418). The emergence of controlling behavior in the child can lead to a helpless stance by their parent, which may be related to the parent's sense of failure to provide protection or reassurance for the child. Other times both the parent and the child seem helpless in the face of the mother losing control in some manner. Or the parent may report feeling helpless to manage the child's behavior (Lyons-Ruth & Jacobvitz, 1999).

Both of these controlling types are at high risk for externalizing behav-

ior problems. Moreover, these insecurely attached, disorganized children
are considerably less likely than securely attached children to have accurate
and positive views of themselves, interact with others empathically and sensitively, regulate their emotions, and describe their feelings accurately. This
is concerning given that these qualities are also notably absent in individuals
who sexually offend (Marshall, 1993).

A history of severe sexual abuse is prominently mentioned as a primary
contributor to disorganized attachment (Main & Solomon, 1990). The incidence of prior sexual abuse in the parents that I work with is quite high. Disturbances in the parent-child relationship are reflected in several of the risk factors
identified by Hall and her colleagues (1998; see Table 1.1). Each of these is
closely related to the attachment process. For example, having an intrusive
or enmeshed parent-child relationship, which includes role reversal, are two
risk factors from Table 1.1 that are closely related to the insecure attachment.
In addition, PTSD symptoms in the mother—also listed as a risk factor—certainly suggest an elevated probability of disorganized attachment.

AFFECT, COGNITION, AND PSYCHOPATHOLOGY

In contrast to Ainsworth's categorical description, Crittenden has designed
a dimensional model. I spend extra time describing this model—the Dynamic
Maturation Model (DMM)—because it provides a useful way to think about
the diversity of the children you see and what their treatment needs are. Her
model illustrates the nuances in the relationship between parental behavior
and child outcomes (a version of it appears in Figure 2.1). According to Crittenden (1995, 1997, 2006), there is more variability in attachment styles than
the big four of secure, insecure-avoidant, insecure-resistant, and insecure-disorganized. The variability comes from the child's inherent differences as well
as the degree to which the child has integrated affect and cognition. This
variability emerges over time, and some of her categories are not seen until
the child is older. Successful integration of thought, affect, and behavior is
a hallmark of developmental maturity (Sroufe, 1996). The DMM, however,
is incompatible with a model of disorganization (Crittenden, Clausen, &
Kozlowska, 2007) because the distortions described by Crittenden function to
make endangered children safer. The distortions are, in other words, extreme
self-protective strategies that are suited to specific dangerous contexts.

Figure 2.1 Crittenden's Dynamic Maturation Model of Patterns of Attachment in Adulthood (1997)

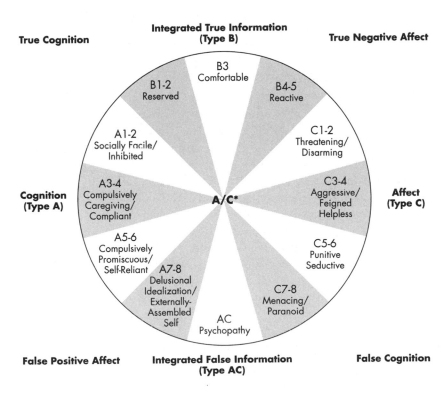

True Cognition — **Integrated True Information (Type B)** — **True Negative Affect**

B3 Comfortable

B1-2 Reserved — B4-5 Reactive

A1-2 Socially Facile/ Inhibited — C1-2 Threatening/ Disarming

Cognition (Type A) — A3-4 Compulsively Caregiving/ Compliant — **A/C*** — C3-4 Aggressive/ Feigned Helpless — **Affect (Type C)**

A5-6 Compulsively Promiscuous/ Self-Reliant — C5-6 Punitive Seductive

A7-8 Delusional Idealization/ Externally- Assembled Self — C7-8 Menacing/ Paranoid

AC Psychopathy

False Positive Affect — **Integrated False Information (Type AC)** — **False Cognition**

Source. From Crittendon (1997).

At the top of Figure 2.1, one can see that the secure (B) children have accurate or truly predictive negative affect and cognition and that these components are integrated (e.g., a secure child might feel and display anger when left by the parent). There is some variability among secure children (i.e., B1–2 reserved, B3 comfortable, and B4 reactive). The reserved group of children possibly reflects some combination of temperament (e.g., slower to warm up), and also maternal affective behavior that mildly discourages children's display of negative states.

---

*A/C is an alternation of any Type A strategy with any Type C strategy. AC (psychopathy) refers to an integraton of A7–8 with C7–8.

Moving down the left side are examples of defended (A) children (called *avoidant* only in infancy). In the DMM, all Type A children inhibit the display of negative affect. Crittenden uses the term *defended* for Type A because these children have learned that close relationships are painful and are defended against them. Because these children still need protection, they develop dispositional representations that enable these relational needs to be met through indirect channels. The A1–2 inhibited group is more likely to have parents who reject unnecessary displays of negative affect, and with whom the child learns to be superficially close but not intimate. Furthermore, the displayed affect of the compulsively Type A child is often false. For example, even when such toddlers are smiling or indifferent at the absence of the caregiver in the Strange Situation, elevated stress-related chemicals in the child's blood system suggest that the child is actually highly aroused with negative affect (Nichols, Gergely, & Fonagy, 2001). The compulsively caregiving A3 children have parents who are often withdrawn and truly unavailable (e.g., neglectful, depressed, psychologically unavailable) and thus need to be actively solicited into the parenting process. A3 children have to work particularly hard to elicit maternal caregiving by functioning as caregivers to their attachment figures.

In a separate study, Crittenden described a group of abused children that she labeled compulsively compliant (A4) (Crittenden & DiLalla, 1988). These children are vigilant, jumping at a parent's smallest cue, and on the surface appear to be remarkably well behaved. This comes at a high price. The child must inhibit accurate, negative affect and substitute false positive behavior. Type A children inhibit the display of the mixture of distressing negative affect that is a natural outcome of harsh or isolating parenting. Often they become unaware of their true feelings.

The experience I have when interviewing these hypercompliant children is that I do not know what they are feeling. During the interview, they do not provide an accurate emotional response to my questions. I am often confused because they present a positive veneer but yet their history and occasional meltdowns with their primary parents, which Crittenden treats as unregulated "intrusions of forbidden negative affect" (2006), suggest otherwise. However, Type A children have more accurate cognitions about what is likely to occur in interpersonal relationships or how they need to behave.

Compulsive promiscuity (social or sexual) and compulsive self-reliance develop in adolescence when no strategy has made the parent safe and comforting. A5-6 adolescents deny their true feelings, including even pain, and either idealize strangers (A5) or avoid intimacy altogether (A6). Often promiscuous sexual displays are false; the individual only wants to attract another person who will end their isolation, however briefly.

Defended children typically do not feel accurately and will deny feeling anger, fear, desire for comfort, and sometimes even pain. Consequently, they engage in much less integration of cognition with affect than Type B (balanced) children. They are well behaved and sometimes socially engaging children who behave in ways that reflect adults' standards well. As a result, adults, including teachers and other professionals, are not made uncomfortable by these children and refer them for psychological services far less than other insecure children. Depression and anxiety, together with psychosomatic disorders, are common, however. In extreme cases, sudden loss of control in a formerly obedient or competent child can lead to diagnoses of psychosis. Because their parents have punished displays of negative affect, either directly or through withdrawal of love, it can be very difficult in treatment to tempt these children to even show negative affect. Until that occurs, the child cannot learn that negative displays have, in moderation, communicative value. That is why both children and their parents must be given a protected context in which to first *experience* displaying negative affect and, later, *regulate* it.

The right side of Crittenden's model in Figure 2.1 illustrates what occurs when the parent's unpredictability makes cognitive prediction suspect but affective responses are more predictable and understandable. Coercive children (Type C), according to Crittenden (1995), alternate coy (passive) and angry (resistant) displays that function to manipulate their parents' response. The angry outbursts of the C1–2 threatening/disarming child, designed to elicit parental response, may be modulated by a quick and disarming smile if the parent responds angrily. A classic example of an exchange between a C1–2 child and the parent that displays evidence of the child's false cognition is when a frustrated parent asks, "Why did you do that?" to which the coercive child replies, "It wasn't me," giving a charming smile.

In fact, coercive children experience anger concurrently with fear and desire for comfort. However, the aggressive (C3) child is much more likely to use very intense anger with only slight modulation, and runs the risk of angry parental retaliation, which will only further solidify the child's angry behavior. By 2 years, this creates a new group of children at risk for abuse. In some cases, caregivers describe passive-aggressive behavior in these children; this may be a version of C4, feigned helplessness.

C5 children are punitively obsessed with revenge; these are typically the bullies, members of gangs, and, in adulthood, potentially abusive to their partners. The persisting bullies from the study by Keller and colleagues (2005) would likely be C5–6 in Crittenden's model because they exaggerate the display of negative affect and dismiss the feelings of others. C6 children, on the other hand, are seductively obsessed with rescue; many take passive aggression to the level of an art form, while others have self-destructive disorders (e.g., eating disorders; Ringer & Crittenden, 2007). C5–6 children (and adults) often use deceptive false cognition to deflect others' attacks.

Coercive children typically do not think accurately about the consequences of their behavior and will deny even the obvious when confronted. Consequently, they engage in much less integration of affect with cognition than Type B (balanced) children. They are tyrants at home but may be fearful about school, new situations, and so on. They exhibit minimal reorganization of their behavior in response to new information, for example, when the parent has genuinely started to change as a result of therapy and become more predictable. Because their parents have used unpredictable, intermittant positive reinforcement of their negative affect, these children regard much speech as unreliable and often fail to respond to new contingencies, thus failing to reorganize their attachment strategy to integrate new information. That is why parents must repeatedly demonstrate new behaviors and articulate the new sequences before any real change occurs in these children.

Crittenden's (1997) DMM also includes two very severe conditions, A7–8 (delusional idealization and externally assembled self) and C7–8 (menacing/paranoid). These individuals use falsified information and are extremely unintegrated with regard to affect and cognition; they are often found in mental hospitals and prisons. On the other hand, when individuals have been very endangered and are also very intelligent, they may integrate the false information, an anti-integration if you will, yielding a dangerously flexible psychopathic strategy (AC). This does not occur before the transition to adulthood (i.e., late teens and early 20s).

There are two key elements to the individuals represented at the bottom of the circumflex in Figure 2.1. First, they are the most likely to have unresolved traumas and losses that will render their behavior non-strategic. Often, this initiates referrals for psychotherapy. Second, when these teenagers and adults utilize false positive affect and false cognition, they struggle with the seemingly impossible task of living in a safe world. Their strategies are adapted to dangerous conditions in which dissociation, a normal function of the prefrontal cortex, keeps them safe. Under safe conditions, dissociation leads to exclusion of important information and (for them) inexplicable outcomes. A particular advantage of the DMM is that it includes sexuality as a component of attachment strategies after puberty. Prior to puberty, it has its roots in (1) arousal regulation through genital stimulation (both calming and arousing) and (2) coy/submissive and angry/dominant signals that function to elicit attention. After puberty, these same signals are used to show sexual interest, i.e., to flirt, thus creating the possibility of misattributions of meaning in the observer. Submissive sexual posturing in young children is particularly common when children are desperate to induce underesponsive parents to take appropriate control, but when viewed by outsiders, it can be misunderstood (by both professionals and perpetrators, albeit differently).

These variations in attachment style, especially A5–6 and C5–6, have the most relevance to our discussion of sexually intrusive children, given the ease with which seeking comfort can translate into sexually seeking contact and comfort. The transition into seductive and promiscuous behavior is hastened with the addition of sexual abuse or an isolating home environment that causes children to seek contact with strangers. For example, I have had a number of unnerving experiences during interviews with preteen victims of sexual abuse where the child was openly flirtatious; it is impossible to know the degree to which their behavior is or is not intended to elicit a sexual response.

In addition to the attachment quality the child has with the parents, we must also consider the socialization of the siblings in these families. In one study of family dynamics, older siblings were found to interact with the infant sibling in a manner similar to that of their mothers. This suggested that they had learned their style of interaction from their mothers. In addition, as the siblings matured, the well-adjusted ones increased their sensitivity to their younger siblings, but the maltreated siblings did not (Crittenden, 1984). The clinical implications for this are clear. Therapy has much more to offer the child with sexual behavior problems when the siblings and parents are also present, and the overall quality of family relations can be addressed and improved.

There is considerable utility in Crittenden's (2006) expanded version of the varieties of children that are subsumed under the labels *secure* and *insecure*. These are children you are more likely to meet clinically. Foster and adoptive parents will tell you, after knowing a child for more than a year, that they still do not truly know this child, or that he or she is sneaky or shows no physical pain or guilt. The reason behind this is often the presence of simultaneous and unintegrated false affect and cognition. This is very different than avoidantly attached children (A), who seem to keep their emotions to themselves, but who clearly brighten as the parent becomes more positive and enthusiastic. This child may still spend some energy worrying about the parent taking antidepressants, but significantly less so.

The disorganized child is also very different from a resistant child (C) who whines about the time and lies about the parent's behavior during the week. However, after successful family therapy, these children will exhibit more mastery of their emotions and will be generally more resilient in the face of minor stressors that in the past would have resulted in a tantrum or other affective display.

CONNECTION BETWEEN ATTACHMENT AND ABUSE

As the previous section described, research has firmly established the vital role that attachment plays in the adaptive functioning of the child. In particular, a secure attachment is central to the development of a positive and accurate view of oneself, empathic and sensitive interactions with others, and adaptive and flexible emotion regulation skills (Cassidy & Shaver, 1999). Unfortunately, children who have been maltreated are at a unique risk for problems in their attachment relationships (Cicchetti & Toth, 1995). In fact, the probability of a child being sexually abused increases with each of the following risk factors: a parent who has been sexually abused, a sexualized home environment or one in which sexuality is avoided, or the experience of other forms of abuse (Friedrich & Sim, 2003). In addition, maternal sexual abuse tends to be associated with psychopathology, limited self-knowledge, and unresolved feelings of anger and sexuality (Dozier et al., 1999). Of special concern is the disorganized and profoundly disturbing parenting that occurs when a parent has a history of unresolved abuse, in which they are frightened by or frightening to the child.

Clearly, these problems place a child at risk for insecure and disorganized attachment relationships and corresponding behavior problems. These problems in functioning can include subsequent victimization, sexual behavior problems, and even sexually intrusive behavior, particularly when predisposing factors such as cumulative adversity, modeling of coercion, and proneness to acting out are present (Friedrich et al., 2003). As such, personal or parental sexual abuse is typically one of several factors in the lives of victimized children that place them at risk for problems in later life.

What does this mean for readers of this book who will subsequently work with these children and their parents? It is important to consider the high frequency of parental histories of sexual abuse. Is this addressed as part of treatment? Is the parent referred elsewhere? If the history of abuse is severe, the parent typically aborts therapy. If such parents can stay in therapy, I make a point of behaving with extra sensitivity, referring to their experiences as such, and helping them use their newfound wisdom about their child in the best way possible. Once I asked a parent, "Is what I just told you something that would have helped you and your mom out if someone had said it back when you were abused?" The parent replied, "I've wished she could be here in these meetings since we started."

There are many ways that sexual abuse in parents' own history can contribute to impaired attachment in their children. The obvious first pathway is true for families in which a child has been sexually abused by another family member. It is impossible to imagine how an incest perpetrator can have anything other than a disturbed pattern of relating with the child victim. In fact, it has been reported that at least 95% of all maltreated children have insecure attachment with the maltreating parent (Cicchetti & Toth, 1995).

One would hope that a child's attachment quality with the nonoffending parent is secure, to balance out the child's insecure attachment with the offending parent. However, there is little systematic research using appropriate assessment techniques (e.g., Strange Situation) that examines the attachment quality of sexually abused children and their nonoffending parents. Nevertheless, there is ample evidence to suggest that many nonoffending parents have their own psychiatric difficulties and abuse histories, factors that can seriously interfere with their quality of attachment with their child (Alexander, 1992; Leifer, Kilbane, & Grossman, 2001).

Two studies come from longitudinal research by the Mother-Child Project at the Institute of Child Development, University of Minnesota. The first study prospectively examined maltreated children in a high-risk sample (Erickson & Egeland, 1987). In particular, this study found that sexually abused children invariably were victims of other types of abuse in their home environment, including neglect and emotional and physical abuse. Presumably, the mother inflicted some of the other abuses, but equally important is the suggestion that sexual abuse is rarely the only adversity in a maltreated child's life.

A second set of studies from this project found a subset of mothers who, during a play observation, exhibited seductive behavior with their children (Sroufe & Ward, 1980). Interestingly, these mothers typically reported a history of sexual maltreatment that had never been treated. Followed over time, children with seductive mothers were rated as the most disturbed subset of children in the sample; indeed, some of the mothers admitted to actually sexually abusing their children (Sroufe, Jacobvitz, Mangelsdorf, DeAngelo, & Ward, 1985). Clearly, the presence of a sexual abuse history in the mother suggests unresolved victimization and disorganized attachment, which hinders a mother's ability to relate nonsexually with her own children.

The Adult Attachment Interview (AAI) was developed from attachment theory and has become a widely accepted and remarkably powerful strategy for retrospectively assessing the attachment status of parents while they were growing up. For example, parents answer questions about characteristics of their own parents, who they turned to in times of stress, their perceptions of their parent's views of them, and so on. Research on mothers' responses to the AAI found that those with unresolved trauma, including sexual abuse, provided narratives in the AAI that violated the numerous criteria that are used to score the quality of attachment (Hesse, 1999). In particular, this research showed that these mothers had disorganized infants and children, failed to see their children accurately, and viewed both their parents and their children in contradictory and even incoherent ways. Consequently, the state of mind of disorganized mothers did not provide the type of reference points that allow their children to think accurately about themselves or be aware of the motivations behind their behavior (Siegel, 1999). I say this since the infant "borrows" from the maternal state of mind to manage relational issues that emerge during development (e.g., "What does that behavior from you mean?" "Am I safe?").

Several studies have been published that report observations of parent-child interaction without utilizing an attachment paradigm. For example, one observational study of children whose mothers had a sexual abuse history found that these mothers tended to be self-focused rather than child focused (Burkett, 1991). They appeared to use their children as a source of emotional support. This reflects role reversal, a dynamic that is often observed in incestuous families. Role reversal appears to be present even when the abuse occurred in the previous generation, once again implicating the "ghosts in the nursery" (Fraiberg, Adelson, & Shapiro, 1975).

However, two publications have raised the possibility of far more variability in the parenting capabilities of women with a history of childhood sexual abuse. For example, one study found that if the mother's life was stable and she reported neither depression nor domestic violence, then her parenting outcomes during the preschool period were not particularly disturbed (Schuetze & Eiden, 2005). The addition of any of these risk factors was related to more punitive parenting by the mother. This opened the door for more behavior problems in the child.

A second study utilized observation of the mother-child dyad during a problem-solving task. These authors found that although abuse survivors rated themselves as less efficacious in parenting, their interactional styles with their children were comparable to those of nonabused mothers (Fitzgerald, Shipman, Jackson, McMahon, & Hanley, 2005).

It is data of this type that helps clinicians understand why some of the families they work with make genuine changes, while others find the accumulation of previous maltreatment in the parenting generation along with current adversity too much to manage. It should give all of us additional hope that our efforts can be successful.

PARENT SEXUAL ABUSE HISTORY AND CHILD OUTCOMES

A number of studies have examined the victimization history and related psychopathology in parents of children who have been sexually abused or have sexual behavior problems. These studies are relevant since psychopathology interferes with normal parenting (Rutter & Quinton, 1984). Parents can influence their child's functioning along several pathways: (1) dyadic interaction between parent and child, (2) coaching and teaching about relationships, and (3) providing an environment that nurtures social activities (Dodge, 1990). Dyadic interaction between parents who are depressed or who have other psychopathologies and their children is likely to be frustrating. They may not offer their children sufficient models of how to solve conflict, share with others, and be empathic. Clearly, parental psychopathology interferes with the quality of parental teaching and coaching, and can even affect the child's willingness to share failures and then together learn from experience. Finally, it can be a formidable task for a single, overwhelmed, and depressed or personality-disordered parent to expose the child to positive peer influences and structure the child's schedule to accommodate social and academic concerns.

George and Main's (1979) research with the children of physically abusive parents comes to mind at this point. These children were often physically aggressive with their parents. The parallel between a child striking a caregiver and physical abuse by the caregiver should be clear. Physically abused children have learned how to behave in a coercive and physical manner with the adults who were coercive and overly harsh with them. I believe this parallel is directly supportive for a similar relationship between sexual exposure of the child via abuse or distorted family sexuality and subsequent sexual acting out. This would be particularly true in those children who fall into the more severe categories developed by Hall and her colleagues, which are discussed in Chapter 1 (Hall et al., 2002).

A study of the Minnesota Multiphasic Personality Inventory (MMPI) profiles of three groups of mothers compared mothers of sexually abused children to mothers who were receiving outpatient mental health services or mothers with no psychiatric history. The study found that mothers of sexually abused children were more likely to have a profile characterized by elevations on

Scales 4 (Hysteria) and 3 (Psychopathic Deviate), including 4–3 and spike-4 profiles (Friedrich, 1991). This was particularly true for mothers of sexually abused children who also had a personal history of sexual abuse. The MMPI code types of these parents have implications for attachment. In particular, the elevation on Scale 4 is often related to issues with sexuality, as well as the expression of anger. The addition of Scale 3 to Scale 4 reflects problems with self-understanding, particularly with regard to understanding one's anger and sexual feelings. Patterson (1980) has found that this latter group of mothers is also incredibly difficult to keep in treatment since they act superficially compliant but then bolt from therapy.

A child's self-knowledge emerges via attachment with a parent who modulates the child (Fonagy et al., 1995; Fonagy & Target, 1997). Clearly, any unresolved parental anger or sexual issues might translate into coercive parent-child behavior. Since the parents have problems understanding themselves and others, they are also likely to have problems understanding the world from their children's point of view, which is a central component of attunement. In particular, a child's normal sexual behavior can be quite provocative to a parent with unresolved sexual issues. As a result, the parent may overrespond or become quite punitive to a child's normal sexual behavior, thus setting the stage for a negative series of interactions. Moreover, these parents may also have partners who sexualize relationships, thus modeling overt sexuality in the home.

In addition, parents with a sexual abuse history may take one of two routes to their own sexuality: hypersexual or inhibited (Downs, 1993; Merrill et al., 2003). Each path may have unique effects on child outcome. For example, hypersexual parents may contribute to a sexualized home environment. In particular, they may either misinterpret normative sexual behaviors exhibited by their child, or, conversely, their relationship with their child may become sexualized. In addition, hypersexual parents are likely to have a history of unresolved abuse, which may affect their relationship with their child (as described earlier). In contrast, parents who respond to their sexual abuse histories through inhibited sexuality (Merrill et al., 2003) are at risk for rejecting their children, because the parenting relationship is so intimate that it can be dysregulating for the parent. They may also further reject their child for exhibiting normative sexual behaviors. This rejection may be a primary component in the creation of coercive interactions between the parent and the child.

To illustrate, New and her colleagues (1999) studied the mothers of boys, aged 11 to 15, who had either victimized other children or had a history of sexual abuse. Mothers of perpetrators reported higher rates of sexual victimization in their own childhood (55%) than mothers of victims (30%). Moreover, both mothers of perpetrators (72%) and mothers of victims (50%) reported high rates of domestic violence. The authors also found a surprisingly high frequency of what they called "repressive coping style" in these mothers. This was defined by the mother's lack of awareness of the needs of those in their care. The authors believed that repressive coping style contributed to these mother's psychological absence.

A colleague and I have examined the relationship between maternal victimization history and child outcome (Friedrich & Sim, 2003) with a consecutive sample of 391 children and adolescents admitted to a psychiatric unit. These children and their parents were assessed with a standard set of screening measures (outlined in Chapter 4). This battery enabled us to assess critical aspects of the parent-child relationship, including child internalizing and externalizing behavior, child sexual behaviors, maternal victimization history, maternal depression, and maternal social support, as well as discipline tactics used by the mother, and maternal negative attributions toward the child.

Overall, we found that mothers with a sexual abuse history, compared to those without one, perceived themselves as having lower levels of social support and higher levels of depression. They also reported more negative feelings toward their children and used more coercive discipline techniques (Table 2.1). In addition, the children of mothers with a sexual abuse history were more likely to have been sexually abused (35%) than those whose mothers did not have a sexual abuse history (17.8%; $\chi^2 = 13.58$, $p < .001$). The children of sexually abused mothers also had experienced more negative life events and exhibited more symptoms of PTSD, as well as increased externalizing and internalizing behaviors, than children whose mothers were not abused (Table 2.1). The groups showed no difference in child sexual behavior, which may have been due to the fact that some victimized mothers are avoidant of sexuality and less likely to report problematic sexual behavior in their children.

Our findings underscore the need to clinically assess the multigenerational symptoms in the families of disturbed children. For there to be improvement in a disturbed child's behavior, parents must correct both their cognitions about their child and the disciplinary strategies they use. Rejecting cognitions and harsh discipline are indicative of attachment problems, which cannot be corrected in individual therapy with the child.

Table 2.1 Means and Standard Deviations of Maternal Characteristics for Mothers With and Without a History of Child Sexual Abuse

	GROUP		T VALUE	df
	No Maternal History of Sexual Abuse (N = 222)	Maternal History of Sexual Abuse (N = 132)		
Coercive discipline tactics (CTS)	.99 (.74)	1.21 (.82)	−2.58**	348
Maternal negative attributions (PCS)	3.31 (.74)	3.15 (.66)	−2.12*	350
Maternal social support (satisfaction item)	2.38 (.79)	1.92 (.97)	4.81***	237
Depression (Brief BDI)	.28 (.37)	.52 (.44)	−5.37***	234
Child life events (LEC)	.14 (.14)	.22 (.14)	−4.88***	352
Child sexual behavior (CSBI)	.21 (.31)	.29 (.38)	−1.25	112
Child intrusive sexual behavior (CSBI–Intrusive behavior items)	.00 (.23)	.18 (.37)	−1.53	112
Child externalizing behavior (CBCL–Externalizing subscale)	60.6 (12.92)	64.3 (12.27)	2.37*	287
Child internalizing behavior (CBCL–Internalizing subscale)	64.1 (11.92)	67.80 (10.45)	−2.67**	287
Child PTSD symptoms (CBCL–PTSD scale)	.58 (.43)	.70 (.43)	−2.34*	294

Note. Means are presented followed by standard deviations in parentheses. CTS = Conflict Tactics Scale (Straus et al., 1998); PCS = Parentification of Children Scale (Friedrich & Reams, 1987); Brief BDI = 13 Items from Beck Depression Inventory (Beck, 1996); LEC = Coddington Life Events Scales (Coddington, 1999); CSBI = Child Sexual Behavior Inventory (Friedrich, 1997); CSBI–Intrusive = Intrusive items from the Child Sexual Behavior Inventory (Friedrich, 1997); CBCL = Child Behavior Checklist–Parent Report (Achenbach, 1991a).
*$p < .05$, **$p < .01$, ***$p < .001$.

ATTACHMENT AND VICTIMIZATION OR VICTIM BEHAVIOR

Insecure attachment is also directly related to subsequent victimization or perpetration, a topic that is certainly relevant to this book (DeMulder, Denham, Schmidt, & Mitchell, 2000; Troy & Sroufe, 1987). The study by Troy and Sroufe is particularly interesting and worth summarizing. They studied pairs of preschoolers who were known to each other and who were observed in free play interactions. Victimization was defined as the presence of an asymmetrical relationship in which one child was actively exploitative and the other child was vulnerable; this dynamic could be readily identified. The victimization behavior observed varied from one dyad to another and included both verbal and physical types. When at least one member of the dyad had a history of secure attachment in infancy, victimization was never observed. When the other member was secure, the play was reciprocal. When the partner was vulnerable, the secure member behaved in a nurturing manner. When the partner was prone to aggression, secure children did not allow themselves to be victimized. In contrast, when at least one member had a history of avoidant attachment, and the partner was vulnerable, victimization ensued. Troy and Sroufe hypothesized that an avoidant child, who was more familiar with rejection and rebuff, would be most likely to act out with another child who was anxiously attached. Keller and his colleagues (2005) also found that avoidantly attached preschoolers were the most likely to persist along a conduct-disordered trajectory, including aggression toward peers.

These findings suggest that if a pattern of distorted sexual interaction is added into the victim-victimizer equation, the interaction can go in a more sexual and pathological direction. This is even more likely to be the case in the presence of predisposing factors, such as cumulative adversity, modeling of coercion, and proneness to acting out (Friedrich et al., 2003).

A variety of other studies have also examined attachment-related variables in the parents of sexually abused children. For example, mothers with a sexual abuse history whose children were also sexually abused had more disturbed relationships with their victimized children and a more negative rearing history, compared to mothers with a sexual abuse history whose children had not been sexually abused, and mothers without a sexual abuse history whose children were sexually abused (Leifer et al., 2001; Leifer, Kilbane, & Kalick, 2004; Paredes, Leifer, & Kilbane, 2001). In addition, parental support has been consistently associated with a sexually abused child's adjustment (for a review, see Elliott & Carnes, 2001). Clearly, parental history of sexual abuse, attachment problems, or current psychopathology can significantly interfere with the level of support they can offer their sexually abused child.

EVIDENCE THAT ATTACHMENT QUALITY CAN BE ALTERED

Hopefully I have impressed upon you the power of parent-child attachment in setting the stage for relationships and behavior problems, particularly those that are related to self-control and the pursuit of intimacy. The point of this chapter is to also provide information about how to improve the attachment quality of the parent and child in front of you. So what does research say about the stability of attachment types over time?

As a matter of fact, attachment stability has been the subject of much research. In fact, there are some findings that are very useful to any of us who intervene with these children and their parents. For example, in the Mother-Child Project at the University of Minnesota, which assessed attachment quality using the Infant Strange Situation, movement of the child from an insecure classification at Time 1 to a secure classification at Time 2 was reliably related to a number of factors. One of the most frequently cited variables was improvement in the mother's overall level of positive social support from Time 1 to Time 2. Her increase in felt support made her a more attentive and attuned parent (Vaughn, Egeland, Sroufe, & Waters, 1979). This certainly suggests that, first and foremost, the parents we work with need to think of us as a supportive presence.

Other research suggests that experience with psychotherapy focusing on prior abuse is also helpful in preventing parents who were maltreated as children from abusing their own children (Egeland, Jacobvitz, & Sroufe, 1988). Research also suggests that insecure attachment may change with positive life experiences, such as becoming a parent or finding healthy friendships and romances (Lichtenstein, Belsky, & Crnic, 1998).

Another study examined foster and adoptive mothers of severely maltreated 4- to 6-year-old children (Steele, Hodges, Kaniuk, Hillman, & Henderson, 2003). Because they were maltreated, these children had been removed from the home of their biological parents. The authors interviewed each of the adoptive mothers with the AAI (George, Kaplan, & Main, 1985) to examine their attachment security. Results showed that after only 3 months of placement, maltreated children gave solid evidence that they were influenced by their adoptive mothers' security of attachment. In particular, children of securely attached adoptive mothers were significantly less likely to generate stories about relationships that had themes of aggressivity and catastrophe than children with insecurely attached adoptive mothers. The children placed with the adoptive parents who were rated as secure on the AAI showed a decrease of close to 70%, whereas no change was noted in the children adopted by parents who were rated as insecure on the AAI.

This is one of those research studies that clinicians love to read. The results showed that after only 3 months of living with a parent who was attuned, calming, noncontrolling, and comfortable with relationships, the children were affected in a profoundly positive manner. They were literally able to borrow from their new mother's state of mind and began to view the world in a new manner; furthermore, their internal map of relationships became more positive. This study provides some of the first direct empirical support suggesting that parental behavior will alter the child's schema of relationships, which is the first step needed for behavioral change to occur. This study also explains in part why it is that some children who may struggle in one foster home will thrive in another, a phenomenon that is well known by therapists and caseworkers.

CONCLUSION

The attachment literature reviewed in the first portion of this chapter illustrates that attachment security dictates relational quality and is affected by parental histories of maltreatment and parental psychopathology. Depending on the parent, the differences emerge in relatively predictable ways. Interventions are needed to help parents realize they need to change their manner of interaction, view their child more accurately, and interact with them less intrusively. The parenting that occurs with insecurely attached and maltreated dyads is also associated with the relative overall reduction in positive interaction between parent and child. In addition, the degree to which parents are supported and can alter their view of relationships will predict the changes children are able to make. Relationship history is related to sexual history, and by improving attachment, we can facilitate improvement in both how children think about relationships and the sexual connotations they place on these relationships.

In addition, maltreated and insecurely attached children exhibit their own set of behavior problems, many of which are truly controlling and punishing of the parent (Kolko, 1996). This can only lead to further distance in the parent-child relationship. An air of hopelessness often pervades these families when you meet them, since they routinely experience frustrations when they do try to connect. They will not be able to change unless they are provided with a detailed road map and receive ample support along the way.

3

THE ROLE OF FAMILY SEXUALITY IN SEXUAL BEHAVIOR PROBLEMS

DISTURBED SEXUAL BEHAVIOR is typically present not only in the child that is referred to you, but also in the child's primary socializing environment, the family. Bolton, Morris, and MacEachron (1989) created an extremely useful model presenting a hierarchy of the family sexual environment. He suggests that two key processes comprise family sexuality. The first is the degree that the parents are both emotionally and physically nurturing to the child. For example, are they child centered and attentive? Do they respond to their child in a growth-enhancing manner? Do they touch, pat, or hug their child appropriately and with some frequency? The parents' optimal actions reflect the best needs of their child and are neither exploitive (e.g., hugging the child does not satisfy any unmet sexual needs of the parent) nor aggressive (e.g., the parent does not hug the child too tightly).

The second process pertains to expressions of romantic love between the parent figures (this includes all variety of parent combinations). It is reflective of the degree to which the parents are comfortable with their own sexuality and physical intimacy. For example, do they appropriately express affection for their partner in front of the child? Is the child heartened by the fact that the parents are close and show their closeness in a way that is not overwhelming? Or are these romantic expressions either excessive or nonexistent? Table 3.1 illustrates the range of family sexuality and also offers a suggestion about whether or not a particular type is abusive (Bolton et al., 1989).

Family sexuality can become confusing and even abusive to the child at either extreme of these processes (e.g., rigid/puritanical or overly provocative/exhibitionistic). In Table 3.1, the environmental vacuum eschews both processes of nurturing and appropriate expressions of romantic love while Level 8 is characterized by a high tolerance for overt sexual behavior between adults

79

TABLE 3.1 Bolton et al.'s Family Sexuality Model: The Abuse of Sexuality

DEVELOPMENTAL ENVIRONMENT	DEGREE OF VICTIMIZATION
1. The ideal environment	
2. The predominantly nurturing environment	Nonabusive
3. The evasive environment	
4. The environmental vacuum	
5. The permissive environment	Abuse of sexuality
6. The negative environment	
7. The seductive environment	
8. The overtly sexual environment	Sexual victimization

Source. From Bolton et al. (1989).

as well as between adults and children. However, there can also be subtle messages sent to children that either reinforce provocative male behavior or diminish and shame females. These messages can take several forms, such as a derisive response when a teenage sibling starts her menses, or fathers putting down mothers in front of their children. Both of these examples communicate very clearly that females have a reduced status in that home.

A related process is the degree to which children are exposed to adult sexuality via the Internet, television, or video pornography. Sometimes this occurs because of poor monitoring by the parent figures. Other times, the parents are cavalier and nonprotective about what their child is exposed to. Often, the longer you work with children who have been exposed to adult sexuality, the more deviations you will observe from what you have long thought to be normal. For example, one 9-year-old began sexually touching younger girls after frequently viewing his young teenage sister having intercourse with a man in his twenties. The sister's behavior was occurring with the full knowledge of the single-parent mother, who became upset with me when I filed an abuse report on the young man. Another 5-year-old revealed that on several occasions he had ridden "horsey" on the back of his mother's boyfriend while this man was having sex with his mother. The mother later confirmed this, and to her credit was appropriately embarrassed when I brought it up.

However, there are other, less overt violations, and the amount of inappropriate sexuality needed to affect a child's behavior will vary from child to child. The "dose" of inappropriate sexuality needed is typically a function of what the child has already experienced in terms of cumulative adversity. For example, if the child has already been exposed to physical abuse or domestic violence, or lived with a depressed parent, a smaller dose may be all that is needed. In all of these cases, family sexuality—not only what children experience or witness but also how they are reinforced when they exhibit typical child behaviors, is extremely relevant in the development of sexual behavior problems.

REVIEW OF RESEARCH

Research indicates that many of the family members of sexually aggressive children were also sexually victimized as children. For example, Gray and her colleagues wrote that even when excluding the index child, 72% of the families in their outcome study included at least one additional sexual abuse victim, with an average of 1.9 ($SD = 1.8$) additional victims. Typically, one of the additional victims was the mother (Gray et al., 1997).

Hall and her colleagues (2002) studied several relevant maternal variables including sexualized appearance and history of sexual abuse, as well as family variables, problematic sexual attitudes, and sexualized interactions. Each of these was examined with regard to the severity of child sexual behavior problems as determined by a five-group typology. None of the mothers in the two least severe groups, that is, "developmentally expected" and "interpersonal, unplanned," were reported to have had a sexualized appearance. However, 65% of the mothers in the most severe group, "interpersonal, planned and coercive," were rated as such.

Maternal sexual abuse history was high across all groups in Hall's study, ranging from 56% to 100%. Neither problematic sexual attitudes nor sexualized interaction were an issue with the two least severe groups, but variably present in the other three groups. For example, sexualized interactions in the home setting were reported for 20% of the self-focused group, 42% of the interpersonal planned group, and 100% of the interpersonal planned and coercive groups.

New and her colleagues (1999) found that mothers of sexually aggressive boys were 1.8 times more likely to have been sexually abused than the mothers of non–sexually aggressive boys (55% vs. 30%). The MMPI profiles of mothers of sexually abused children with a history of sexual abuse, when compared to the mothers without a history of sexual abuse, indicated a greater frequency of profiles associated with sexual impulsivity and sexual acting out in the former group (Friedrich, 1991). These results correspond with research that finds disturbed sexual behavior and distorted perceptions about sexuality to be the most common short-term and long-term consequences of sexual abuse (Widom & Kuhns, 1996).

Finally, in my own database ($N = 305$) of children with sexual behavior problems, over two thirds of the mothers report contact sexual abuse experiences prior to age 18. Information is available on a smaller number of fathers ($N = 78$), but over one third of the fathers reported a similar history. This is slightly more than three times the rate for an upper Midwest male sample (Friedrich, Talley, Panser, Zinsmeister, & Fett, 1997). Slightly fewer than 90% of the mothers reported at least one of the three types of maltreatment screened for (emotional, physical, and sexual).

This research indicates that sexual behavior problems in children are not simply about the child having been molested or having a maternal history of sexual abuse, but rather that they result from different complications of variables that are in part categorized as family sexuality. Paternal history of sexual abuse and its effect on parenting has not been studied systematically, but not only can it distort father-child interactions (in a manner similar to its maternal counterpart), it may also represent additional family risk that the child must face.

Deviance and appropriateness occur in all family types, including heterosexual, homosexual, and bisexually parented families. While heterosexual parents comprise the bulk of the parents I see, the clinician must be cognizant of whether the combination of parents in front of them may contribute to both sexual behavior problems and the family sexual climate. Caregivers whose adult sexual issues intrude precociously and in an overwhelming manner into the lives of their children are those who concern me, and whose sexual behavior in front of their children must be challenged.

It is very important to add here that the first representative and comprehensive study drawn from a national sample found that 12- to 18-year-olds, raised by same- or opposite-sex parents and matched on key demographic variables, did not differ on psychosocial adjustment or school outcomes (Wainwright, Russell, & Patterson, 2004). The study also examined romantic relationships in the 12- to 18-year-olds and found no between-group differences. Not surprisingly, adolescents whose parents described closer relationships with them reported better adjustment.

What the developing research cited above indicates is the frequency of children with sexual behavior problems living in home environments in which problematic sexual behavior is modeled and serves as a template for interpersonal relationships. The poor personal boundaries that are often cited as present in women reporting a history of childhood sexual abuse are likely to serve as one of the models that are imitated by some of their children (DeLillo & Damashek, 2003).

The following case illustrates the need to be both persistent while respectful with parents where you continue to suspect that undiscussed issues of family sexuality are operative.

The A. Family

I started work with A.A., an 11-year-old, and his mother. He had sexually touched his 6-year-old half sister on numerous occasions. It wasn't until his sister finally complained to her teacher that protective services were notified and an appointment was arranged. His mother had been a reluctant participant at the onset of therapy. I was very concerned about her differing views of her children from the outset. For example, during my first meeting with her, she asked several times if I did not think social services were exaggerating the seriousness of A.A.'s actions.

A.A.'s behavior with his mother was extremely variable. For example, during the first child-directed interaction portion of parent-child interaction therapy (Hembree-Kigin & McNeil, 1995), he was very critical of her efforts to praise him. Yet during the same coaching session, he draped his arms around her, occasionally gave her a loud kiss, and typically pushed his chair to be right next to her. To me, they felt like a couple—one with a highly conflicted and ambivalent relationship.

She had earlier denied that either of her children slept with her or that there were any problems with family nudity. These were in response to questions from the Safety Checklist. By the sixth session, she seemed to be more invested in therapy, and I took a risk and asked her again, without A.A. present, about the most recent cosleeping and cobathing with him that she could recall. She became embarrassed and looked ashamed. She never fully shared the exact frequency with me but she did admit that for the sake of convenience she and A.A. would "sometimes" shower together. The pattern had started at the beginning of the school year to prevent him from being late for the school bus. The current frequency appeared be one or two times per month at a minimum.

I reiterated the need for reducing his confusion about boundaries, but I adopted a one-down stance when I confronted her. I started off by saying that I knew I had emphasized the need for her to repair their relationship. I added that she was doing some of that by putting up with my coaching of her. I then said that maybe she was trying to help out the relationship with this behavior. I also added that I should have been clearer that parental nudity was probably confusing to him while we were also teaching him sexual rules.

Despite my tact, she did not return for another appointment. Finally, at the urging of the caseworker, she returned over a month later and we were able to have a more frank discussion about privacy and the need to stop both the joint showering and his occasional grabbing at her, which was also disclosed.

Once A.A. rejoined us, I did have to remind him twice in the first coaching session about no hugging or kissing without permission. I was very pleased to see that their ambivalent dynamic had altered somewhat by the time we decided to take a break from treatment due to the mother's work schedule changes. A.A. was able to tolerate her praises and redirection more easily. She reported greater compliance at times that previously had triggered anxious attachment behavior, for example, when she went out with friends, suppertime, and going to bed. A.A. was more respectful of his sister as well, and the first family goals of learning sexual rules and increasing family safety and appropriate closeness had been achieved.

However, this mother had only started to address her history of abuse and her problems with mood. I believe only the first few steps were taken in what will undoubtedly be a long path for this family.

This case, and similar cases, have taught me about the significant role of family sexuality in shaping the sexual behavior of a child. I have learned that parents with behavior like A.A.'s mother are often secretive; what they initially say may not be true, and you should watch for subtle cues. This mother was quite different from others I have confronted in that she was able to return to therapy and make some changes. If the mother-son pattern had been more entrenched, or if she had a history of antisocial behavior, then my experience and that of others is that therapy would have ended abruptly (Stoolmiller, Duncan, Bank, & Patterson, 1993).

HOW A PARENTAL SEXUAL ABUSE HISTORY AFFECTS PARENTING

The family-based treatment approach recommended by this book emerged in part because I became aware that my child clients with sexual behavior problems were being raised in families with sexual "ghosts" (Fraiberg et al., 1975). My use of the term *ghosts* comes from Selma Fraiberg, who wrote extensively about a variety of unconscious issues (i.e., ghosts) that persisted into the parent-child relationship. These ghosts can include a history of sexual abuse in one or both parents.

If left unresolved, a parent's sexual abuse history is often a clear contributor to the child's sexual behavior problems. This history of abuse increases the probability that the parent has a disturbed attachment relationship with the child (Main & Hesse, 1990). A second contributor is that insecure attachment often translates into increased behavior problems in the child (Cassidy & Shaver, 1999; Greenberg et al., 1993). For example, a child may have greater problems with self-regulation because the parent typically has not been the secure, modulating base the child needs. Consequently, the child becomes more impulsive and less self-controlled, and as a further result, is more likely to be reactive to aggressive or sexual parental behavior. In addition, the child's working model will contain coercive and distorted perceptions about relationships. He or she will not be as effective at judging how to become close with others and meet affectional needs in healthy ways.

There are other dynamics as well. However, severe sexual abuse in a father or mother interferes with their capacity to think accurately about their child's sexual behavior or objectively answer questions about it. They may be unaware of how their past has influenced their parenting behaviors and interactions. The inability of these parents to view their children accurately reflects impaired attachment (Bowlby, 1969). Failure to observe includes: (1) a lack of awareness of the parent's provocative behavior; (2) inability to accurately observe the nature and type of sexual behavior the child exhibits; (3) objectifying the child, with the result that children often become precociously sexual; and (4) poor monitoring of the child in general. This blindness regarding these emotionally charged topics probably correlates with their lack of attunement to their child. In fact, this blindness is also consistent with most people who exhibit provocative behavior. They seem to have either an absent or temporarily suspended capacity to observe how they appear to others.

In addition, severe and unresolved sexual abuse in adult women appears to lead primarily to one of two outcomes (Merrill et al., 2003). These have been labeled as *avoidant* and *promiscuous/preoccupied*. The authors of this study derived this formulation based in part on the number of sexual partners in a large sample of female naval recruits. It seems fair to surmise that this typology would also be related to the type and quality of response that these parents make to a child's behavior or comments. My thoughts about both of these two types and their relationship to parenting are outlined next. This dichotomy also seems to fit for the fathers I have seen clinically.

AVOIDANT

Parents with unresolved sexual abuse histories who handle it through avoidance will vary depending on how avoidant they are. For example, some avoidant parents may simply not be able to recognize sexual behavior in their child. When you ask them to rate its frequency or monitor its occurrence, they may be unable to do so with any level of accuracy. If you ask them to fill out a CSBI, it comes back with mainly zeroes.

As avoidance increases in severity, you will notice that these parents are often unaware of both safety issues and their own intimacy needs. Shame and depression are activated by intimacy of any sort, and therapists have to be aware of this. If these parents do have awareness of their need for closeness, they are still quite ambivalent about meeting this need openly.

Another type of avoidant parent may actually be hypervigilant and respond harshly to even normative manifestations of sexual behavior in the child, for example, if a preschooler touches his or her parts while at home. The parental coercive response may trigger the onset of a coercive cycle between the parent and child (Patterson, 1980). While it may initially revolve around sexual behavior, the cycle is likely to then expand to include other behaviors, often aggressive. Over time, such a child may begin to exhibit provocative behavior not only at home but also in other arenas. Regrettably, the child's persistence in these behaviors only serves to solidify and even elaborate the parent's negative attributions (e.g., "He's so sexed up," "He's a future rapist").

The following case example captures this dynamic, in this case, avoidant mother and provocative son, and illustrates both the origins and treatment of the child's behavior.

The B. Family

B.B., a 5-year-old boy, came to my office in midsummer because his parents were worried that his sexualized behavior at home would interfere with his successful entry into kindergarten. For example, B.B. had created a game that he called the whizzie dance. The game consisted of him exposing himself to his mother as often as one to two times per day. He then made his penis or "whizzie" dance as he jumped around the room and would yell at her to look at his whizzie. She typically overreacted emotionally and often chased him to ensure his compliance.

Both of B.B.'s parents had sexual abuse histories. The mother's abuse included fondling but began with exposure by two teenage relatives. Evidence that she was still affected by her abuse came in response to my question about whether B.B. had ever witnessed sexual intercourse. She told me that she was relieved that she and the boy's father were rarely intimate. In fact, although the two lived together, they maintained separate bedrooms and had never married.

The mother's emotional response to the whizzie dance was a powerful reinforcer to her son. To her credit, her interaction with him in the intake session was generally appropriate; she described him in generally positive terms and he was well behaved in her presence. He also looked distressed and asked her to stop when she specifically started to describe the game to me. Both of them reported doing several enjoyable things together each day. He had impressed me in my initial time with him as a fun-loving, non-sexualized, and generally resilient child, and as a result, I did not believe sexual abuse was a motivator for his behavior. Consequently, I opted to intervene toward the end of the first 90-minute session, rather than more thoroughly interviewing B.B. about sexual abuse.

I brought them back together and asked B.B. to demonstrate the whizzie game to me. He refused and became even more embarrassed. I then used two small dolls to superficially role-play the mother-son interaction and asked the mother to provide her own sound effects. By using the dolls, I showed her how to turn away during the next doll role-play and say, "I was hoping we could play right now, but I see we have to wait."

She was able to do this several times in the session. I wrote the suggested phrase down as a script, and both agreed that she would read it whenever he played the whizzie game. She and I scheduled an appointment for 10 days later. When she came in, she reported that the frequency had dropped to less than once per day. She agreed that she had not been able to completely alter her response. We talked about her relationship with one of the relatives who had been abusive to her and who she still saw with some frequency. I praised her ability to set limits with this relative about another family issue. She didn't want to talk about him further, so we then role-played her withdrawal of attention from B.B. once more. We also discussed some of the elements from parent-child interaction therapy, including generic and labeled or more specific praise and the overuse of questions and commands (Hembree-Kigin & McNeil, 1995; described in Chapter 8, Form O).

Two weeks later, she and B.B. came in and reported that he had been symptom-free for the previous 6 days. We decided together that he "had grown tired" of the game and needed to be "old enough" for kindergarten. Via a phone call roughly 3 months later, I heard that the behavior had completely extinguished. I again suggested that she enroll in a group for victims, but she reported that she still was not ready.

This case clearly illustrates the etiology and resolution of a specific dynamic, that is, reactivity triggered by the avoidant resolution to a history of sexual abuse. This was a quickly resolvable issue because the mother-son coercion did not extend beyond his sexually provocative behavior; no maltreatment was evident in the boy; and his mother had other strengths, including a commitment to her son. In the presence of other risk factors and greater overall coercion and rejection, this would have been a more challenging case.

Provocative/Promiscuous

Variability also exists in the provocative/promiscuous group of parents, but the underlying feature is that sexuality is a component of most of their relationships. These are the parents who dress provocatively, have a history of many brief relationships, and, although most seem able to talk about their sexual history, often quite openly, are still fairly poor observers of their child's sexual behavior. This can happen either because the parents exaggerate the behavior or because the behaviors do not seem deviant to the parents and they miss them (e.g., the child touching their breasts or standing too close).

Children raised by these parents experience the full gamut of dysregulating emotions, since many of them, in addition to being overstimulated by the higher level of sexuality in the home, are also neglected or physically abused. Other parenting features may include intrusiveness in the child's activities, which I believe reflects poor boundaries and has been documented in parents with an abuse history (Burkett, 1991). However, there is often a great deal of shame in these parents, and this can be one reason why the rate of therapy dropout is very high with this group. Another contributor to the lack of engagement in therapy is that despite your efforts, it can be difficult for these parents to understand that there is a problem with their child's behavior.

The next case was a referral from the courts for an extended evaluation of C.C., a 9-year-old boy (Carnes, Wilson, & Nelson-Gardell, 1994). Connie Carnes and her colleagues from the National Children's Advocacy Center have demonstrated how spending more time with children who are difficult to assess, as well as obtaining rating scales and other information, leads to a greater likelihood of determining prior abuse.

The C. Family

This particular situation came to the court's attention as part of a visitation dispute. For the past two years, C.C. had touched his mother's breasts. This grew more persistent over time and now occurred at least daily. During my interview with the mother, she also reported that C.C. now asked her to touch his butt and occasionally asked to touch her butt.

The mother was concerned that her son had been molested. One possible perpetrator was a day care employee who was later convicted as a sex offender and whose employment overlapped with C.C.'s enrollment. The mother was also concerned that her ex-husband, whom she described as a sex addict, was another possible perpetrator. However, she could identify nothing concrete that pointed specifically at either the day care worker or her ex-husband.

She reported having been sexually abused at multiple times in her life, and had been in therapy for years because of her "addiction" to males. She was provocatively dressed at all appointments, and I noticed that when she and her son were seated in the waiting room, she often had her arm around him. She also reported that she was occasionally partially undressed in front of him. She typically responded to his touching of her breasts by telling him to stop and occasionally sending him to his room. However, the frequency had actually increased but had not extended to other females.

Over a 3-week extended interview with C.C., he denied ever having been sexually touched by anyone. He seemed to enjoy his visits with his father. He was immature but generally exhibited good boundaries with me, although he provided sexualized stories in response to several projective pictures from the Roberts Apperception Test for Children (McArthur & Roberts, 1982). He did reveal that he might have seen his mother doing something that was "bad touch," but he gave me no clear details.

I spoke to his mother after this interview. She earlier had denied that her son had seen her engaged in intercourse. I asked her to think hard and let me know if there was a remote possibility that C.C. could have seen her engaged in sexual behavior. This time she quickly recalled something and admitted that two years earlier, C.C. had seen her engaged in oral sex with a male friend. Both of them were nude and in the living room.

This event was the only potential trigger described by both C.C. and his mother, and it had occurred roughly around the onset of the behavior. It also seemed quite possible that she had not made the connection due to her inability to think accurately about herself and her sexual behavior.

I saw this more clearly after both were referred for treatment. Although on one level she could verbalize that she was increasingly concerned about his touching her, on another level, she was not extra vigilant about being completely clothed in his presence. She also had considerable difficulty realizing that that her snuggling with him was more her own wish than his.

In my sessions with them, I helped C.C. and his mother establish sexual rules that included her behavior as much as his. For example, two of his rules were "I do not ask my mom if I can touch her butt" and "I do not touch my mother's breasts." I told her directly that two rules needed to be written with her in mind, so that everyone in the family got the message of privacy. These included "I let others see me only when I have all my clothes on" and "In our family, we hug each other only when asked to." C.C.'s problematic touching was eliminated and therapy ended successfully.

The origin of C.C.'s behavior was different than that of A.A. A.A. was more purely provocative, while C.C.'s origins reflected the sexual exposure in combination with fewer personal boundaries in the home and subtle sexual reinforcement by the mother.

MATERNAL BOUNDARY PROBLEMS

Parenting is a highly intimate activity. Secure parents open themselves up fully to tiny infants, love them unconditionally, smell their skin, change their diapers, and have many tactile and visual sensations that are not that far removed from the visual and tactile stimuli of sexuality. It should not be surprising that when parents are confused about intimacy, problems can emerge in their relationship with their child. For example, disorganized attachment was first associated with severe, unresolved sexual abuse (Main & Solomon, 1990).

One paper about preschoolers from the Minnesota Longitudinal Project (Sroufe & Ward, 1980) illustrates this. Mother-child interaction was videotaped in a toy cleanup situation. The raters observed both overt and covert adult-child sexuality in a small percentage (9%) of the mother and child pairs in this longitudinal study. The behaviors included a variety of sensual physical contact, such as prolonged kissing, caressing, sensual teasing, promises of affection, and maternal requests for affection. This behavior was directed almost exclusively to males, was associated with significantly more physical punishment and threats of punishment, and was unrelated to cooperation, encouragement, or emotional support. As a group, these mothers were less supportive and effective in guiding their children's behavior.

One can see that sexual intrusiveness was not the only concern about these mothers. They were also more harsh physically, less supportive, and did not seem to respond very sensitively or reciprocally to their children. So when we see maternal issues with sexuality, it is also important to think that there are other psychopathologies that often operate to accentuate the impact of disturbed sexuality.

A follow-up to that study was completed when these children were school age (Sroufe et al., 1985). The authors found that these mothers were more derisive of their daughters and that their boys were among the most disturbed children in the sample. The maternal sexuality had become one more dysregulating variable for these children, over and above the usual in this disadvantaged sample, and further tipped the balance into pathology.

This research suggests that while some parents exhibit overt sexuality and others are more rejecting, parents can also behave in a combination of these two styles (Merrill et al., 2003). Sexualized interaction, along with the other disadvantages that are often present, contribute to the child's dysregulation and confusion about intimacy. The mothers (and fathers) who do this do not have a map for intimacy, and thus their children are also left without a roadmap of the most appropriate path to obtaining closeness. Sroufe and his colleagues (1985) did not study fathers, but it is likely that similar issues operate for them.

Denov (2004) suggested that the majority of fathers and mothers with a sexual abuse history struggle with how best to interact with their children. Many report sexual arousal in the presence of the child and respond by increasing their avoidance of the child. To the child, this withdrawal is likely to be processed as rejection and unavailability. In fact, the fear of sexually abusing children was present for 86% of the fathers and mothers in her study, and the fear was particularly apparent for those who were raising children on their own.

TRANSMISSION OF DISTURBED SEXUALITY ACROSS GENERATIONS

Zeanah and Zeanah (1989) utilized an attachment paradigm to examine the process whereby abuse in one generation manifests itself in a subsequent generation. They suggested that it was not the exact type of abuse that was transmitted, but rather the processes of role reversal, fear, and rejection. These processes constitute an organizing theme of the parent-child relationship, which is manifested in a way of living and experiencing the internal working model.

I believe other processes are involved in transmission of disturbed behavior, derived from research on the onset of juvenile delinquency (Loeber & Stouthamer-Loeber, 1998; Patterson et al., 1992). These include poor monitoring and modeling of aggression, or in this case, parental sexuality. Other research on the relationship of maternal depression to antisocial behavior is also informative. For example, depressed mothers provide inadequate parenting, poor-quality interactions, and stressful family contexts that promote behavioral problems in their children (Dodge, 1990; Jacobsen & Miller, 1999). In addition, their choice of mate may add to the stress level of the family or raise the potential for maltreatment (Kim-Cohen, Moffitt, Taylor, Pawlby, & Caspi, 2005).

ROLE REVERSAL

Although these authors (Zeanah & Zeanah, 1989) did not specifically write about the theme of sexuality, the concept of theme transmission seems to hold for how family sexuality, particularly parental history of abuse, manifests itself in sexual acting out in the child. For example, role reversal teaches a child a pattern of relationships in which the needs of the parent are primary. Role reversal may be the child's resolution to disorganized attachment, and if so may be seen more accurately as controlling or caregiving (Jacobvitz & Hazen, 1999). It has also been described as one outcome of avoidant attachment (Alexander, 1992; Crittenden, 1995).

Several potential contributors to sexualization are as follows (Zeanah & Zeanah, 1989):

1. Role reversal: Relationship rules are distorted; the child's needs are not met directly; the caregiving may assume a sexual connotation.
2. Fear: Child's dysregulation contributes to impulsive behavior; child learns self-soothing rather than being soothed by a caregiver.
3. Rejection: Child seeks other avenues for closeness; child incorporates sexual elements into coercive cycle.
4. Poor monitoring: Child has increased opportunity for exposure to sexuality or victimization.
5. Modeling of parental sexuality: Sibling incest.

If there is a sexual tinge to parental needs, such as the child rubbing the parent's back after work or watching a favorite, sexually charged TV show with the parent, then the child has a routine model of introducing sexuality into relationships. This phenomenon has been documented as a contributing factor with adolescent females who sexually offend against children in their care (Mathews, Hunter, & Vuz, 1997).

I worked with one 12-year-old boy who was a surrogate parent to his mother and also had fondled at least two children in his apartment building. These incidents had occurred while he was babysitting these children. When I asked his mother what the two of them did together for fun, she shared that they watched her evening soaps together. All of these soaps had sexual themes, and the mother strongly identified with a few female leads. When I interviewed the boy, he could tell me all about the plots, the characters, and so on. The mother had no appreciation that their shared activity was inappropriate given the paucity of nurturing interaction directed to her son.

FEAR

Fear has a central role in attachment theory, given the theory's emphasis on the child's need for a secure base (Ainsworth et al., 1978; Bowlby, 1969). It is also a manifestation of the dysregulatory experience of being raised by a parent who is less skilled at soothing a child than is optimal. Manifestations of overwhelming fear in the very young child include such disparate self-soothing behaviors such as rumination, self-injury, and self-stimulation. In my visits to several Eastern European orphanages, I was struck by the number of children of all ages with their hands in their pants or giving other more obvious signs of self-stimulation. Their genitalia had become a primary reference point for them and in some ways an attachment object. My perspective is that this could then lead to a genital focus in relationships, starting extremely early in childhood. However, I do not have data to support this.

REJECTION

Rejection takes many forms, but at its core it is the inaccurate perception of the child. Consequently, the attributions are typically a parent's mixture of overly negative and occasionally overly positive public statements about the child (Jacobsen & Miller, 1999). But all of these attributions fail to the degree that they are inaccurate. For example, I often hear "But he's very smart" from the parent of a child with sexual behavior problems. However, the child will be doing poorly in school and will seem at best to have average intelligence when interacting with you. Overly positive and inaccurate attributions about the child will still leave the child feeling misunderstood. This is one reason why generic praise (e.g., "You're great") is less effective than specific praise (e.g., "You are so good at numbers"; Hembree-Kigin & McNeil, 1995).

Rejection by the parent in response to a benign behavior, such as a 5-year-old touching his crotch, can inhibit or exaggerate sexual behavior that would be viewed by other parents as normative. It signals to the child that this is a sensitive topic, and introduces an element of uncertainty into the parent-child relationship about this issue. Children will act out until clarity is provided; some may respond by inhibiting their behavior until parental supervision is over, while others react with provocation. It also interferes with future efforts by the parent to be appropriately educative, since the child has learned not to trust what the parent says. Recall the frequency of parental rejection noted by the Vermont study (Gray, Pithers, Busconi, & Houchens, 1999) and by caregivers of sexually reactive children in care (Friedrich et al., 2005).

POOR MONITORING

Several researchers have identified poor monitoring as a direct contribution to the emergence of juvenile delinquent behavior (Biglan, Mrazek, Carnine, & Flay, 2003). Children who are poorly monitored are more apt to roam their environment and eventually engage in small criminal acts like vandalism. One can also speculate about the effect of going hours without parental support and the negative effect this has on school achievement. In the children with sexual behavior problems that I have seen, poor monitoring is usually another manifestation of rejection. However, it typically occurs in families that have far less structure and internal support than, for example, families that are rejecting but have rigid rules of behavior.

For example, I saw an 11-year-old boy who, along with a younger peer, had been raped. The younger boy was the only child who reported it to his parent. My patient, the 11-year-old, was a reluctant therapy participant but did agree that the event had happened. This boy's mother participated minimally in his treatment and had her own childhood maltreatment and substance abuse problems to manage. The boy was raped by an offender who showed him pornography, allowed him to smoke cigarettes, and bribed him with CDs and some clothing. His mother had no awareness of their relationship, and I believe her ignorance spoke clearly about her poor monitoring. My patient acted out sexually during my treatment of him and was sent to a residential facility for juvenile sex offenders.

PARENTAL MODELING

Interesting research from the sibling incest field suggests the various ways that overt parental sexuality loosens the strictures on sexuality between siblings. For example, one Colorado study found a relationship between extramarital affairs by the mother and daughters who were incestuous with a sibling (Smith & Israel, 1987). Another found a 46% combined incidence rate of sexual abuse in the mothers and fathers of sibling incest families (O'Brien, 1991). Presumably some of these parents may have fallen into the preoccupied category described by Merrill (Merrill et al., 2003) and in this manner affected the sexual climate. Both of these underscore the effect of parental modeling of sexuality as a key contributor to the tenor of sexuality in the family. Social learning theory clearly explains the function and process of modeling (Bandura, 1986). Much of the modeling will be less direct and can include put-downs of females by older male and female caregivers. This modeling also includes domestic violence, which is an even more powerful statement of male or female dominance and the use of aggression to solve problems.

COGNITIVE DISTORTION

Parental selectivity and cognitive distortion are also contributory to sexual behavior problems in children. For example, it is the parent who decides what is sexual, not the child. A child may simply touch himself because his penis is there; it is the parent who interprets that the child is sexually focused and masturbatory, and is then in a position to shape the behavior.

The relative contribution of family sexuality to the emergence of sexual behavior problems in children is central to understanding the child sitting in front of you. Family sexuality operates on both macroecological and micro-ecological levels in the child's environment. An example of a macrolevel contribution is the underlying input that comes from growing up in a home characterized by domestic violence. Not only does domestic violence serve as a model of intrusive and coercive interaction, it also gives children a model for who has less status. Mothers who are victims cannot provide the secure base the child needs for secure attachment (Jacobsen & Miller, 1999; Main & Solomon, 1990). Consequently, parents in these situations predispose their children to insecure attachment of one form or the other.

Now let's add an additional microfeature of the child's emotional climate. In the following case example, it is exposure to pornography, and the user is someone who is elevated in the hierarchy and with whom the child has a frustrating and ambivalent relationship, a father or older brother. Relationships characterized by frustration and ambivalence are harder to both resolve and ignore. The child expends a great deal of energy trying to both fit in and be on his guard. Identification with the frustrating individual and consuming pornography becomes a solution in the same way that identification with the aggressor is the solution for many victims.

The D. Family

I will never know the full story of one boy whom I saw at different times over a 3-year period. He now is in residential treatment for adolescent sex offenders. D.D. was referred at the age of 8 years by his local school for sexual harassment of female peers. His mother grew up in a family characterized by multigenerational neglect. For example, she reported that she lived for 2 years in a car with her mother and half siblings. She was involved in the juvenile justice system as a teenager. She was chronically depressed and often physically victimized by her boyfriends, including D.D.'s father. In my various interviews with her, she would contradict herself in the same session, alternatively stating that she loved D.D. and then asking to have him removed from her care. She could never remain in treatment for very long despite ample support from local county and school authorities.

When D.D. returned to my office at the age of 10 because he had pulled down the pants of several girls, I found out that he was also being exposed to pornography by an older male relative, who had earlier been investigated for physical abuse of both D.D. and his half sibling.

D.D. was also accused of sexually touching several preschoolers who were neighbors in his community later that year, but after this event, his mother only brought him in a total of two times.

After being caught molesting a kindergartner at age 11, D.D. was expelled from his elementary school and placed in a separate building for emotionally disturbed children. A year later, after having met with him for a number of evaluation sessions and obtaining input from the school setting, I too was advocating for an out-of-home placement.

I try to remain optimistic about the children I see who have sexual behavior problems, and I believe this optimism is warranted for the majority of the children. But D.D. is one of several I see each year that immediately make me concerned about their long-term prognosis. In addition to his insecure attachment with his mother, the primary contributors to his behavior were features of the family sexual climate.

At the start of this section, fear, rejection, and role reversal were suggested to be the processes whereby the effects of sexual abuse in one generation are transmitted to the next generation (Zeanah & Zeanah, 1989). Each of these processes reflects a basic impediment to attachment security, and in the context of a coercive, aggressive, or sexualized home environment, provide the basis for future problems with intimate relationships. Not only do these processes place the origin of sexual behavior problems in attachment insecurity, they are also processes that can be identified as the clinician evaluates and treats these children and their parents.

ASSESSING FAMILY SEXUALITY

It is helpful to keep Bolton's (Bolton et al., 1989) two constructs, parental romantic behavior and parental affection to the child, in mind during your evaluation. This will assist you in calculating the degree to which the parents are fostering an environment in which the child's affectional needs can be met in healthy ways rather than via sexual contact with another child or by repetitive self-stimulation.

Interviews about safety and family sexuality, in combination with observation of overt behavior, are the primary means to understanding the sexual dynamics of families. The interview is focused and specific, educational, and also supportive. Completing the Safety Checklist discussed in the prior section makes for an excellent start. The Family Sexuality Index (Chapter 8, Form C) can provide other information. I often have parents complete it while I talk to their child and then review the endorsed items with them later.

Families also offer insight in terms of overt sexual behavior. A parent's provocative dress certainly suggests a more sexually permissive home environment, but by itself it is not conclusive. However, dress may indicate that you need to ask appropriate questions on this topic.

A parent's history of frequent romantic partners is also important to consider as a potential risk factor. The use of touch when parents are in your office, as well as respect for boundaries, can also be illuminating. This is particularly noticeable when the whole family is together in your office. Siblings who hit and shove each other, or parents who adopt similar strategies when their children are getting out of hand, indicate an intrusive style that may have served as an early model in developing intrusive sexual behavior.

The wording of questions is also important. For example, provocative dress may lead me to first educate the parent about the need for privacy in the treatment of children with sexual behavior problems. However, I will then ask, "How many times has Junior seen (heard) you and any of your boyfriends having sex?" rather than, "Has Junior ever seen you and your boyfriend having sex?"

My belief is that the bulk of your interactions with therapy-naive parents in this sensitive arena should be both educative and positive. Education facilitates change and can be absorbed by parents and applied later (Miller & Rollnick, 1991). A direct result of this belief is to frame questions as part of education either about the importance of being honest ("so we can figure out why your child does this") or why a risk factor is so concerning. For example, you could preface a series of questions by saying, "People like me wonder all the time about where kids get these ideas."

INCREASING PARENTS' CAPACITY TO OBSERVE AND MONITOR SEXUALITY

I believe that families with a child with sexual behavior problems, and parents who have their own sexual abuse history, must have a central, but treatable, issue over and above their inherent provocation to a child with sexual behavior problems. That issue is their inability to accurately observe their own or their child's sexuality. Sexualized parents are rarely fully aware of the sexual nature of their comments or interactions with their children. They are also unable to accurately observe their child's behavior.

So how do you increase a parent's observation capacity? First, you need to know that it is a problem and observe how it is manifested. Often my most objective indicator of problems in this area comes from how parents complete the CSBI (Friedrich, 1997). The avoidant-preoccupied dichotomy pattern often correlates with either underendorsement or overendorsement of items, respectively. For example, it is not uncommon for a sexually intrusive young child to run up to me in the first appointment and give me a big hug, although the parent does not endorse CSBI Item 26, "Overly friendly with men they do not know well." Other parents fail to endorse CSBI Item 2, "Stands too close to people," even when their child practically sits on your lap or you observe the child leaning on or sitting on the laps of people in the waiting room.

You move parents into the observing role via repeated, friendly, and targeted education that is tactful. For example, you might start saying early on, as you are interviewing the parent about safety, "Some kids who touch other kids seem to get really stirred up by seeing naked adults. These same kids might get very bothered by grown-ups who are kissing. This seems kind of crazy, doesn't it? But I know you want your son to stop his behavior. So what you will want to keep in mind is whether he sees you kissing anyone. Does that make sense?"

As you continue the safety interview, you might ask about the parents being naked in front of the child. I'll say things like, "He probably should not hear any loud, smacking kissing. Kissing and nudity are things that stir him up and that he should not be observing. Doesn't that make sense? Is that something you can agree to? Not being naked. No kissing in front of him. Is it something that your partner can follow through with as well?"

The above questions may need to be spread out for some parents, but by asking them, you are helping them (1) identify a problem and (2) see a solution.

Brainstorming how to create the solution is also necessary. Questions such as the following can be helpful: "So what would that mean you would have to do in your house? When and where does he see you naked? How could we make sure that he's not sneaking a peek at you having sex? What would that take? What would you have to do to prevent that?"

This is where it can be useful for you to create a list of potentially excitatory behaviors so that the parent can see them as a group and not be overwhelmed by any individual one. You can then follow up this list by drawing connections for the parent (see Figure 3.1 for a very simple example). I have created this for a number of parents and forgotten about it, but then heard them refer to it in subsequent sessions. This fact makes me believe that writing, in addition to speaking, is critical for these parents in learning new rules and improving their capacity to observe.

FIGURE 3.1 Sample sequence of connections between child exposure and behavior.

Jay sees your boyfriend naked ──────────────▶	Exposure
Jay thinks it's cool to show off his unit ──────▶	Thought
"I could flash kids on the school bus" ─────────▶	Related Thought
Exposes to kids on the school bus ─────────────▶	Behavior

I try to employ list making and simple drawings of this type in every session. Many parents are visual learners; these topics require repetition if you wish to see change, and besides, a therapist's language can be confusing. My drawings help to reiterate the main points in a visual mode. I also think that giving any list or drawing to parents as they leave your office allows them the opportunity to look it over a few times, and the message can sink in.

Early on in therapy, when I am talking with parents about establishing sexual rules, I say something similar to the following to parents: "You know we are making sure he follows some sexual rules. For the time being, it might be useful if you give yourself some sexual and privacy rules. I am not trying to criticize you. You weren't the one who did (the child's behavior). I am just telling you what I know can work. If he is no longer seeing you naked, then he is less likely to expose himself to your daughter."

CONCLUSION

This chapter suggests that clinicians need to look beyond a child's history of sexual abuse and consider how sexuality and intimacy are expressed in the family. Parental sexual behavior influences children in a variety of ways. Some of these are more active, such as overt sexuality, and others, like poor monitoring and neglect, reflect passivity.

Identifying sexual abuse in the history of a sexually intrusive child is difficult. For some children, you will never know their abuse status. There are several possible reasons why it cannot always be substantiated. The first is that the child has never been overtly sexually abused, but suspicions linger for one reason or another. The second is that there is a suspicious early history, and sexual contact probably did occur, but there is no way for the child to inform you accurately since he or she was so young at the time. A third reason is that you are dealing with a child who will not disclose actual abuse because he or she denies it out of fear of the consequences. Finally, the child is a preschooler and for developmental reasons cannot articulate any abuse that happened.

Rather than persist in questioning the child about possible abuse, clinicians should expand their focus and consider major contributors to child's sexual behavior, such as exposure to adult sexuality, domestic violence, or exposure to pornography. All cases of sexual behavior problems require a multigenerational focus regarding the father and mother for both assessment and treatment. These problems do not develop and persist without additional interpersonal forces that often have existed for several generations.

Unresolved sexual abuse in the parental generation does seem to lead to parenting processes that can interfere with how the child learns about closeness, intimacy, and nurturing. For example, parents who have been violated only by males may fail to appreciate their rejecting behavior or attributions about a male child. They may also fail to appreciate how dysregulating their behavior is to a child who needs to learn self-modulation as he or she gets old enough to enter school.

Establishing sexual rules is one strategy (described in Chapter 8, Form K) that puts sexuality in the forefront and provides an initial framework for family sexuality to be corrected. These rules articulate a territory that is uncharted for these families, and in this way help to make clear what has been ambiguous.

Establishing these rules provides an excellent example of how assessment and therapy can be made seamless, a particularly desirable strategy with treatment-naïve or treatment-resistant families. By inquiring about family sexuality in a manner that is educational and nonblaming, you put the parents in a better place to think about what is unsafe about their family and make the first, critical changes that can reduce the frequency of their child's behavior.

4

SCREENING, DIAGNOSIS, AND TREATMENT PLANNING

THE INFORMATION IN the previous chapters has provided you with sufficient facts and theory to understand the origins of sexual behavior problems. We now know that children arrive at inappropriate and intrusive sexual behavior by various pathways. We now are in a position to understand why one child might frequently touch his genitals because of PTSD or a variant, another child relates sexually to other children because of disturbed relational patterns in her family, and a third is coercively sexual because of a conduct disorder. This knowledge aids the evaluation process.

However, to evaluate, you need data. All parties involved in the evaluation of a sexually intrusive child have varying levels of difficulty with providing the data that are needed to plan for treatment. Parents, for example, have difficulty talking about their children's sexual behavior. Children are typically averse to talking to adults about sexual behavior, especially behavior that may have caused them difficulty. Finally, clinicians must work very hard to become facile at asking the type of direct questions needed to obtain accurate information about the behavior, potential contributors, and risk and protective factors in the home, while also establishing rapport by being accepting. This initial task is arduous for all.

Routinely obtaining information through a standardized set of screening measures will assist this process. However, bear in mind that defensive parents can easily distort the results of these face-valid measures. In addition, many of these parents have not had the time or capacity to think about their child's experiences and behavior until they answer your questions and complete the objective questionnaires. Despite these conditions, the majority of parents I meet still provide useful and valid information.

101

It is also important that your screening process facilitates the therapy process and is not burdensome (Friedrich, 2002). Assessment and treatment can be seamless if you educate and support both the parent and child while gathering the information needed. For example, if parents reveal their own abuse history, thank them for their openness, be supportive of any emotional reaction, and start treatment by saying, "You probably already know that parents who have been sexually abused sometimes have stronger emotional reactions to their child's sexual behaviors. We'll figure all of this out as we go along."

The goals of screening are to (1) inform the parent about the range of behavior problems that the child exhibits, and (2) begin to make the parent aware of the various contributors to the child's behavior. In return, the clinician will learn about (1) the openness of the parent, (2) the scope of the problem, (3) potential moderators of the problem behavior, and (4) treatment needs.

This chapter initially focuses on outlining a perspective that will enable you to more efficiently sort the information you gather as you determine a diagnosis and then develop a plan for treatment. Case material will help you appreciate how selected standardized measures can aid in this process. The most relevant standardized measures—which enable you to assess the potential array of issues that accompany each case—are reviewed. Additional suggestions for treatment planning are also provided.

PERSPECTIVES ON DIAGNOSIS AND DECISIONS REGARDING TREATMENT

It is important to go into each first interview thinking about the type and amount of treatment that will be needed, and to focus on how the interview process can respectfully inform the parents and start the treatment process. Several issues must be reviewed and determined during the initial sessions. First, does the child have a sexual behavior problem, and if so, what is the nature and severity of the problem? If it is decided that the child does not have a problem, educating the parent about normal versus problematic sexual behavior would be suggested; one to three sessions should be sufficient. If it is determined that a sexual behavior problem exists, the following issues need to be addressed during the first session or two:

1. Is the child safe from maltreatment?
2. Do other children need protection?
3. Is there reason to think that sexual abuse or exposure to adult sexuality is a contributing factor?

4. What is the nature of the parent-child relationship and the balance of acceptance and rejection of the child?
5. Are other behavior problems present?
6. How open is the family to treatment?
7. What barriers to treatment success are present?

For example, with experience you will learn that if a young (aged 4 to 7) child is in your office because his sole problem is that he has either played doctor or exhibited self-stimulation without masturbation, then it is less likely that maltreatment, exposure to adult sexual behavior, severe parent-child problems, or comorbid behavior problems are contributors. A list of assessment foci is as follows:

1. Nature and severity of sexual behavior problems
2. Safety from future maltreatment
3. People in need of protection
4. Role of sexual abuse or exposure to adult sexuality to SBP
5. Quality of parent-child relationship
6. Presence of comorbid behavior problems in child
7. Family's openness to treatment
8. Barriers to treatment success

More of the issues identified above become evident as the sexual behavior problem in question increases in severity. For example, you will be much more likely to see evidence of disturbed parent-child relationships, adversity, comorbid behavior problems, and maltreatment. Furthermore, as the severity of the problem increases, it can be accompanied by more barriers and less openness to treatment (Hall et al., 2002). The child's sexual behavior is more likely to be persistent, premeditated, interpersonal, and even coercive. The parents are more likely to be defensive, and it can be more difficult to obtain a comprehensive history from them.

At the outset, I consider treatment options ranging from no treatment to prolonged treatment and monitoring. Some children's behavior, when viewed in the context of their family, is completely understandable, and one to three contacts are all that is needed. In these cases, the parent will benefit from your education, the child will clearly hear the message that the behavior is causing concern and needs to stop, and you will be reassured at a follow-up visit that your decision was correct.

From this point, length of treatment expands in varying degrees. The evaluation may uncover some safety or sexual exposure issue that needs to be corrected and followed over a period of several weeks to several months, if the family is cooperative. Other families are in and out of therapy and present ongoing concerns. In other cases a child is already out of the home, and foster parents are minimally involved; in these cases the child becomes your treatment focus, even though it might not be the most appropriate option.

The initial data are critical to planning. Interviews and screening measures should each contribute usable data that are used to plan treatment interventions. This point is illustrated in the next example.

The E. Family

Ms. E. was a divorced mother who came into my office with her 9-year-old son, E.E. I had asked her to come to the first appointment alone, but she brought her son. She glared at me when I came to meet her in the waiting room and insisted that the two be seen together. I opted not to fight that battle and brought the two back to my office.

She clearly resented being in my office and told me that she still was not convinced that there was a problem. She attributed the blame for the referral to her former sister-in-law, and went on to tell me that her sister-in-law would call me so that I got the "real story, but it will be a bunch of lies."

I said a few things about in-laws. She laughed a bit and I asked Ms. E. what had happened that made everybody so upset. She started to talk and then turned to her son and said, "I think you need to be the person to tell the doctor." E.E. looked away and reddened. He made one or two attempts to talk and looked at his mother to help him out. When she refused, he talked about his 5-year-old female cousin and her pregnant mother. "She didn't know anything about babies. I told her how babies are made."

He stopped at that point and I asked if there was anything else he needed to say. He looked at his mother, and she firmly told him, "Go on, tell what else happened." He muttered that on that same day, in an effort to tell her how babies are made, he exposed himself to the cousin. He also asked her to expose herself to him. "But she wouldn't. She just told her mom."

I immediately praised Ms. E. for raising a son who tried to be honest about embarrassing things. Although she promptly offered some criticism of his other problems, she seemed pleased to hear this from me.

At this point, I was fully aware that I did not know the complete story, and that neither mother nor son wished to be in my office, but (1) the boy had spoken at the mom's urging, (2) she had not been intrusive with him or overtly dismissing of the girl, (3) at the age of 9 he was a bit more experienced than the usual child (reported for 4.7% of the 6- to 9-year-old boys; Friedrich, 1997) when it came to playing doctor, and (4) it was a good sign of overall maturity that the mother both asked her son to talk and softened when I praised and supported her.

However, Ms. E. and her son were at the precontemplation stage of change (Miller & Rollnick, 1991). Neither had even begun to think that there were any concerns that warranted therapy or behavioral change. Miller and Rollnick (1991) argued that education is one strategy to move a person from precontemplation to contemplation; the contemplation stage is prior to taking action. Screening educates the parent and facilitates therapy. It is part of treatment.

At this point, I broke up the interview and gave Ms. E. some questionnaires to complete, and asked her to be as honest in her answers as she could. I told her I always saw honesty as a sign of overall family strength. She returned to the waiting room and I remained to talk further with E.E.

The very act of answering the screening measures helped Ms. E. realize a number of things about her son. After completing a 38-item scale of sexual behaviors (CSBI; Friedrich, 1997), she saw that of the 38, E.E. had only shown 2 of these behaviors, one time each, in the past 6 months. These were No. 33, "Shows sex parts to children," and No. 38 (Other sexual behavior), "Asked his younger cousin to take off her clothes."

The next scale she completed was the Strengths and Difficulties scale (Goodman, 1997), a 25-item measure that assesses generic behavior in children. Because it is briefer and not as consistently negative as either the Child Behavior Checklist (Achenbach, 1991a) or the Behavior Assessment System for Children (BASC; Reynolds & Kamphaus, 1998), she appreciated that E. E. frequently exhibited positive behaviors (e.g., "considerate of other people's feelings" from the five Prosocial items), and occasionally some negative behaviors (e.g., "temper tantrums," "lies" from the five Conduct items). However, as she read the other 15 items on the scale, she endorsed none of them at any level. Later when she returned to my office, I reviewed the results with her and was able to help her appreciate that E.E. was relatively well behaved.

Ms. E. completed two other screening questionnaires. The first reviewed any traumas E.E. had experienced (Traumatic Event Screening Inventory, TESI; Ford et al., 2000). The second asked her about the various conflicts she had with E.E. and how she resolved them (Parent-Child Conflict Tactics Scale, Chapter 8, Form E; Strauss, Hamby, Finkelhor, Moore, & Runyan, 1998). On the TESI, Ms. E. reported that E.E. had observed adults striking each other in the family and that he had been picked on while riding the school bus. She also reported that although she used time out and explained what was wrong, she frequently yelled and screamed, occasionally insulted E.E. and, at times, had threatened her son with corporal punishment.

The four measures that she completed provided the type of quantifiable information that will aid you in planning treatment of the parent-child dyad.

Although the validity of screening measures is always subject to parental distortion, the data added to the emerging picture of E.E.

While his mother was completing the measures, I spent time with E.E. He was friendly and sociable, exhibited appropriate boundaries, and was not demanding or disruptive. I opted not to ask further about the incident with the younger girl, since I planned on obtaining input from the girl's mother and also from Ms. E.

First, as I scanned the questionnaires, I saw that she could have been far more nondisclosive. In actuality, she was very precise on the CSBI. I have seen many parents in similar situations; for one of several reasons, they will deny all sexual behaviors, despite what has been publicly acknowledged. Ms. E.'s relative openness was a very good sign for future treatment. It also suggested that she was capable of having a balanced perspective about her son.

Ms. E. reported the occasional temper tantrum and some lying from E.E., but when summed together as part of the Conduct scale, it was not in the clinical range. She also described E.E. as a relatively caring and supportive child, which reflected her positive attributions about her child, a suggestion of secure attachment.

The two CSBI items she endorsed earned him a SASI T score of 64, which just missed the clinical range (this score is described in more detail later in this chapter). After hearing more information, I may have changed my mind, but at this point she had reported relatively little concerning sexual behavior, given what I knew of the context. I also had information that E.E. functioned reasonably well despite the fact that he had received a moderate amount of overly critical parenting and had experienced two other traumas, that is, domestic violence that led to the divorce, and peer harassment.

The framework provided by the CSBI and a behavior problem rating scale educated Ms. E. about the full range of behavior problems that children can exhibit. In fact, this was the start of treatment. At this point, parents can appreciate the fact that their child does not have "all those other problems." Disadvantaged parents are not used to thinking about their own or their child's emotions and behaviors, and your assistance will be needed to help them appreciate that their child exhibits some positives.

How do you help parents think more accurately and complexly about their child? You inform them that the measures they completed help you plan treatment. You also spend some time reviewing their answers with them, helping them appreciate the results and what this says about their child and their relationship.

I may ask parents what they have learned after completing the questionnaires. It is always a good sign when parents mention a mixture of positives and negatives. As I reviewed the results with Ms. E., I praised her son, particularly given all he had struggled with. I mentioned that he could have been a lot angrier after having a father who was abusive to her. I also thanked her for her honesty about her disciplinary strategies, and she offered that she was embarrassed to admit that she was a "yeller."

Before the session was over, I was able to tell her that compared to other boys his age, E.E. had only mild behavior problems, and even though he could have been a bit of a bully, he wasn't. I buttressed these comments by referring to some of her behavior in the room as responsible for him being a generally "okay" boy. I told her that I would need to obtain permission to talk to the former sister-in-law to get any other information, and she assured me she would sign a release. However, the entire process helped her to move on to contemplation. I was able to nudge her into deciding to do less screaming and threatening and helped her realize that I had some useful strategies that I could teach her. Both assessment and treatment occurred in this initial session.

As I review the questions with parents, I ask new questions to help them understand what their answers say about their child and their relationship. For example, I will ask, "What was it like to fill out that questionnaire?" "What new thoughts did you have about your son?" "Are there any changes in your parenting you might want to consider?" You can comment on any positives they mention, and these comments work best if they are presented in an interpersonal framework, for example, "I can see you have really worked hard to get him to be kind to other children." By adopting this stance, you are helping parents be more open (if they minimized some problems) and also assess for both defensiveness and exaggeration of the child's problems.

SCREENING BATTERIES

The four brief questionnaires described in the case study with E.E. are discussed in more detail in this section, along with other useful, brief screening scales. It is important to become familiar with several scales so that you can interpret them utilizing the accumulated knowledge that comes with regular usage. I typically use briefer rather than longer versions of these measures since they place fewer time demands on the parent. These scales assess those variables that are critical to understanding children with sexual behavior problems. When the data are combined with a review of family sexuality, the risk and protective factors listed in Table 1.3, and a review of the risk factors in Table 1.2 (Hall et al., 1998), you are in an excellent position to judge the severity of the behavior in question. The content of your initial interviews will typically round out the essential data that need to be collected, such as substance abuse, psychiatric history of the parent, and parental history of maltreatment.

The parent-completed measures in the battery I suggest include a measure of generic behavior problems, the child's trauma history, the child's sexual behavior, and also family sexuality. I am very interested in the discipline strategies the parent uses and how the parent perceives the child (i.e., attributions). I think all of these are easily assessed with valid measures that are widely used and readily available.

Other topics that are important are the parent's current mood, the substance abuse history of the parent figures, the presence of domestic violence, and safety in the home (including triggers to sexual acting out). This last dimension is one that is immediately relevant since the best therapy cannot curtail acting out when sexual triggers persist in the home.

In addition, I use some standard measures with older children; these are reviewed later in this chapter. Self-report is less likely to be valid with children who feel unsupported by parents and are wary of disclosure, are younger than 10, or come from families who do not talk about their feelings.

Elements of Screening Battery: Parents

A battery of screening instruments can be used to obtain initial information about how a child is functioning in areas such as general behavior, trauma history, and sexual behavior problems. It is also useful to interview parents regarding their own history of trauma or maltreatment. Instruments that I typically used are described below.

Generic Behavior Problems

Since I use a number of measures in my screening battery, I prefer the short, 25-item Strengths and Difficulties Questionnaire (SDQ; Goodman, 1997). The parent version, teacher version, and self-report versions, as well as scoring information, are available on the Internet without charge at http://www. sdqinfo.com. It has five 5-item scales: Prosocial, Hyperactivity, Emotion, Conduct, and Peer Problems. The inclusion of the Prosocial scale allows the parent to report on empathetic and caring behaviors exhibited by the child, for example, "Kind to younger children." This scale also enables the parent to present a more comprehensive portrait of the child than a simple recounting of problematic behaviors.

I add three PTSD items to the end of the SDQ and can screen this domain as well. These three items are (1) seems to be reliving a past trauma (one described on the TESI), (2) avoids places or people that remind him or her of a past trauma, and (3) has nightmares about previous scary events. The sum of these three items correlated significantly with whether or not a child was diagnosed with PTSD after discharge from a psychiatric hospital (Friedrich & Malat, 2005), and a discriminant analysis was significant in terms of overall hit rate.

Literature also suggests that the SDQ does as well as the 113-item Achenbach Child Behavior Checklist (Goodman & Scott, 1999) and presumably the even longer BASC (Reynolds & Kamphaus, 1998), although a direct comparison with the BASC has not been conducted. Consequently, a 25-item scale is a big improvement when you ask defensive parents to fill out some measures and they are unsure how the information will be used. The results from the SDQ indicate what the parent sees as positive about their child, and whether comorbid behaviors exist that may explain or exacerbate the sexual behavior problem.

Three subscales of the SDQ—Hyperactivity, Conduct, and Peer Relations—have particular relevance. These are even more relevant if teachers corroborate the concerns. For example, elevations on the Hyperactivity subscale could mean that the sexual behavior in question is related to impulsivity. Elevations on the Conduct subscale are particularly worrisome since these behaviors are oftentimes more long-standing and suggest a more aggressive child. In addition, conduct problems more often than not speak to ongoing parent-child coercion-rejection issues (Patterson et al., 1992). When they are present, insecure attachment is even more likely. I also am concerned when problems are reported in peer relations, since this suggests that the behavior may reflect the child's social immaturity and absence of appropriate friendships.

Let's consider another possible profile. This comes from a parent who reports positive things about the child on the Prosocial scale, but endorses several of the PTSD items. In addition, there is an elevation on the Emotion subscale. In this case, you are more likely to be looking at an acute reaction by a sensitive and empathic child to a specific stressor. This suggests a more positive outcome than for the child who has more conduct problems.

Parent Self-Report

There are times when you need to evaluate the parent more specifically. For example, over a dozen of the parents of the children treated with this manual received additional treatment, most often for unresolved prior trauma that was activated by their child's behavior. With some parents, it may be productive to screen and refer them to another provider who can address their problems more specifically. The quality of the parent-child relationship and unresolved trauma, as well as the parent's competence and problem-solving capabilities, are appropriate evaluation foci. The clinician needs to determine whether the parent is motivated to improve the parent-child relationship, can keep personal issues from intruding on the child's adjustment, and can monitor the child and administer behavior management plans designed to reduce the child's sexual behavior problems.

Research indicates that the majority of mothers of sexually aggressive boys aged 11 to 15 were sexually victimized as children (Gray et al., 1997; Hall et al., 1998; New et al., 1999). Consequently, it behooves the clinician to determine parents' level of compromise from earlier trauma, their attitudes toward sexuality, whether these attitudes make them less objective about their child's sexual behavior, and their sexual satisfaction in their current relationship, if any.

A relatively brief measure that efficiently addresses these issues is the Trauma Symptom Inventory (Briere, 1995). The scales Anger/Irritability, Intrusive Experiences, Defensive Avoidance, and Sexual Concerns specifically address the above questions. If a parent is elevated on any of these subscales, it is important to then assess the degree to which these issues interfere with the monitoring and management of the child. However, defensive and antagonistic parents, that is, the parents of children with oppositional-defiant disorder and conduct disorder diagnoses, will disclose minimally (Pithers et al., 1998) and yield normal-limits Trauma Symptom Inventory profiles.

A semistructured clinical interview with the parents of sexually aggressive children would include the following:

1. Is it okay if we talk about sexuality? Does that make you uncomfortable?
2. You have told me that you were sexually abused. So what does it feel like to have a son (daughter) who does sexual things to other children?
3. Are you now thinking even more about your past abuse?
4. Is he ever sexual with you? Even in subtle ways?
5. Do you worry about him being sexual with your other children?
6. Do you worry that he will be sexual with children in the neighborhood?
7. Do you ever think he's doing this to "get you"? That he knows this is a weak spot?
8. How often are you hugging him?
9. Is it as easy to hug him now that you know what he has done to other kids?
10. How often do you get angry at him when you see him doing these sexual things?

11. When you get angry, what do you do?
12. How do you control your feelings of being hurt? Of being angry?
13. Does your child's sexual behavior with other children interfere with your ability to be sexual with your significant other?

The parent's responses to the above questions cannot be scored systematically. However, parents with an unresolved history of victimization who then deny distress, minimize any natural worries about their child, and claim not to be affected are the parents who struggle to respond adequately to the child's problems. A sexual abuse history in the mother has been associated with more negative attributions about the child's behavior (Friedrich & Sim, 2003; New et al., 1999). This suggests that the parent's response to Question 7 (above) is worth examining. A positive answer to this question strongly suggests that the parent interacts with the child as if he or she were deliberately victimizing the parent.

Trauma History

When I am completing a more extended evaluation and need more information than that provided by the three SDQ questions on PTSD, I use two short scales to assess the child's history of trauma, an important moderator of outcome. The first measure is available in the Assessment and Treatment Manual, an abbreviated parent-report 12-item version of Julian Ford's TESI (the longer version is available from http://www.ncptsd.org). The TESI screens for bullying, domestic violence, assaults (experienced and witnessed), and natural disasters. When parents elaborate on the ones they have checked, you also obtain a quick introduction to the many other entanglements these families may have; for example, the child witnessed an assault between his father and uncle while both were intoxicated.

An optional scale is a 30-item life events checklist that was created with children in mind (Coddington, 1999). This informs the clinician about separations, divorces, mood problems in parents, parental death and illness, and other recent events germane to children.

Sexual Behavior Problems

The 38-item CSBI (Friedrich, 1997) is recommended for this domain, particularly when the four additional sexual aggression items suggested by the manual (and listed on page 28) are included. The CSBI is available from www.parinc.com and generates three scores, Total Sexual Behavior, Developmentally Related Sexual Behavior (DRSB), and Sexual Abuse Specific Items (SASI) for six different age-gender groups: boys and girls ages 2 to 5, 6 to 9, and 10 to 12. It allows the user to compare the child to other children of the same age group. Some parents will report little behavior other than the problem behavior that resulted in the referral. Other parents will report many other sexual behaviors, and if this report is valid, it will suggest that the child's intrusive sexual behavior is part of a larger behavioral repertoire.

The DRSB items were endorsed by at least 20% of parents for a particular age and gender group. For example, "Stands too close to people" was endorsed by 29.4% of the mothers of 2- to 5-year-old nonabused boys and 25.7% of 2- to 5-year-old nonabused girls. For example, elevations on this scale are positively correlated with reports of playing doctor in the two younger age groups.

The SASI items were derived empirically and discriminated sexually abused from nonabused children after controlling for a number of demographic factors. However, they are more appropriately called Sexual Abuse Related Items. I say this because the relationships are correlational. Simply because a child is elevated on the SASI does not mean that child was sexually abused. These items are also significantly correlated with exposure to pornography, adult sexuality, violence in the home, and maltreatment. However, when this scale is elevated in a child with sexually intrusive behavior, you do have more reason to be concerned about prior sexual abuse as an etiological factor in the current behavior.

The CSBI items have been factor analyzed and five very similar factors have been generated for each age group. The four most consistent factors are boundary problems, sexual knowledge, sexual intrusiveness, and self-stimulation. The items that reflect sexual knowledge that is atypical for a child that age are the items that are most likely to indicate whether or not a child has been sexually abused (Brilleslijper-Kater, Friedrich, & Corwin, 2004).

These authors also found that sexually abused children share the aforementioned approach-avoidance dichotomy related to sexual behavior and sexual stimuli (Downs, 1993; Merrill et al., 2003; Noll et al., 2003). For example, sexually abused children are more likely than nonabused children to show emotional reactions suggesting that they find visual sexual stimuli aversive. At the same time, they are also more likely to report more sophisticated sexual information. This dichotomy most likely reflects some of the variability of sexually abused children in the level to which they exhibit sexual behavior.

At the start of reviewing the CSBI items with parents, reiterate that they were rating their child over the last 6 months and behaviors observed outside of that time span should not be included. This may result in some reduction of score. It is important to listen to how the parent felt when answering sexual questions. Some parents are made anxious by the items because of their own abuse history.

You may also hear for the first time the depth of the parents' anger at their child for having touched another child. When this happens, you become even more aware of the family's sexual ghosts. Their accompanying anger and rejection will need to be addressed and altered for treatment to be successful.

Research has found that the CSBI questions typically elicit more reports of behavior than does an interview. For example, a study of children in foster care found that using the CSBI revealed more incidents of sexual behavior than had been described in an open-ended interview with the care provider (Farmer & Pollock, 1998). This is further support for incorporating at least a few objective measures in your intake process.

CSBI questions will sometimes lead to a more serious take on the child's behavior. A common referral is for a child, age 8 and under, who has touched another similarly aged child. If this is in the context of playing doctor, something that parents report for at least 25% of children in this age range (Larsson et al., 2000), then the usual CSBI item that is endorsed is "No. 9. Touches another child's sexual parts," or "No. 33. Shows sex parts to other children." However, if many other items are endorsed, the parent appears to have rated them validly, and the SDQ has elevations of one or two clinical scales, you are presented with a different picture than just playing doctor.

Data with a normative sample collected as part of the test-retest reliability study with the CSBI found that no parents ($N = 131$) of the nonabused children endorsed the four sexual aggression items (listed on page 28 and at the end of Form B). Until recently, they had only been reported in children with a sexual abuse history, but Jane Silovsky and her colleagues of the University of Oklahoma Health Sciences Center have found that parents of preschool-age children with sexual behavior problems, most without a clear history of sexual abuse, do report these behaviors (Silovsky & Niec, 2002). For example, 54% (20 of 37) of her sample persisted in touching another child sexually "after being told not to." These behaviors are also typically reported more often by children with externalizing problems than they are by those with a sexual abuse history (Friedrich et al., 2003).

In addition to the discrete behaviors contained on the CSBI, it is critical that the evaluator ask about two other variables. The first is the context of the behavior, and the second is the parent's typical response to the behavior. For example, does the 8-year-old girl put on her bikini only when strange men come to the house? Do the parents have a difficult time responding calmly and in a nonpunitive manner to the sexual behaviors they observe in their child? One question that I have found useful is, "Have you ever found yourself very angry because you are scared about your child's behavior?"

The Q. Family

An example of the clarifying process is outlined in the case of Q.Q., a 5-year-old who had been expelled from day care for making sexual comments to the provider. His mother described numerous instances of unusual sexual behavior, much of it directed at her. However, she said that he had also been removed from an earlier day care for grabbing the provider's breasts. Q.Q.'s total raw score on the CSBI was 67 (T score > 110), an extremely high score for a 38-item scale, even for children with very severe and eroticizing abuse experiences.

When I asked the mother to tell me when, in the prior 6 months, Q.Q. had exhibited these behaviors, the score dropped immediately, since she had failed to use the 6-month timeline as a gauge. For the majority of the other behaviors, she often could report only one instance, despite the greater frequency she endorsed. Finally, I got the impression that she was probably subtly reinforcing the boy's behavior, with her style of dress and her exaggerated emotional responses to his behavior.

I was given permission to contact the previous two day care providers. Each of these women was primarily concerned about Q.Q.'s aggressive and immature behavior toward peers. He was only rarely sexualized in his actions or comments to them, although that had been a contributing factor to his expulsion.

The home versus day care difference did not mean that Q.Q.'s behavior was solely a function of his mother's behavior. However, I could see that Ms. Q. had a very distorted view of her son. I eventually conceptualized the case as primarily related to attachment and not sexualized behavior.

This case illustrates the importance of carefully assessing the context, nature, and frequency of the child's sexual behavior. Children are quite context bound, and if, for example, abuse occurred at bedtime, they might not display much sexual talk or behavior except at bedtime, particularly if they are younger (Hewitt, 1999). Bedtime is not likely to be observed by a day care provider. The treatment plan for such a child will be different from that of a child who primarily has overt sexual behaviors at day care.

Family Sexuality

Family sexuality is a critical but complex domain to assess. You may wish to interview parents or start by having them complete a screening scale (see Chapter 8, Form C) and use that to follow up with additional questions. The true picture may not emerge until, with time, parents learn to trust you and reveal more. However, the sexual attitudes of the parents (e.g., nudity, cobathing, the availability of pornography) and their specific sexual behaviors (e.g., intercourse witnessed by their child) correlate with the total CSBI score. These correlations have been found for all versions of the CSBI (Friedrich, 1997).

When I first started to study sexual behavior, I created a family sexuality subscale that consisted of six items. Two of these assessed for cosleeping or bathing between parent and child, and others looked at family nudity and opportunities to witness actual intercourse or observe sexually explicit movies or TV. I did not screen for Internet pornography, which was nonexistent when I first began to research child sexual behavior. However, more and more children are now exposed to Internet images and even become preoccupied with seeking them out.

I now use the longer questionnaire for all intakes (Chapter 8, Form C). (Norms are not available, but every item correlates with overall sexual behavior, with the direct exposure items the most relevant.) Parents tolerate it quite well. Some of the items are redundant with questions on the Safety Checklist (Form B in Chapter 8) or with the parental maltreatment screening questions I refer to later. However, safety and sexuality need to be assessed thoroughly with these families and redundancy can be useful. When you review their answers to the sexuality index, you can also help them talk about some of the stimuli that may be related to the child's acting out.

It is noteworthy that cosleeping and cobathing with parents, as well as parental nudity, prior to school age, in the absence of other risk factors in the home, is not associated with elevated sexual behavior in the child (Friedrich, 2002). Since other risk factors are routine with families of children with sexual behavior problems, creating sexual rules about privacy and nudity are typically necessary. Occasional cosleeping through the age of 8 does not worry me when the family has good boundaries and there are no sexual ghosts. The same is true for cobathing, although American families typically stop this practice in preschool.

Discipline Strategies

Parents are immediately educated about their role in their child's life when you have them rate their parenting behaviors. Most parents start to think that there are things they could do differently after completing the Parent-Child Family Conflict Tactics Scale published by Straus and his colleagues (1998). The entire scale was published in an issue of *Child Abuse and Neglect* and is available in the Assessment and Treatment Manual (Chapter 8, Form E). It assesses appropriate parenting strategies, like use of time out, as well as inappropriate strategies that are both emotional (e.g., screaming, insulting) and physical (e.g., slapping, shoving).

Parents typically become defensive when asked about their discipline techniques, and the most defensive ones are those who do not return for follow-up appointments. However, this scale is still extremely useful for several reasons. For instance, after parents complete the scale and you review their responses with them, their subsequent self-examination will be very educational for them. Furthermore, by reviewing their responses, you are in a position to do a tremendous amount of therapy. You quite often will hear parents make decisions to be more positive. You can support this decision and your use of a family focus is then justified in their minds. They may reveal behaviors that necessitate filing an abuse report, an issue you should have discussed fully with the parent when you reviewed confidentiality. You can reassure them that protective services will be pleased that they are doing something already by working with you.

Parental Attributions

Parents' beliefs about their child determine whether the child feels accepted or rejected, and consequently provide an indirect measure of attachment security. These beliefs are also related to the child's emotional and behavioral problems. In fact, children in foster care who also had sexual behavior problems were more likely to be viewed negatively by care providers (Friedrich et al., 2005).

Attributions can be assessed with the brief Parenting Stress Inventory (Abidin, 1995). This is a 36-item scale that includes a subscale titled Difficult Child. The items in this subscale concern times when parents view their children in a very negative light. When this subscale is elevated, parents fail to see much goodness in their children. For example, they think of them as being deliberately mean. In these cases, an early treatment goal should be to help alter these perspectives.

If you have any concerns about negative attributions, then there is a good chance that the child feels rejected. It is not surprising to me to have a parent report that he or she "feels better when the child is out of the room," and then be faced with a child whose social skills are described as coercive, and who derives some relational needs via occasional sexual touching of another child.

While parents may have certain attributions about their child in general, they can also have different attributions about their child's sexual acting out. The questions below were specifically directed at the mother of a boy who masturbated frequently. She was very upset at how distressed she became whenever she observed him doing this. The following questions, although specific to this particular child's sexual behavior, can be tailored depending on the issue at hand and expanded as you see fit (Friedrich, 2002).

1. What happens to your gut when you see him do that?
2. What's your theory about why he does that?
3. Do you think he'll just stop on his own?
4. Is there a part of him that is just doing this to drive you nuts?
5. What would happen if you just told him to stop?
6. Do you think he'll grow into a sexual offender?
7. What would it take for him to realize that he just needs to stop doing that?

These questions fall into the categories of powerlessness over the child, belief that the child is being willful, and negative future outcome.

Parental History of Maltreatment

Previous maltreatment contributes to parenting problems and the probability of insecure attachment. This history increases the probability of ghosts that make the parent more reactive to such topics as sexuality.

You may feel very comfortable asking parents about their abuse history via interview. However, screening measures are available, including one titled Problems in Your Family When Growing Up (published in Friedrich, 2002). These questions are more likely to be valid since they typically ask about specific events and acts, for example, "Made you touch the sex organs of their body when you didn't want this?" Regrettably, the questions do not address emotional neglect, an important construct related to feeling unloved and unsupported. However, asking parents if they felt "that there was an adult who was truly there for them" as they were growing up can suffice to screen for this.

If you rely on the interview to obtain information about prior maltreatment, you run the risk of not asking parents about their maltreatment history in a consistent or sensitive manner. For example, you will have fewer acknowledgments of past sexual abuse if you simply ask, "Were you ever sexually abused?" You will obtain a higher yield if you ask, "Think back prior to the age of 18. Did you ever have any type of unwanted sexual experience with peers, family members, friends of your parents, or simple acquaintances?" These differences provide further justification for using screening measures at the beginning of the therapy.

One paper studied the most valid strategy to assess for prior abuse (Harned, 2004). Researchers and clinicians typically use one of two methods: asking people if they were ever abused or assessing if the person has experienced any unwanted sexual acts. It is probably not surprising that assessing for unwanted sexual acts was more valid and more directly related to symptoms. The same strategy also appears to be valid for emotional and physical abuse (Friedrich et al., 1997).

Parental Mood Problems

Depressed parents are less available to their children and more critical of them (Dodge, 1990). They are also likely to have reduced energy for parenting and are often more pessimistic. All of these factors interfere with treatment that relies on heavy parental involvement. If I am concerned about depression, I will administer one of the versions of the Beck Depression Inventory (Beck, 1996). Over 35% of the parents of children with sexual behavior problems that I have seen report at least mild to moderate depressive symptoms on this scale. Some can be helped by medication and can then be more available to their child.

Substance Abuse History

Almost one of four parents (custodial and noncustodial included) of children with sexually intrusive behavior that I have assessed report a current or prior problem with substance abuse, including alcohol. These figures certainly support screening for this problem area. Typically one or two questions will suffice if they include the following: "One or more persons in my family or at my work have said they were concerned about my drinking/drug use," and "I have gotten into trouble because of my drinking/drug use."

Social Support

The parents of children with externalizing problems are often entrapped (Wahler, 1980) and conflicted in their own families, and frequently have few friends in the community. Support by close friends has been shown to facilitate the quality of attachment in young parents with their children (Egeland et al., 1988). Be sure to ask parents about the balance (positive and negative) of support they feel from family and friends. The majority of the parents I see feel undersupported.

Domestic Violence

The TESI (Ford et al., 2000) contains several questions about physical threat (e.g., have they seen "people in your family physically fighting, beating up, or attacking each other?" as well as people outside the family). However, admitting to the presence of violence in the home is difficult for many parents. Consequently, as you review the TESI, it is often useful to requestion parents about these behaviors, and their child's age and level of fear at the time they witnessed this. Domestic violence makes children feel insecure with their caregiver and can explain why a family is struggling. It is also a model of coercive behavior.

Family Safety

The Safety Checklist (Friedrich, 2002) is a semistructured interview (see Chapter 8, Form B) that is typically completed in the first two to three sessions. The Safety Checklist assesses a number of areas that can contribute to sexual acting out. These include cosleeping, cobathing, family nudity, aggressive behavior, family sexuality, pornography, PTSD triggers, community violence, and the quality of monitoring by the parent of the child. This measure makes sense to parents and serves to both interview and educate them about key issues that may need to change.

For example, the questions help the parent see the relationship between overt family violence or sexuality and the child's sexual behavior problems. By using the checklist as a semistructured interview, you have many opportunities to plant seeds about the need to change risky behaviors. You are also in a position to create links between one safety area and the child's behavior, such as witnessing sexuality and subsequent sexual behavior.

Parents who grew up in unsafe homes often struggle to provide safety for their children. If safety was poorly modeled for them, it is not part of their internal working model. Furthermore, they often have trouble believing that their life experiences do not have to be the same as their children's (Fonagy & Target, 1997). For example, neglectful parents are very good at ignoring their child's needs, dangerous situations, and so on. Their parenting creates many unsafe circumstances for children. Neglectful parents are also particularly difficult to change (Friedrich, Tyler, & Clark, 1985), since they often do not become anxious about situations that would distress many parents.

When I first started to use the Safety Checklist, I was struck by the number of parents who did not see a connection between sexual exposure or seeing violence and their child's subsequent behavior. Consequently, I systematically interviewed 31 consecutive parents—before interviewing them with the Safety Checklist—about why they thought their child was acting out sexually. Almost 40% replied with an answer that suggested the child was "bad" or "mean" or deliberately provocative to them personally. Another 20% mentioned impulsivity, and most of the remainder mentioned probable sexual abuse. Very few talked about safety issues, such as family nudity or parental intercourse being witnessed as a possible cause. This is one more reason why screening for safety can be therapeutic; parents now have a clearer perspective on possible reasons why their child is having these problems.

Since parents do not automatically think about safety, these questions not only educate them but also assess for additional risk. For example, it is not uncommon for parents to allow an older sibling with sexual behavior problems to continue sleeping in the same room with the preschool sibling she had touched. Several other parents allowed an older child with sexual behavior problems to bathe with the younger sister with whom he had engaged in repeated sexual play.

Monitoring as Assessment

I often ask parents to keep track of one of the concerning and relatively frequent behaviors between the first and the second session (see Chapter 8, Form I). This exercise can be very useful at determining their ability to cooperate with an important part of treatment—the follow-up after sessions. It is important for the success of treatment that the parent be involved in tracking and monitoring the child's behavior between sessions, providing encouragement and praise when the child follows the rules and therapeutic suggestions, and intervening quickly when the child slips into problematic patterns. Through this tracking system, you will obtain additional information on the extent of the problem.

Parental Response Style

After meeting the parent and reviewing the completed measures, you are in a position to tell whether the parent is able to report honestly or is defensive or prone to exaggeration. The perceptions of the latter two groups of parents will interfere with subsequent treatment and need to be addressed early on. I typically reframe defensiveness as protectiveness of their child and praise them for it. When parents exaggerate, you may reply with a reframe that goes like, "You really wanted to make sure I saw all the problems you are dealing with. But I also want you to see his positives when they show up."

ELEMENTS OF SCREENING BATTERY: CHILD

Assessment involves the child and includes observations, interviews, and, for older children, the selective use of self-report measures. The child's assessment has some elements that are evaluated by the parent, such as the child's PTSD symptoms and the extent of the sexual behavior problems. It is important to understand both how the parent views the child's behavior and how the child perceives and reports the behavior. The views may be similar or quite different, and this will influence how you will work with the family. If the reports are similar and appear to be reasonably accurate, this is a sign that interventions will progress well. If they are highly dissimilar, for example, the parent exaggerates and the child does not recognize the problem, or the parent denies and the child appears to be significantly minimizing the problem, this can alert the therapist that intervention needs to focus on moving the parent and child to more similar views of the child's problematic behavior. Assessment domains include personal boundaries, developmental level, PTSD, and sexual behavior or sexual preoccupation. I also obtain information from older children about the nature of their intrusive sexual behavior.

Boundaries

Assessment of younger children, whose capacity to self-report is compromised, is usually derived from parent input and your observations of the child's interaction with you and their parent or caregiver. All children, regardless of age, should be carefully observed along the dimensions of personal boundaries and overt sexuality. As children get older, they are less and less likely to exhibit overt problems in these domains with you, a relative stranger. However, it is not too uncommon for an older latency-age female and even the occasional boy to show some boundary problems as the interview progresses. When this occurs, I am very concerned about future vulnerability to victimization. For example, I have asked children to draw pictures, and before they are done, they have tapped me with the pencil, bumped their shoe into my leg, and asked me a personal question. All of these suggest problems with personal boundaries and increased intrusiveness.

I created a Therapist's Rating Scale (Friedrich, 2002; see Chapter 8, Form D), which provides a guidelines for the two domains of boundaries and sexual behavior. Behaviors to be aware of include self-stimulating behavior, or if the child touches you for no reason and makes sexual comments. Other children show their distress by grabbing their crotch or touching other parts of their body during questioning or play activity. I have observed a number of sexually abused females who sit in a manner that exposes their underwear. Rarely, children become aroused as they talk about their abuse or what they have done to other children. Boys may have an erection or touch their crotch. I have also seen an occasional girl touch her chest or wedge her hands between her legs at these times. These behaviors are extremely concerning to me, and in my experience they suggest that these children are more highly sexualized. As adults and other children can view these behaviors in school settings, it is suggested that treatment focus on reducing or eliminating them as quickly as possible.

Developmental Level

The prevalence of developmental delay and learning problems increases in clinical samples (Webster-Stratton & Reid, 2003) and this is also true with preschoolers who exhibit concerning sexual behavior (Hewitt, 1999; Silovsky & Niec, 2002). Typically you ask the parent about developmental level and school performance in the first interview. However, when a developmentally delayed child has been accused of touching a younger child, and the court system is now involved, it can be helpful to obtain a more formal assessment of the child's developmental level and IQ. I have used this information several times to influence the courts to act more sensitively because of the child's developmental delay. For example, an 11-year-old boy with an IQ in the mildly retarded range was actually less mature than the 7-year-old he was reported to have sexually touched.

Post-Traumatic Stress Disorder

It is important to assess for trauma-related symptoms. The most reliable source about these symptoms will be the parent, at least for children ages 10 and under. However, after that age, children are in a better position to self-report and in fact data exist showing that children are better at identifying internal symptoms than are parents (Stone & Lemanek, 1990). PTSD scales for children exist, and several of these are discussed in Friedrich (2002). I prefer to use the Trauma Symptom Checklist for Children (TSCC; Briere, 1996) since this 52-item scale also asks questions not only about PTSD components but also about sexual distress and other affective symptoms. The existence of PTSD in a child with sexual behavior problems will amplify and expand your treatment focus, since PTSD by itself warrants intervention. The percentage of sexually abused children who report PTSD varies widely from one study to the next (Friedrich, 2002) but in my experience, the percentage is even higher in children with intrusive sexual behavior.

Sexual Behavior and Sexual Preoccupation

It is also important to assess for children's sexual focus and the degree to which sexual thoughts dominate their mentation. Once again, interviews are not that useful at assessing sexual focus. In addition, no self-report measure exists for very young children to report on their sexual behavior.

The Sexual Concerns items from the TSCC (Briere, 1996) are variably useful for older children. Two clusters of items are included in this scale, sexual preoccupation and sexual distress. Sometimes it is the child's behavioral response to the items that is most illuminating. For example, a child may express disgust with these items while completing the test in my office and make comments such as, "These are nasty." The child may not endorse any items but the comments suggest otherwise. These are important cues that should invite you to query further. Even if the child denies any issue, the topic is broached when you comment, "You really want to let me know what you think about sex," or "I knew a kid who told me he thought sex was disgusting, but later I found out he thought about it all the time."

If I am interacting with children who have touched several children, or made sexual comments in my office, I often tell them a therapeutic story about another, similar-aged child who was preoccupied with sexuality. After I have created the story, I will state that this child seemed to have "sex on the brain. They couldn't stop thinking about sex." I might then say that "when you talk like that, I wonder if you think about sex sometimes or even a lot of the time." I then help them answer this question by using a circle diagram to create a percentage of the time or a number of times each day that they think about sex. Such children may clam up and tell you little, but what you now have is a metaphor and permission for this topic to be discussed at a later date. This type of groundwork early on can open up children to being more forthcoming with some of their sexual thoughts.

I believe the majority of children with sexual behavior problems do not persist with these problems as adults. However, children who think about sex or their sexual experiences and are over 9 years old are concerning to me. These children are more likely to maintain their sexual preoccupation. They warrant a more significant individual treatment focus, combined with the family-based approach that is emphasized here.

Drawings and selected projective picture cards are things that some clinicians use with these children. Drawings from such series as the Roberts Apperception Test for Children (MacArthur & Roberts, 1982) are a way to assess a child's sexual focus more precisely. Card 5 from the Roberts depicts a child looking at a couple who appear to be close to kissing. Card 15 shows a woman sitting in a bathtub with a boy looking through a crack in the door. If the child makes comments about "doing it" or "peeping" or demonstrates agitation in response to either of these cards, this also suggests to you that benign pictures are seen as sexual by the child (Brilleslijper-Kater et al., 2004). This child has more information on sexual behavior than his or her peers, and addressing it is an important therapy focus (Friedrich & Share, 1997).

There are number of features of drawings that can be indicative of sexual preoccupation, including secondary sexual characteristics, particularly from younger children; adding detail below the waist in the form of a zipper or other details that have a genital focus; and the drawing of provocative dress. I have also observed young severely abused children spontaneously drawing sexual acts when asked to draw a picture of their family or of a person. This is an indication of the degree to which their own abuse dominates their life and most likely contributes to their subsequent sexual behavior. Older children are often better able to keep their drawings benign.

Problematic Sexual Behavior

Over the years, I grew very frustrated at asking children to talk about any sexual things that had happened to them and what sexual things they had done to another child. I believe that older children should talk about their behavior with you and make it an important part of therapy. To talk about a shameful action exposes the anxiety and opens the door to inhibition of future behavior. However, this process was typically painful and characterized by long silences, lots of "I don't know," and "I can't remember," and a breakdown in the therapeutic alliance. There was a period of time when I either variably or rarely asked for this information since I had met with so much resistance.

However, I hit upon a strategy to make the process more open and collaborative. I came up with a list of 21 questions. I share a copy of these questions with the child at the onset of the interviews that I plan on having with the child to obtain this information (see Chapter 8, Form F). I often show the list to parents as well, especially if I am asking them to encourage their child to talk to me. By proceeding in this way, children have a copy of each question and know exactly what is expected of them. They also know what questions have been asked and which ones remain. When I can address these topics conversationally and stay away from asking one question after the other, I have been struck by the degree to which children become partners in the process. They have been more open with me about their history and what they did with other children. With some children, I will negotiate how many questions we address per session and occasionally reinforce their efforts with an extra activity or reward. I do not expect that all of these questions will be answered, although I do not share that expectation with children at the onset of my interviewing. However, with older children, I believe that the majority of them can and should be answered. Asking and answering these questions is therapeutic and provides another strategy for combining assessment and therapy into one process.

Child Self-Report

The validity of input from the child depends upon both the child's developmental age and how much you need to know about the abuse. How important is it for you to have children spell out specifically what they did to another child? I make a judgment call with each child, but adolescent and adult treatment programs are vehement about the need for their patients to take ownership of their behavior and describe it fully. Does that make it imperative that preteens are dealt with in the same manner? No, it does not.

Reviewing a child's sexual behavior is a different matter when a child is very young. For example, a 5-year-old might assume that adults already know what happened. Young children's reports of their own sexual behavior are likely to be faulty and incomplete, and often cannot be completely verified. If pressured, the child is likely to feel coerced and even more distant from you. This interferes with the first stage of therapy, and the data you obtain will add little to the treatment process.

Older children also vary in their capacity to self-report on standardized measures. Accurate self-report requires training in the understanding of emotions, trust that children have permission to report their feelings, and trust in the evaluator. However, metacognition is reduced in insecurely attached children (Fonagy & Target, 1997) and abused children have fewer words for feelings than do nonabused children (Beeghly & Cicchetti, 1994; Toth et al., 1997). Children who lack training in the identification and reporting of feelings will tell you very little, even when they are old enough to be able to (Aldridge & Wood, 1997). Insignificant elevations are far more common on a self-report measure such as the TSCC (Briere, 1996) than are significant elevations for children with sexual behavior problems. As a group, these children appear to be more compromised in their self-report capacity.

Shame

One of the risk factors listed by Hall and her colleagues (1998) pertains to children blaming themselves for the abuse. This is related to feelings of shame about both their own abuse and the behavior they exhibited to another child. Some degree of shame about their behavior with the other child is probably more therapeutic than not, since it suggests a degree of self-responsibility and empathy.

A paper by Schore (1996) linked the concept of shame to both attachment security and dysregulation. He stated that shame is a "primary social emotion" (p. 69) and makes its appearance at 14 to 16 months. Schore attributes its emergence to a break in affective attunement with the primary caregiver and elaborates further when he writes, "shame represents this rapid state transition from a preexisting positive state to a negative state" (p. 69). Shame then becomes an attachment emotion, and is the reaction "to an important other's unexpected refusal to enter into a dyadic system that can recreate an attachment bond" (p. 69). How long and how frequently a child remains in this state is an important factor in his or her ongoing emotional development.

Shame clearly is tied to both attachment and self-regulation. The already tenuous parent-child relationship is now frayed further due to the shameful reactions of both the parent and the child to the child's inappropriate behavior. Items to assess shame are in the Assessment and Treatment Manual (Chapter 8, Form N), and can also be incorporated into the therapy session at a later date.

Shame and guilt correlate with the emergence of postabuse sexual behavior problems (Hall & Mathews, 1996) and the persistence of symptoms in victims (Deblinger & Hefflin, 1996; Feiring, Taska, & Lewis, 1996). However, a 10-year follow-up of official reports on these factors seems to clearly indicate inaccurate perception of trauma, a history of impaired attachment, and a lack of training or modeling of self-regulation.

Risk for Reoffense

Children with sexual behavior problems prompt questions about safety with siblings and potential for reoffense. According to parental reports, the recidivism rate for another inappropriate sexual behavior was 15% after 2 years in the Oklahoma Study (Bonner et al., 2000). While there is some agreement about risk factors for adolescent offenders (Prentky, Harris, Frizzell, & Right-hand, 2000), no validated risk assessment exists for the preteen age group. Subsequent research may identify factors that elevate the potential to reoffend, but that is not yet available.

If you are asked about future risk for a preteen, begin by stating that it is nearly impossible to do this on an individual basis. However, there are times when you may have concerns. In these cases, I suggest looking closely at Hall's risk factors (Hall et al., 1998) and calculating the degree to which the child meets them. However, remember that these risk factors were developed with sexually abused children. Other variables that are not included in Hall's risk factors (see Table 1.1; Hall et al., 1998) but are likely to contribute to reoffense include a longer history of exposure to sexuality, earlier onset of sexual abuse, multigenerational history of sexual abuse in the family, violence in the home, and severe externalizing behavior in the child.

There is an additional measure that I have used with some very disturbed 12-year-olds in the past several years. The Antisocial Process Screening Device (APSD; Frick & Hare, 2002) is a juvenile version of the Psychopathy Checklist–Revised (Hare, 1991), an instrument used with adult sex offenders. On several occasions, I have received congruent data on the APSD from both parents and teachers and used the data to argue for or against outpatient treatment. Caution should be used when interpreting information from this instrument, as multiple informants are necessary for a valid assessment on this face-valid measure.

OTHER ASSESSMENT CONSIDERATIONS

Sexually abused children vary in the nature and degree of sexual reactivity to abuse. For example, children's trauma-based sexualized responses may be gender-specific; that is, children may only behave in certain sexually inappropriate ways with one sex or another (Hewitt, 1999). This explains why female children molested by males may engage in highly sexualized behaviors with males but behave appropriately with females. In rare cases, if the child's sexual behavior toward a male therapist persists after appropriate intervention, it may be useful to include a female therapist in the treatment to assess the incidence of inappropriate sexual behavior with the opposite gender. With these children, the perspective of both male and female caregivers and therapists can be useful.

A second factor, more important than in other areas of assessment described in this book, is that the evaluator must be comfortable asking very personal, sexual questions. Can you ask a 10-year-old boy who has sexually touched several other children such questions as "How often do you rub your penis to make it feel good?" "To make it get hard?" "What do you think about when you rub your penis?" "What did it feel like to touch so-and-so's private parts, and you can't just say I don't know?" Now imagine asking related questions of an 11-year-old girl who fondled a child while babysitting. Questions of this type yield information useful to the evaluator. Remember, the goal is to have a conversation in which the child feels comfortable, not an inquisition. When done in this manner, your questions begin the important process of allowing children to examine and discuss their experiences, which helps correct behavior and thinking.

In summary, the assessment of children with sexual behavior problems must take into consideration some variables that are not commonly evaluated in children who have been sexually abused but have not developed sexual behavior problems. These include the nature of children's abusive experiences; their history of rule-violating behavior; contextual limits on future behavior; parent discipline practices; and the quality of the parent-child relationship. The assessment of these domains does not necessarily involve any of the new approaches that have been already outlined. However, the evaluator must have a sharp appreciation of the abuse-aggression link, the variability of these children, and the problems inherent in predicting behavior, particularly aggressive behavior.

GOAL SETTING

Establishing treatment goals also helps speed up the treatment process. Let's imagine that you have now met with the parent and child for a couple of sessions. You have a good idea about what is going on and the challenges that the parent faces in managing the child's behavior. Ask parents what would have to change for them to feel that the child is improving. The better-functioning and less resistant parents will actually answer that question with some quantifiable goals. Other parents will need your guidance in arriving at treatment goals. The key is for these parents to adopt them for themselves.

Three clusters of goals are imperative: (1) improved safety in the home; (2) reducing the problem behaviors that have been identified; and (3) enhancing the parent-child relationship. Safety is immediately reflected in the establishment of sexual rules for the child, as well as for other individuals in the home who might behave in ways that reflect problems with boundaries and sexuality. The child's sexual behavior may be the first sexual goal set, particularly if it is self-focused behavior (e.g., masturbation), and the child is fairly persistent or even self-injurious. If this is the case, treatment needs to focus on this problematic behavior immediately. In cases in which the child touched or was sexually aggressive with another child some time ago and the behavior has not reoccurred since it was reported, this behavior may not be the immediate focus of therapy. Consequently it does not make a very useful treatment goal. Other frequent behaviors that are more appropriate include noncompliance with the parent, sexual talk, tantrums, failure to follow a sleep schedule, or difficulty turning in homework.

The parent-child relationship is also a primary focus, and at the very least, parents need to set a goal to learn some strategies so that they can spend more positive time with their child and repair the relationship. More information about using these goals in treatment in provided in the Assessment and Treatment Manual, (Chapter 8, Form J).

The F. Family

F.F. was a 10-year-old girl who was referred because she sexually touched Cassie, a 4-year-old girl, in a day care setting. During her 3 months at this day care center, she had established herself in a parental role and frequently helped serve snacks and get children packed up when parents arrived; additionally, she helped two younger children with toileting. One of these was Cassie, who was reportedly sexually touched during toileting.

F.F. was adopted at the age of 4. She lived with her adoptive parents and had a 17-year-old sister, the biological daughter of her parents. Neither of her adoptive parents had a history of sexual abuse, and both had generally good relationships with their families of origin. F.F.'s postadoption adjustment was characterized as uneventful, and she had never been identified as a behavior problem. For example, her grades in school were typically above average. Her preadoptive experiences, however, included neglect and physical abuse. Sexual abuse was never confirmed, although it was probable given her rearing circumstances, wherein her mother had numerous male companions.

Ms. F., the adoptive mother, reported that F.F. had exhibited a 9- to 12-month history of greater sexual interest and daily genital touching after the adoption, but this had faded before she entered kindergarten. For example, she had often come into the bathroom when her mother was there and, at those times, would point to different body parts on her mother. However, the mother had used some mild limit setting and the behavior had stopped. More recently, F.F. had started talking about boyfriends, and Ms. F. felt that F.F. had a long-standing problem of being overly friendly with adult males. However, this had never presented itself as a problem in their home. She also wondered if the interest in boyfriends was due to the fact that her 17-year-old daughter had a boyfriend.

Ms. F. also reported that she and her husband were in marital therapy and would most likely be separating. Her return to full-time employment was in response to this likelihood and was why F.F. was now in after-school day care. She agreed that F.F. had a very helpful side and thought this varied directly with her own anxiety.

Ms. F. wondered whether F.F. was adversely affected by the upsurge in family tension over the previous 6 months. She was also concerned about Cassie, whom she knew from having observed her at the day care. Ms. F. described a number of incidents suggesting that Cassie was an impulsive, aggressive, and provocative child. She cited a situation where she had seen Cassie hitting another 4-year-old female at the day care. It was her opinion that F.F. was in a vulnerable position with her and regretted that the two had been together unsupervised in the bathroom.

At the end of this first meeting, Ms. F. completed the Child Behavior Checklist (Achenbach, 1991a), the Parenting Stress Inventory–Short Form (Abidin, 1995), the CSBI (Friedrich, 1997), and the Parent-Child Conflict Tactics Scale (Straus et al., 1998). She signed a release to have F.F.'s teacher complete a Teacher Report Form (Achenbach, 1991b), which I typically modify by adding three additional sexual items: (1) plays with sex parts in public; (2) sex play with peers; and (3) sex problems (describe) (Friedrich, 1997). Ms. F. also agreed to ask the day care provider to complete a Child Behavior Checklist and CSBI on F.F.

F.F. was very subdued when I first met with her and exhibited some separation anxiety in the waiting area, which persisted into the first few minutes of the interview. She had little recollection of her preadoptive life, although she had been told that she was hospitalized once as a baby for not gaining weight. She liked school and wanted to be a teacher when she grew up. She identified her best friend as a 7-year-old girl in the neighborhood.

She was highly uncomfortable speaking about the incident with Cassie, becoming flushed and squirming in the chair during this portion of the interview. She agreed that she had touched Cassie's "potty" three times, and volunteered that Cassie had asked her to touch her the first time and that Cassie "told me to use my two fingers like this and move them like that." Cassie asked to see her "privates," but she only showed them to her once. She felt "funny" when this happened, but after looking over a feelings poster, was able to elaborate that she had felt scared, excited, ashamed, and anxious. She knew it was wrong and assured the interviewer that it would never happen again because "Cassie can use the bathroom herself." She completed the Multidimensional Anxiety Schedule for Children (MASC; March, 1997), the Child Depression Inventory (Kovacs, 1991), and the TSCC (Briere, 1996), after agreeing to my request that she read each item carefully and answer honestly. I was available during this time to decipher any confusing words, but she did not need any help with words, although she often referenced the feelings poster.

Parent-Caregiver Reports

Ms. F.'s responses to the Child Behavior Checklist (Achenbach, 1991a) suggested social competence scores within normal limits, including Social, a subscale measuring relationships with friends. Two mild clinical elevations were noted, on Anxious/Depression ($T = 66$) and also on Withdrawal ($T = 65$). She endorsed such items as "cries," "nervous," "fearful," "guilty," and "self-conscious" for Anxious/Depressed and "secretive," "shy," and "withdrawn" for Withdrawal. She endorsed four items on the CSBI. These were "stands too close to others," "overly friendly with men they don't know well," "touches another child's sex parts," and "interested in the opposite sex." This translated into T scores of 67 on Total Sexual Behavior, 71 on Developmentally Related Sexual Behavior, and 60 on Sexual Abuse Specific Items. On the Parenting Stress Index–Short Form (Abidin, 1995), she answered validly and nondefensively, with her defensive responding score at the 45th percentile. Scores ranged from 15% on Parental Distress to 51% on Parent-Child Dysfunctional Interaction, and 44 percent on Difficult Child. This resulted in a total stress score at the 40th percentile. This was in keeping with what I saw: a mother who did not feel overly distressed, generally felt positively about F.F., and enjoyed the parenting process. Finally, she reported primarily positive parenting strategies on the Conflict Tactics Scale (e.g., use of time out, positive reinforcement), but also admitted to occasional shouting and slapping on the hand.

Further support for the accuracy of Ms. F.'s perceptions of F.F. came from the Teacher Report Form (Achenbach, 1991b) completed by F.F.'s fifth grade teacher. Adaptive Functioning scores were in the normal range. Clinical scales were also in the normal range with the exception of a mild elevation on Withdrawn ($T = 63$). The teacher did not endorse any of the three sexual behavior items.

The day care provider had only known F.F. for 3 months. Consequently, she was less sure of many items on Social Competence. However, she did not report any clinical problems. On the CSBI, she endorsed two of the four items that Ms. F. had identified: "stands too close to others" and "touches another child's sexual parts." This translated into a Total Sexual Behavior of $T = 52$, $T = 45$ for Developmentally Related Sexual Behavior, and $T = 45$ for Sexual Abuse Specific Items. At the bottom of the measure she wrote that had she rated Cassie, she would have endorsed 15 to 20 items. This comment suggested that Cassie was far more sexually focused than was F.F.

Child Report

F.F. did report a clinically significant elevation ($T = 67$) on Social Anxiety from the MASC (March, 1997), with a secondary elevation on Humiliation/Rejection, a subscale from that domain. A sample item from Humiliation/Rejection is, "I'm afraid other people will think I'm stupid." However, she did not report a significant level of Physical Symptoms or Harm Avoidance, and her MASC total score was $T - 57$.

On the Child Depression Inventory (Kovacs, 1991), she was clinically elevated on Negative Self-Esteem ($T = 68$), for example, "I do not like myself," and Interpersonal Problems ($T = 67$), for example, "I am bad many times." On the TSCC (Briere, 1996), she answered validly, and most T scores were in the 52-58 range, with the exception of Sexual Concerns ($T = 72$) and the related subscale, Sexual Distress ($T = 87$).

Parent and caregiver ratings of F.F.'s general behavior suggested a girl who felt less sure with peers and responded to this uncertainty with some withdrawal. She also tended to be more anxious, emotional, and self-critical than average. Some of her sexual behaviors were more specific to the incident with Cassie, but others suggested a needy girl whose interpersonal boundaries needed shoring up. Her adoptive mother did not report that F.F. was overly challenging to parent; she described her in a generally positive tone and generally employed very appropriate disciplinary techniques.

It is not very common, but always heartening, to see overlap between parent and child report. F.F. reported a significant level of peer insecurity and feelings of being bad. When I questioned her later, the Negative Self-Esteem items from the Child Depression Inventory were related to her behavior with Cassie and suggested some elevation in shame. In addition, her report of elevated Sexual Concerns is appropriate to the situation and reflects a girl who is not denying her vulnerability in this domain. The fact that other trauma-related scales from the TSCC were not elevated is also a positive and in keeping with her report that she remembers very little of her life prior to her adoption.

This screening data allowed us to suggest that F.F.'s preference for caretaking and befriending younger children put her in a vulnerable situation with a provocative and sexualized girl. Additionally, her adoptive parents' potential separation and divorce most likely was contributing to her behavioral reactivity. Treatment suggestions included a greater focus on developing peer relations via play dates (Frankel, 1996), helping F.F. see herself more accurately and with less shame, and increasing overall positive parent-child interactions (Hembree-Kigin & McNeil, 1995). In addition, Ms. F. and her husband were advised to work even harder on providing reassurances to F.F. about her continued well-being despite their problems. Both parents agreed to learn the child-directed interaction portion of parent-child interaction therapy (Hembree-Kigin & McNeil, 1995) and, in addition, we established several rules about personal boundaries and intrusive sexual behavior. I also spent several individual sessions with F.F.

At a 7-month follow up, F.F.'s mother expressed appreciation for the sexual rules. She had started to date, and F.F. had initially made one of her male friends uncomfortable but had stopped the behavior after being privately reminded of the rules. There had been no further instances of sexual touching, and Ms. F. reported that she and F.F. were closer as a result of the child-directed interaction. I suggested that sometime in her teen years, it would be useful for F.F. to spend a few sessions with a therapist, with a focus on helping her understand how her "unknown past" may or may not be activated as she grows into a young adult and, eventually, a parent.

CONCLUSION

Two often-competing forces operate when working with families of children with sexual behavior problems. The first is that troubled families are difficult to keep in therapy long enough to create an impact. The second is that the greater-than-usual complexity and variability of the families of children with sexual behavior problems require careful assessment. These two competing forces are best answered if the assessment and treatment process are seamless and begin at the first contact.

A seamless process can occur when the therapist immediately focuses on the alliance by being empathic and supportive, responding to parents with education, encouragement, and a clear road map of how to proceed. The use of selected screening instruments also speeds this process along, since they inform the therapist and parent about key issues (e.g., parent-child relationship and safety) and make the rationale and focus of therapy understandable.

Ideally, assessment should be understandable and part of treatment. I have found that when therapy-naive and therapy-resistant parents appreciate what your purpose is, understand why you are asking the questions you ask, and feel respected in the process, therapy can often proceed long enough so that there is an impact.

5

PARENT-CHILD INTERACTION THERAPY AS AN ATTACHMENT-BASED INTERVENTION

MOST CLINICIANS READING this book have had a mixture of positive and frustrating experiences with behavioral family therapy and the behavioral management programs that typically accompany this type of therapy. With mildly disturbed children, these techniques can bring an end to symptoms quite rapidly. However, with more entrenched children, the change can be quite slow, especially if the child responds with increased coercion and other strategies are not employed. Maltreated children can be particularly oppositional and aggressive in response to beleaguered parents and may present with a mixture of internalizing and aggressive symptoms that reflect their PTSD (Kolko, 1996).

One example of a frustration you may encounter is as follows. You have explained the use of a point system to the parents or role-played the use of time-out in your office. However, in the week between sessions, the parents have revised the program so that it is punitive, or they announce to you that they have tried everything but it is not working. Over the years I learned not to rush in too early, but so often the child's behavior was so difficult to manage and the parent's story so compelling that I still succumbed to the urge to "try something."

What I have appreciated so much about parent-child interaction therapy PCIT (Hembree-Kigin & McNeil, 1995), and the reason it is the central component of family treatment described in the Assessment and Treatment Manual, is that it pays close attention to the fact that before beleaguered or abusive parents can interact successfully with their child, we need to help them repair the parent-child relationship. The repair begins by having them spend more positive time with their child—a very common deficiency. The PCIT framework provides the necessary rationale for parents to wait before intervening too quickly. It also helps parents to appreciate that the change process requires that they change as well. Other management programs, such as positive parenting, have the same philosophy, but extensive, in-session time spent coaching parents in how to be more positive with their child and how to avoid getting caught in old traps sets PCIT apart from these other systems.

Although developed for oppositional preschoolers, PCIT has been used successfully with older, physically abused children whose parents have been court referred for treatment (Chaffin et al., 2004; Timmer, Urquiza, Zebell, & McGrath, 2005). It has two essential components, child-directed interaction (CDI), which occurs in the first phase of treatment, and parent-directed interaction (PDI), the second phase of treatment, which is addressed after CDI has been successfully completed. CDI is where parents learn the selective attention and play skills necessary for establishing a warm and loving relationship with their child. They are taught to recognize their child's unique and special qualities, and learn how to avoid falling back into prior behaviors including coercion, criticism, and control. They will begin to view their child more positively and start to discard previous, erroneous attributions. As parents grow to like their child more, they will become less demanding and more child sensitive. PCIT has afforded me more direct examples of parents who say "I like my child for the first time!" than any other treatment strategy I have used over my many years of doing therapy.

The direct coaching, either via bug-in-the-ear or the low-tech system I use, which is to sit next to the parent, enables you to reinforce essential points of the intervention while you are lending your mind to the parent and creating a supportive presence. For example, I typically have already met the parent and spent some time with the parent and child together, so that I have a sense of their interaction. I will spend part of another session introducing the basic elements of PCIT to the parent, and role-play the parts that the parent seems to have difficulty understanding. The following week, the parent will bring in the child; the parent and I will have already reached an understanding that the focus this session will be on praise, one of the PRIDE skills (praise, reflect, imitate, describe, and enthusiasm). I will set a few ground rules for the next 10 minutes (e.g., staying seated).

Let's say a boy decides to start with Legos. Before the parent can say anything controlling or critical, have her imitate you and say, "Legos! A great choice." The child may be initially put off by the fact that the mom is now an echo of you, but he will quickly fall into the process because it will be so nice for him to hear four to five praises a minute when his typical diet is sometimes as few as one to two per day or even less.

If this child is very estranged from the parent, then he may start to act out fairly quickly. Rather than get ruffled when the parent turns to you with a look that says, "What did I tell you," have the parent either turn away from the child to ignore his actions or have her say, "I'd love to play with you but not until I hear your inside voice." With older children, I may create a praise list for the parent to use in the coaching session and at home. During coaching sessions, until we are ready to move on to other PRIDE skills, I will simply point to one of the praises. The key with any skill is to practice it outside of the session. It is important to spend some time with the parent figuring out when and where it can occur and how often each week. You will also need to determine whether there are other children in the family who will need to receive attention and figure out how to handle the logistics of that.

The process of in-session coaching should be an example of attuned and respectful behavior with the parent. Parents will typically feel scrutinized and uncomfortable, and it is up to you to help them get past this. While I often try to teach both praise and enthusiasm during the first session of coaching, if parents are subdued or appear depressed, I will not expect them to be enthusiastic that day or even the next week.

The skills that are taught with CDI are directly related to attachment theory. For example, praise helps to correct the positive–negative imbalance that exists in abusive families. This will help the child perceive the parent as a secure base. Reflection helps the child develop the internal state lexicon (Beeghly & Cicchetti, 1994) that is sorely lacking in maltreated children; as the internal state lexicon develops, the child will improve at identifying feelings and describing them to others. This will increase children's awareness of who they are with respect to other people. Reflection is also a function of attunement and can represent an exquisite meeting of minds between parent and child. Imitation requires some skill and should be practiced sensitively with older children to avoid insulting them. However, it is similar to praise in that it allows the parent to acknowledge that the child has done something very worthwhile that warrants imitation. Describe also adds to the intensity of connection between parent and child. When children hear their parents describe their actions, it reinforces the children's sense that they are being attended to in a positive manner. Because the attention is modulated, the child is better able to incorporate it. Enthusiasm also helps to resolve the positive–negative imbalance in the parent-child exchanges and will brighten the child's affective world, a very important correlate of secure attachment.

As you can see from the manual, one of the elements under praise is "touch."

This is not in the PCIT text (Hembree-Kigin & McNeil, 1995), but I believe that not only is it correlated with praise, it also provides a direct opportunity to teach parents how to touch their child appropriately and get them used to doing this. It is especially critical for children with intrusive sexual behavior to learn that their needs for affection can be met in appropriate ways by their parents. However, it is important to prepare the parent for this in the first session by teaching the techniques of praise. The parent's comfort level, current practice of touch, and the child's responses all need to be reviewed and processed so the practice can proceed in a way that is helpful for both of them.

Another aspect of CDI that facilitates attachment is the in-session coaching. If you approach this sensitively, you are in a position to serve as the good, wise parent that these parents typically did not have. Most parents will overcome their reluctance to be observed. It is very important for you to appreciate it when parents are really on the spot, especially if social services are involved. I typically intersperse positive comments to the parent, either indirectly to the child ("Your mom is doing great today!") or more directly to the parent ("I should get you to help some of the other people I work with," or "That was an outstanding reflection").

It is critical to be attuned to parents' discomfort with the process and modulate your behavior in accordance to what they can manage. I worked with one oppositional parent who could not reveal a glimpse of softness. Each praise I suggested was met with "I would never say it that way," and the result was that the child was never praised. So I shifted to having her say, "Dr. F. wants me to say . . ." which she generally complied with. When the end of the session came, I said, "I know you thought I was just blowing smoke in there, but you said it anyway. I greatly appreciated you hanging in there with me today." She calmly agreed with my assessment but came the next session and was more cooperative. This was also the mother who smiled when I told her children, "Your mom is no wimp."

The second component, PDI, is designed to teach parents how to use discipline strategies effectively. This phase of treatment complements CDI, which enhances the parent-child relationship. The CDI skills continue to be used throughout all phases of PCIT. In PDI, parents are taught several new skills: (1) how to give good instructions, (2) how to set appropriate limits, (3) how to behave in a consistent and predictable way, and (4) how to follow through with what they say. CDI alone is not effective in reducing significant behavior problems. It is the combination of a warm relationship (CDI) and appropriate limit setting (PDI) that is associated with the best outcomes for children, so both components are necessary. Remember, the PDI phase of PCIT comes after parents successfully master the CDI skills. Children will be more likely to comply with parental commands because during CDI they will have received lots of praise for minding and developed a positive relationship with their parents.

Initially, parents are taught to give single commands that are direct, positive, specific, age appropriate, respectful, and necessary. For example, in the session parents may say, "Please hand me a red crayon" or "Please hand me a blue block." If children comply with the command, they are immediately praised, using skills learned in CDI. If they do not comply, parents begin the negative consequence procedure, which begins with a warning and—if the children still do not do what they are expected to do—proceeds to using a 3-minute time-out from positive reinforcement (time-out chair). Parents are taught to use this procedure the same way every time to reinforce the PDI values of predictability, consistency, and follow through while giving minimal attention to the child's misbehavior.

Although this method is recommended in other parenting programs and cited in many parenting books, PCIT strives to ensure its success. So, rather than simply instructing parents to use time-out when their child does not obey a given command or instruction, PCIT increases the understanding and in-session practice of time-out by parents. Parents are taught the learning principles behind time-out, and all components of time-out are practiced: getting to time-out, behaviors likely to occur when the child is in time-out, and staying in time-out. The parents also learn options for how to handle when the child leaves time-out. Each step is designed to close the loopholes that many children find in traditional time-out programs, which are often inconsistent and ineffective.

The PDI procedure always begins with a command and ends with the child being praised for compliance. Once the time-out period is over (3 minutes plus 5 seconds of silence), the child is given an opportunity to mind or obey the instruction again. Compliance is acknowledged, but enthusiastic praise is reserved for the child's immediate compliance with a simple follow-up command. Parents are supported by active coaching, a hallmark of PCIT, as they move through the discipline procedure. In PCIT, parents are never asked to put the discipline skills in place with their child until they have been practiced in a therapy session, increasing both parent compliance with the discipline program and the overall program's success. Parents are taught to know how to handle discipline situations without having to make on-the-spot decisions that may be heavily based on their current emotional state. Once they see their skills working to reduce the child's problematic behaviors, they continue to use them in many settings.

Some of the children I have seen with sexual behavior problems have improved enormously and the results persist simply after CDI. But these children were typically younger. Their behaviors were more isolated, and they never had significant oppositionality or sexual preoccupation. In addition, their parents were able to appreciate that their child was changing due to their efforts. Parental and child pathology will certainly interfere with the success of any intervention, including all aspects of PCIT. When I observe this in the process, I try to back off and spend more time supporting the parent if it is the parent, or changing my focus with the child in the individual time I might be spending with him or her.

PDI seems essential for true change with the more disturbed group. It puts the parents in charge, and this is enormously reassuring to the child. They now feel they can engage their child directly rather than avoid or fight with their child. Parents have more follow though and consistency and this also serves to create a regulatory superstructure to the family.

PCIT forms a core of the Assessment and Treatment Manual outlined in Chapters 7 and 8. To master this invaluable framework, you must do two things: You must read the book thoroughly and you must actually practice coaching sessions with a colleague. Kazdin (2003) believed that a primary failure in translating such skills as PCIT from the lab to the office is that clinicians do not appreciate that it takes effort to really learn how to do this fluently. It also helps greatly to attend a formal PCIT training programs. These are conducted at the University of Florida, where cases and research are discussed and skills can be learned (the Web site is www.pcit.org). The University of California–Davis is also skill focused (the Web site is www.pcittraining.tv). The University of Alabama Health Sciences Center focuses on direct clinical applications (www.okpcit.org). Dr. Cheryl B. McNeil also teaches groups of therapists both on-site and at her home base at West Virginia University's Department of Psychology. As a trainer and human being, she has few equals.

I have utilized PCIT with many parents and children to increase the positive aspects of their relationship and to improve parents' discipline strategies. Several of these are described below. I think these examples will remind you of the clients you work with.

The T. Family

Many attachment-related themes are illuminated in this case study, particularly the multigenerational impact of sexual abuse on parenting. The 19-year-old stepnephew of the T. family, who had joined his mother in the city where the T. family lived, molested their 7-year-old son (T.T.) from an intact family over the course of several months. The abuse of T.T. first came to his parents' attention when the mother was called by the elementary school principal during the second week of school. She informed Mrs. T. that her son had been trying to set up a "sex club" with other boys, typically the older boys in the school. Several fifth graders had informed the principal that T.T. would talk to boys about "sucking his wiener" and him doing the same to them. When interviewed by protective services, he revealed the earlier abuse by the 19-year-old and reported that it typically involved mutual oral sex. He estimated that it had occurred about 10 times.

The family came in to see me and T.T. readily agreed that he was constantly thinking about "wieners." Since the older boy had left, he would aim the shower at his penis and imagine earlier experiences of oral sex. He had not been able to talk any of the boys at school into joining his sex club, but his father reported that T.T. had recently started to come into the parents' bathroom when the father was in there, and twice had asked to shower with him. T.T. also agreed that he would look at the crotches of teenage boys and imagined sexual interaction with these teenagers. He had attempted to find pornography on the Internet, but his parents had a lock on their computer and he had not been successful.

Mrs. T's use of a repressive coping style was first reflected in the results of the screening battery, in which she denied that T.T. had exhibited a single sexual behavior. Mrs. T. also revealed that when she was younger she had been molested by an older cousin over a several-year period but had "pushed it from my head." She had never received any therapy for her abuse, but was being treated for depression with an SSRI by her family physician. She appeared to have an avoidant attachment style with her son. She was not overtly supportive of him while I was interviewing him in front of her. I used a few items from Zeanah's Working Model of the Child Interview (Zeanah, Benoit, & Barton, 1996) and her responses suggested that she thought of her son in stereotypical and not highly individualized terms.

Because T.T. was so verbal and forthcoming and so obviously agitated, it was tempting to focus on him individually. In addition, he was suspended from school until I was able to inform the principal that he was ready to return. For several weeks, I made repeated requests to the parents to start PCIT and begin regular special parent-child time; however, T.T. was dropped off at therapy by an older sibling and the parents did not attend as requested. Mrs. T. then enrolled her son in a different school district. Only after he was suspended from the second school for the same behavior did his parents seem to hear my concern about their son. I told both of them that we had a narrow window of opportunity to make sure that T.T. associated them with normal love and affection and did not associate love and affection with the abuser. I added that the vehicle for doing this was for them to make themselves into the most inviting and special people T.T. had ever met in his life.

To her credit, the mother started to see a therapist who helped her with her abuse, and over time enabled her to be more open with her son. In addition, the father heard my plea and consistently came to therapy with T.T.; he also practiced special time with him, typically five times per week and some weeks even daily. After a few months, T.T.'s mother was able to become more fully involved, and both parents were then on the same page with T.T. They enlisted the aid of an older sibling to spend fun time with T.T. The parents' relationship with T.T. became more positive and exciting. Both parents had been inhibited about physical touch, such as hugging and touching T.T., but with my encouragement and some in-session practice they grew much more comfortable with this as well.

I was also spending weekly individual time with T.T. At the start, he was still thinking with some longing about his perpetrator, and over time grew quite embarrassed when asked to talk about the abuse. We worked on several strategies to help him stop his thoughts when he thought about his abuser or wanted to relive the abuse experiences. By the end of therapy, he was talking about his perpetrator with considerably less enthusiasm and frequency than before. For example, he was able to perceive the abuse as a trauma, and during some PTSD exercises was able to write that he had learned that the abuse "wasn't fun, it was bad" and made him "lose his friends."

I have seen T.T. yearly for follow-up after the initial 11 months of therapy and, several years later, he is a good student, has not been suspended, and reports that he rarely thinks about the abuse. His parents are still quite involved and much more physically affectionate with him than ever before. How he will negotiate adolescence is not known at this time but there is reason to think that we were helpful in correcting his attachment, and that by making it more secure, T.T. disconnected from the relationship he had with the perpetrator.

This case illustrates that parental abuse histories do persist and have an impact on their own families, even if the families are well functioning and report little adversity. The parents' increased involvement was critical in helping this young boy view his abuse more accurately, and enabled the individual work we did to have real meaning.

The L. Family

The L. family illustrates the importance of moving beyond the more typical in-office one-session-per-week format as necessary for many overwhelmed families. Ms. L. was the mother of three boys by three fathers, none of whom she had married: Calvin, age 11; Tom, age 10; and Nick, age 5. Ms. L., a health professional, had received social services support for physically abusing Calvin several years earlier. In fact, she continued a very harsh disciplinary style with the two older boys.

The referral came to me after an investigation substantiated that Calvin had molested Nick on at least three occasions. He had put his mouth on Nick's penis and then had forced Nick to do the same with him. Ms. L. informed me at intake that Calvin had been molested orally by her youngest brother, a teenager who had babysat Calvin when Calvin was 6 years old. Her brother had received therapy and no longer lived in the area.

A decision had not yet been made about Calvin remaining in the home, which was Ms. L.'s desire. However, the boys were poorly supervised for a several-hour period after school, and during this time, the two older boys engaged in extremely physical play. Nick was a target to get hit since his brother perceived him as Ms. L.'s favorite.

Ms. L.'s response to the boys reflected her relationship with their respective fathers. Tom's father was the only one who had visitation with his son. Ms. L. despised Calvin's father and, even though that influenced her view of her son, she didn't want Calvin to be damaged further by contact with him. Ms. L. was also estranged from her family of origin, and she reported that they had been emotionally and physically abusive to her when she was younger. She denied ever being sexually abused as a minor but alluded to a rape attempt when older. Despite this adversity, she was highly valued at her employment place and had worked there for many years. She often put in many extra hours on weekends. This presented a genuine monitoring problem in crafting a plan to keep Calvin in the home.

After two sessions with Ms. L., I felt more comfortable about her ability to parent, until I saw her with her three boys on the day I was to interview Calvin. The family was asked to leave the waiting room because of their pushing and shoving, and this continued even in another, less confined area. Ms. L. alternated between shrugging her shoulders, barking orders, and even deriving some delight that they were so out of control.

Calvin was a sad, anxious, and lonely boy who both appeared this way and endorsed symptoms of depression. He wished he could see his father, blamed his mother for his absence, and explained that hitting was how anyone got what they wanted in their family. He briefly listed what he had done to Nick and knew that he had been molested in the past "because my mom told me."

In order to determine the next steps, I met later in the week with the caseworker and Ms. L. to talk about interim strategies until a decision could be made about Calvin. Ms. L. had not worked weekends since the allegations were made and had paid a babysitter to watch Nick during the after-school hours. However, she felt that this was unfair to Nick and wanted Calvin to have "to pay for something."

Ms. L. was loathe to learn CDI skills with Calvin, but compromised by allowing me to coach her with Tom and then alternating these individual sessions with Calvin. However, despite Tom's eagerness and cooperation, Ms. L. took a break from treatment after three more sessions, claiming that she had a family to support. However, I continued to see Calvin close to weekly.

I continued my e-mails with Ms. L. and the caseworker, and Nick started seeing a school counselor. Ms. L. reported that, because of her new CDI skills, Tom briefly "argued less," but then she returned to working on weekends. For a period of time, no one was absolutely certain about who was monitoring the children over the course of a week.

By this time, I was more certain of Calvin's ability to control himself. He had no other victims, and he was open and eager for adult male attention each week. He also admitted that he could recall his prior sexual abuse and had intrusive thoughts about it. We were able to link it to his abuse of Nick, even though "my uncle was older and he should have known better."

At Tom's urging, his father contacted me a few months into the process. With Ms. L.'s permission, he and I met. He also was concerned about his son and I offered to help him learn some of the tools I had taught Ms. L. He agreed and we then proceeded with several coaching sessions with Tom. Tom's father was able to learn some basic skills. He also expressed concern about Ms. L.'s mistreatment of Calvin and wanted more weekend time with Tom. The caseworker and I were eventually able to convince Ms. L. to set aside her suspicions and agree to allow Tom and Calvin to spend time together with Tom's father on weekends.

I kept up pressure on Ms. L. to continue to use her CDI skills with her children during the week and provided suggestions by e-mail. Calvin's sessions with me also improved, which I believe reflected the extra support he was receiving at home.

After being absent for over 5 months, Ms. L. returned. She was feeling less depressed and now felt that she was "losing" her older boys to Tom's father. The entire family felt calmer, and the boys were more compliant at their return. Now that she was more motivated, Ms. L. was a quick student of the CDI and PDI portions of the training. Chore charts and an allowance were also established and this helped solidify her sons' behavioral change. No further incidents of sexual behavior had occurred, and while Calvin continued to underachieve in school, he was a less frequent visitor to the principal's office.

I spent a total of 43 hours with this family or its individual members in actual therapy sessions. Follow-up 4 months later revealed that Ms. L. was still feeling more positively about her sons and rarely used corporal punishment.

Ms. L. was able to make the changes she made for a number of reasons. She had a committed social worker, a history of successful employment, and was determined to remain the mother to her children. However, I had to be very flexible and creative so that I could continue to maintain a therapeutic presence and provide support that enabled her to return. This required a number of additional hours of time out of session, a frequent requirement in these difficult cases. In addition, Calvin responded to treatment and was at a lower risk to reoffend.

LIMITATIONS WITH PCIT

Every intervention has its limitations, and PCIT is no exception. One potential limitation with PCIT is that it is skill based and requires parents to both respond to your coaching and practice it between sessions. This can quickly activate resistance in some parents, typically the ones who have the most ambivalent relationships with their children. It should not be a surprise that they also have ambivalent relationships with helping professionals. Even if the child improves and is eager for more attention, such parents will not respond to these changes by becoming enthusiastic. They tend to stagnate in the therapy, and you will not see them taking over from your coaching. In fact, given their pathology, these parents are the most likely to prematurely withdraw from treatment. Unfortunately, they are also more likely to have children whose sexual behavior problems are particularly concerning to you.

Another limitation is reflected in those parents who are charming and have good social skills. You may initially fail to appreciate that they also have poor relationships with their children. In fact, their child may have sexual behavior problems related to the parents' sexualized behavior or poor choice of friends or companions. However, underneath the charm can be a lack of follow through. They learn the skills quickly but infrequently practice at home. Their child's PTSD or aggressive behavior will grow worse because it is further activated by the parent's extra attention, while at the same time the child is frustrated by the same inconsistency and rejection they have long experienced.

I believe that both of these limitations reflect long-standing problems of impaired attachment and parental pathology. Ideally, parents realize that they need to change, take the time to change, and then enter parent-child therapy. This does not happen with the more disturbed and disconnected families that live with generations of maltreatment.

Over my years of using many family therapy strategies with families of traumatized children, I do not know that an approach other than PCIT would have been more effective in the long run. What PCIT does that nonbehavioral approaches such as narrative or strategic family therapy do not do is to actively involve the family far more. It also provides a clear set of expectations about what constitutes change, and you can see these changes from one week to the next.

PROBLEMS WITH ATTACHMENT THERAPY

Practitioners who work with severely disturbed children are sometimes attracted to interventions that have no empirical support but have intrinsic appeal. Attachment therapy falls into this category. I would be remiss if I did not add a strongly negative statement against its use by therapists who work with children who have sexual behavior problems. The attachment therapy promulgated by the Attachment Center of Evergreen, Colorado, and its devotees is *not* derived from the attachment theory developed by John Bowlby and Mary Ainsworth. In fact, this approach is counter to attachment theory along a number of critical dimensions. For example, the intervention acts as if the problem is inherent in the child, a highly individual notion, and in direct contrast to attachment as a relational process. That is true whether or not the therapy being described is labeled as the traditional rage reduction approach or its variations (i.e., holding therapy, attachment therapy, or humanistic attachment therapy).

Beverly James was an early critic of rage reduction therapy and its various permutations, and in her seminal text, *Handbook for Treatment of Attachment-Trauma Problems in Children*, she elaborated on this sociological phenomenon (James, 1994). She suggested that mental health practitioners have long held to a hydraulic view of emotional problems. My summary of her perspective is that emotional problems are akin to fluids or pressures that build up and, after a certain point, become "bad things being held inside." The uninformed therapy that flows from this viewpoint aims to "get the bad things out." Some of you may remember primal scream therapy from the early 1970s (Janov, 1970). This therapy, which still has its followers, is directly related to this hydraulic view. James views these naive theories related to the discharge of emotions as an enormous obstacle to thinking accurately about therapy.

Professionals who work with maltreated children know how challenging many of them can be, whether in their birth homes, foster homes, or the homes of adoptive placements. I personally have found a subset of maltreated children some of the most difficult children with whom I have ever attempted therapy. The increase in orphanage-reared Eastern European children now living in the United States and Canada has also created challenges for therapists. It is quite difficult to sit in an office with a warm-hearted and well-meaning couple that adopted a child with a lifelong history of neglect, and then hear their pleas for help, without wishing that behavioral change could be more rapid. These factors, in combination with the highly publicized death of a 10-year-old girl while undergoing holding therapy in Colorado (King, 2000), prompts these comments.

A stunning lack of precision and science abounds in the field of child mental health. The diagnostic labels of reactive attachment disorder and childhood-onset bipolar disorder seem to be used indiscriminately and frequently. ADHD is increasingly viewed solely as a neurological phenomenon, despite the research literature indicating that when ADHD presents in combination with oppositional-defiant disorder or conduct disorder in young children, it quite frequently indicates maltreatment or traumatization (Ford et al., 2000).

This same lack of empiricism extends to psychotherapy with children. Despite the empirical support for relational approaches such as PCIT (Hembree-Kigin & McNeil, 1995) or directive approaches such as cognitive behavioral therapy in the treatment of maltreatment-related symptoms (Deblinger, Lippman, & Steer, 1996), the majority of therapy with children continues to be nondirective and supportive (Friedrich, Jaworski, & Berliner, 1994). I believe that as a field, we should strive to practice at the most empirically supported level possible. The absence of empirical support for attachment therapy is another argument against its utilization. I can think of absolutely no situation where attachment therapy is appropriate.

CONCLUSION

The onset of sexually intrusive behavior in children is often predated by a greater than normal likelihood that one or more parents has a history of sexual abuse, the child lives in a home environment in which sexuality is either overly present or avoided, or that the child has grown up with other types of abuse, including domestic violence. All of these variables contribute to insecure attachment and disrupted parent-child relationships. Of particular concern is the parenting style of parents who have a history of unresolved abuse, with the result that they are either frightened of or frightening to their child. This contributes to disorganized attachment and is characterized in adult life by the overexpression of severe Axis II disorders, substance abuse, unemployment, criminal involvement, and abusive parenting (Lyons-Ruth & Jacobvitz, 1999).

Clinicians are best served when they conceptualize attachment as a multigenerational process and maintain a three-generational perspective in their diagnostic interviews and therapy (Friedrich, 2002). Attachment-related ques-tions that I recommend include the following: (1) Does the child's primary caregiver have a history of sexual abuse or other victimization? (2) If so, has the parent ever received treatment? (3) Does the parent have accurate and generally positive attributions about the child and the child's sexual behav-ior? Clinicians should also pay close attention to how parents describe their relationship with the child's grandparents. A positive relationship with one's parents predisposes individuals to have a more positive relationship with their children (Main, 1995).

Since attachment is a secure-base phenomenon and secure attachment emerges with caregivers that provide safety, it is also important to assess for the safety and security of the child's home. The Safety Checklist (Friedrich, 2002; see Chapter 8, Form B) is one measure that assesses the safety and secu-rity of the child's home environment.

Children's or adolescents' behavior can also provide clues to the nature of their attachment. Controlling behavior by children toward caregivers, the presence of severe externalizing disorders, self-injurious behavior, dissocia-tion, and confusing and contradictory behavior toward or descriptions of their parents all suggest disturbed attachment (Friedrich, 2002). Children who have a failure in empathy and are cruel to others are particularly likely to have dis-turbed attachment relationships and, consequently, are at risk for future sex-ual offending. In fact, one of the reasons why the relationship between prior sexual abuse and subsequent sexual offending is so variable is that research has probably focused on too narrow a sample (i.e., children with a prior his-tory of sexual abuse) and neglected the assessment of internal working models through which sexual abuse is processed. Sexual offending is a classic model of disturbed relating in a manner similar to disturbed attachment, especially disorganized attachment.

A review of the risk factors posited by Hall and her colleagues (1998) underscores the multiple family and individual issues that are relevant to the assessment and management of children with sexually intrusive behavior. I believe that you waste everyone's time, stigmatize the child further, realize small treatment gains, and alienate the family from further therapy if your pri-mary approach is individual therapy with the identified child. In addition to the issues identified by Alexander (1992) that characterize the parent's attach-ment with the sexually abused child, such as rejection, role reversal, and mul-tigenerational transmission of unresolved trauma, you have the added issues of coercive interaction and sexual preoccupation, typically fueled by parents with their own unresolved abuse.

In addition, the treatment goals that make the most sense for these children, such as safety and learning sexual rules, reduce the likelihood of future problematic sexual behavior. Creating new sources of support, for example, teaching them that interpersonal interaction can be nonsexual, is best done in a family-based model.

Families with persistently intrusive, sexually problematic children are typically ambivalent about their children and their need for treatment. These parents are often at what is appropriately called the precontemplation stage of change (Miller & Rollnick, 1991). In other words, they have not really started to think that change of any sort is needed. They will show up to see you in response to external sources such as orders from the court, recommendations from the school, or threats by relatives.

If you immediately focus on the child and do not work hard to engage and educate the parents about the need to intervene, you lose the first critical opportunity to connect with parents and help them appreciate that there is a problem you can help them with. It may take several attempts to get the process underway with the most disturbed families, but you have at least taken an important first step: identifying that there is a problem. When the issue reemerges, parents will recall that you were friendly, helpful, and nonblaming, and they will be more likely to return to your office.

An immediate family focus also helps establish and get several processes underway: a thorough screening and identification of the scope of the problem, understanding the parent-child relationship, activating the parent's appropriate concern for the child, and engaging with the parent, the player that can make the biggest difference. I think the most compelling argument for family-based therapy is that the emergence of sexualized interaction between two children reflects premorbid problems with parent-child interaction, and unless that parent-child relationship is improved, child-child sexual interaction will become the child's primary model for relating and the problem will worsen.

6

INDIVIDUAL THERAPY FOR CHILDREN WITH SEXUAL BEHAVIOR PROBLEMS

A SIGNIFICANT NUMBER of children with sexual behavior problems are very difficult to manage. Many have severe behavior problems that seem to scream for treatment. For a variety of reasons, individual therapy is often the treatment of choice for practitioners working with such children. It is essential for making a valid assessment of the child and determining what the child and family can truly accomplish. One-on-one time with the child gives the clinician insight into a child's boundaries, sexual preoccupation, and the degree to which he or she can demonstrate empathy and relate appropriately. In addition, individual therapy is excellent for helping children begin to make meaning of maltreatment, loss, and their current sexual behavior.

While individual therapy is clearly important, I believe that it is insufficient as the sole component of the treatment process. In most cases, I utilize individual therapy in conjunction with PCIT, depending on both the child's particular problems and the caregivers' availability to participate. Before beginning PCIT, some children may need to be seen individually to reduce their anxiety and prepare them to engage with and respond to their parents. In some cases, however, children may be in foster or residential care, and parent-child treatment may not be an option.

The degree to which individual therapy is critical to the success of treatment will vary from one child to the next. One key variable is the child's level of development. This can affect both the type of therapy the child receives and what the child needs from the therapy. As the child's social and cognitive development increases, there will also be an increase in the utility of

151

group modalities and therapy that involve reflection and the examination of thoughts.

The efficacy of individual therapy will also depend on the family's capacity to provide additional support for the child. The majority of children with sexual behavior problems can utilize the support provided in the individual sessions. They can also benefit from any of your efforts to help them understand their behavior more accurately. However, a number of the more disturbed children will not respond predictably to your support. Some will be overwhelmed either by the intimacy or the content of the therapy. Usually these will be the most disturbed children, coming from the most disturbed families, and often not living with their parents. In these cases, individual therapy is the only option, and the therapist must determine how best to be a supportive, consistent, and reflective presence for an angry and resistant child.

The frequency with which the more disturbed children have been traumatized is striking. Individual therapy directed at their PTSD can assist in working through, or at least taking the first step in working through, these traumas. Demonstrating the efficacy of cognitive therapy for children with PTSD is one of the primary contributions of the treatment literature on outcomes of child maltreatment (Cohen & Mannarino, 1998).

During a course of individual sessions with a child, I keep three guiding principles in mind. Individual treatment needs to be focused on these same principles; however, the strategies and techniques we use will be different.

First, individual therapy with children must facilitate the child's connection to the parent or current parent figure. For example, I know that a child who is stirred up after a session with me will be more difficult to manage at home, and I will have inadvertently given the parents new data to support negative perceptions of their child. My time with the child thus becomes counterproductive, since I want parents to believe children are doing their part to change their behavior.

Second, efforts must be directive and targeted at keeping children focused on the issues that got them into therapy. This type of therapy requires an active and committed therapist capable of seeing both what is possible and what is essential, all the while promoting the child's capacity for self-regulation. Your therapy should not be one unplanned, nondirective session after another.

Third, the clinician must support children and infuse them with good feelings that promote emotional energy and resilience between one session and the next. The clinician should consider: In what way do I have to behave so that children views me as safe, sensitive, and also enjoyable? What about their attachment history do I need to attend to in order to do this?

PROVIDING SUPPORT FOR INSECURELY
ATTACHED CHILDREN

The relationship between the child and the therapist is the foundation on which the therapist relies to effectively intervene with the child. Children who have experienced an acute stressor but are securely attached will view me as another friendly adult and derive support from our interaction. Providing support for children who are insecurely attached, however, is a challenging and crucial aspect of individual therapy.

Some adults have reported that interacting with a supportive clinician makes them aware of what they have never had when interacting with other adults. Their reaction is usually a mixture of sadness and depression. While young children, who generally do not have this cognitive capacity for self-reflection, cannot be expected to articulate the same conundrum, they are likely to experience some anxiety from the positive therapeutic interaction. Children whose attachment styles are severely disturbed, particularly those with disorganized attachment, must exert energy figuring out how to interact with the clinician. The more disturbed the child, the more the two of us will seem at odds and disconnected. Furthermore, the child may not be in a position to understand or benefit from a clinician's support on a consistent basis; some very disturbed children will be stirred up by a supportive presence and may even be aggravated by it.

Too many therapists fail to appreciate that nondirective play in the presence of a nonjudgmental, accepting, and warm adult works for some children simply by infusing them with calm and thereby reducing the parents' concern. Knowing that "their child is now in therapy can have a positive effect on the parents. On the other hand, some children, typically very disturbed, may start to act out and play more and more aggressively and primitively. Their parents may not be actively involved in altering the child's behavior and in fact may resent that their child is receiving support at all.

Therapists may start seeing more of the sexualized or trauma-related behavior that brought the child to their office in the first place. The therapist may initially think, "Now we are getting somewhere." But the play is likely to be perseverative and not productive (Terr, 1981). In other cases, children will be withdrawn from therapy because the family is too compromised to bring them in regularly for very long. Meanwhile, the first steps to help them have not been provided.

Structured and focused therapy is helpful with very disturbed children, when it is provided sensitively and emphasizes containment. In many of these cases, most aspects of functioning, such as cognition, affect, and behavior, are not integrated (Friedrich, 1995). Your job as their therapist is to serve as an integrating influence who explains why events happen, ties behavior in an understandable way to prior life events, and then connects these disparate pieces in a meaningful manner. All of this work needs to be done in a context that is tolerable and understandable for the child. Most helpful to all parties is psychoeducation regarding the origins of the child's behavior problems and what it will take to stop them. This will give you time to support the parent as the child starts to improve. When these links can be made and validation is then provided, there are times when you can interrupt the sexual behavior sequence. This will be demonstrated in the next case example.

By way of background, this case involved a young child's self-insertion of objects into her vagina. I have seen only four girls with this problem. Two of them gave validated reports of sexual abuse, and evidence for sexual abuse in the remaining two cases was overwhelming. I have also seen two boys who put objects other than their fingers into their rectum. One boy reported sexual abuse, and the other boy was developmentally delayed, had limited verbal skills, and exhibited no other sexual behaviors. In addition, this behavior, while not reported by any parents of 6- to 12-year-old girls or boys in the CSBI normative sample, is a Sexual Abuse Specific Item (SASI) for the 2- to 5-year-old boys and girls (Friedrich, 1997). The absence of subjects in the comparison sample makes it statistically impossible for this item to be an SASI for the older groups. Sexually abused children also exhibit this behavior significantly more often than their psychiatric outpatient counterparts for every age and gender (Friedrich, Fisher, et al., 2001). In other words, when you see this behavior, sexual abuse is very likely.

The R. Family

In the case of R.R., a 6-year-old girl, very focused individual therapy appeared to be the central reason why she stopped stuffing foreign objects into her vaginal introitus. She had been taken to the emergency room on several occasions to have foreign bodies removed from her vagina. Her hymen was not intact and the persistence of her behavior led to a referral to the local authorities. However, she was relatively noncommunicative with the protective services interviewers and abuse was unfounded. After she ended up in the ER once again, R.R. was referred to me.

In her mother's presence, R.R. exhibited all the symptoms of ADHD, combined type. She did not stay in her chair, tried to leave the room, variably listened to questions, and acted impulsively. Mrs. R. completed my screening battery and reported significant hyperactivity, but only the items pertaining to the above sexual behavior and "standing too close" were endorsed on the CSBI.

With me, R.R. was generally calm and focused. However, she occasionally intruded into my space and once touched my hand. These intrusive behaviors were concerning to me since they reflected immaturity, poor personal boundaries, and impulsivity.

The primary and most obvious culprit turned out to be a neighbor boy. Her mother described him as a sexually preoccupied elementary-aged boy who had spent some time alone with her daughter just as the behavior started. The mother had moved away because this boy and his family bothered her so much. For example, she had observed this boy chasing her daughter with a short plastic handle. She worried that he had inserted that, or something else, in her daughter. R.R. denied that she had been abused or touched sexually by anyone, including the neighbor boy. However, her nonverbal behavior (e.g., distress, fidgeting), which occurred only when his name came up, suggested that she was very agitated by him.

At our fourth session, I drew a cartoonlike series of pictures that started with a picture of a girl playing and smiling. The next panel had a picture of the same girl "who had never thought about putting anything in her vagina." The third panel depicted a boy chasing her with a stick. R.R. was raptly attentive for each drawing. Before the last two panels of the cartoon, I turned to her and said, "He should never have put that stick in your vagina. That was a naughty thing for him to do." She grabbed her crotch and looked directly at me and was not agitated. So I went on to say, "And it hurted really bad." She nodded her head and I provided some reassurances. I finished the cartoon. One frame showed her thinking about putting things in her vagina and then the last frame had her visiting with me.

We discussed the cartoon panels and why she came to talk to me and what the goal of our therapy was. Then we collaboratively drew pictures of the neighbor boy, which she enjoyed scribbling over. During this time, she became more agitated but then calmed down. R.R. was eager to show her mother the pictures and we took a break to bring her mother back. The rest of the session was spent with all three of us talking about the boy, his family, the mom keeping R.R. safe, and there being no more need to put things in herself, now that we all understood why she had started to do so in the first place. I saw R.R. and her mother for six more sessions. During this time, R. R. was able to talk about being scared by the neighbor boy, and her mother was coached in CDI (Hembree-Kigin & McNeil, 1995). I followed up with the mother after 4 months had passed. No further concerning behaviors were reported.

Research data and the clinical evidence in R.R.'s situation led me to the point where I suggested the name of the perpetrator. I also did so since I was further convinced during my time with her that she was struggling; she could not verbally articulate the trauma and it continued to intrude into her awareness. I believe this intervention worked in the same manner as the cognitive therapy techniques of exposure This technique reintroduces the fear-provoking stimuli but in a manner that makes it tolerable and understandable. The fundamental treatment components of support, increased understanding, and an improved relationship with parents were all enacted. R.R. was validated, and the previously overwhelming experience occurred in the presence of support and understanding.

The more disturbed the child, the more likely he or she is to become anxious with adults who behave in a consistently positive manner. For example, children who have disorganized attachment will view any softness displayed by a therapist as an indication of the same inconsistency exhibited by their parents. Your flexibility becomes a target for manipulation. This suggests that you need to adjust your level of support and acceptance early on until you know the child better. Typically it is very important to start off your work with a disturbed child with a neutral, benign, but highly consistent stance. You need to make yourself into a presence that is not easily controlled.

The Case of U.U.

U.U. was a 10-year-old boy who had witnessed his mother's overt sexuality for a number of years before being placed in foster care. The foster parents had a very tentative relationship with him. It was in this setting that he molested a foster sister.

U.U. took a very controlling stance with adults. My first example of this was that he began to challenge me in the waiting room at the time of our first appointment. I believe that some of his willingness and even eagerness to take me on publicly in that manner was due to his foster parents' frustration with bringing him to therapy. He informed me in the waiting room, on the way back to my office, and as he first sat down across from me that he had already talked to the cops and he was not going to talk to me. This type of greeting hardly generates enthusiasm in the therapist.

Rather than challenging him to talk, I agreed with him, and said, "I bet you've had to talk about this with a lot of people," to which he agreed. I then pulled out a tablet, moved closer to him, and wrote at the top of the page, "A list of all the people I've had to talk to about this." U.U. then provided the names or titles of different people that he had spoken to. I then suggested that he probably had said one thing to one person and another thing to another person and that all of those people needed to get together and figure out what had happened. He eagerly agreed with that and even revealed how he had made up a few stories. We then reviewed the names of the people he had listed and he told me whether I should put "part of the story," "a little bit of the story," or "a lot of the story" next to each one.

After this was over, U.U. volunteered to tell me "all of the story" but only under the condition that I would give him one of the plastic reptiles that I had in my office. On the face of it, this is the type of suggested bargain that a therapist might wish to bite at. However, this type of negotiation is the hallmark of interactions with controlling children, and they arrive at this style from disorganized attachment. These children view the adults in their life as unpredictable, frustrating, and even terrifying and, hence, try to control every interaction.

Rather than denying the request outright, I then turned to another sheet in my notebook and wrote out "First session," "Second session," "Third session," and so on along the left-hand side of each page. I then created a column for the center of the page that read "What I'll need in order to talk" and then on the far right I put a column that read "What Dr. Friedrich will give." U.U. and I then generated different things that he saw that he would want each time he came into my office. By the time we concluded the list, we had 10 sessions covered in which he would essentially strip my office of every remotely desirable object including computer, Rolodex, squeeze toys, plastic reptiles, magnets, and money.

U.U. and I then turned to the column "What Dr. Friedrich will give." In response to each of the demands listed, I wrote a corresponding "Dr. Friedrich is a stingy dooffus" after each session. He and I talked about what stingy meant, and the different ways I was a "dooffus." By the end of the first session, even though he was frustrated that I had not promised him anything, he had talked about his foster sister and, equally important, he had experienced what was likely one of the most prolonged and in-control periods of time he had ever had with an adult outside of school. That was reflected in our next meeting, where he started off much more compliantly.

The interaction described above is directly related to the fact that rapport building is not just about being friendly, open, and giving to a child; it is also about attunement. It relies on the degree to which you and the child can create a fit that matches the child's history, working model of relationships, and the topic between the two of you. With a child whose working model of relationships is less disturbed, I can be far more directly supportive and also directive with my comments. Strategies that facilitate the child's sense of feeling supported are summarized in some of my earlier writings on individual therapy with traumatized and abused children (see Friedrich, 1991, 1995):

1. Be an animal (e.g., bark like a dog, meow like a cat) at times when nothing can be said.
2. Anthropomorphize the inanimate (e.g., "We must walk softly because we don't want to give the carpet an owie"). This works very well with preschoolers.

3. Be conspiratorial; for example, the two of you are partners on an adventure.
4. Show wide-eyed fascination at who children are and what they say.
5. Activate the physical process (but do not overwhelm), for example, burping noises.
6. Use concrete operations, that is, think very simply (e.g., "We do this seven times since you are seven").
7. Use mirroring.
8. Tailor therapeutic persona to child's attachment style.
9. Monitor your effusiveness.
10. Create images of relatedness (e.g., "us," "we").
11. Speak in terms of collaboration involving both of you; for example, "How do we get sexual behavior problems off your property?"

The above techniques are geared toward younger children, but all of them encourage tailoring yourself to the child, which will make therapy sessions not just tolerable but even rewarding and enjoyable for the child. For example, I worked with a resistant-ambivalently attached 10-year-old child who whined that every activity was "too hard" but became much more amenable once I started prefacing all of my requests with some version of this acknowledgment: "I am the type of doctor who works his patients too hard."

Attachment is related as well to the child's facility with self-regulation. In a securely attached parent-child dyad, the child feels safe, emotions are typically not overwhelming, and the child learns from the parent how to understand and process emotions accurately. Good therapy recreates this process and helps the child feel contained and supported, with enough emotional resources to work on important topics.

Because I like children and can be quite playful, some of my early child therapy cases were very dysregulating and overwhelming for the child. I now realize that this was less than optimal. I was already working with children prone to dyscontrol, and they taught me that silliness can be too much. When I review more recent recordings of my interviews and therapy sessions with children, I am struck by the degree to which I have simplified my speech, implemented long pauses, acted self-deprecating, and taken opportunities for mutual time-outs, drawing and writing activities. I learned to rely less on verbal exchanges.

A Destructive Boy

I saw an adopted 12-year-old who had sexually touched his adopted sibling. His parents used time-out, but he was routinely very destructive during these times. In a prior therapy experience, he had recounted his "bad" behavior for the week as part of each session, and he insisted on continuing this in our sessions. During the recounting, he became agitated and would stand or walk around the room. I did not see this as useful and wanted to modify this practice.

So I took a different strategy by insisting that previous talk therapy had not helped and we were just to write and draw. We spent the majority of our sessions taking turns writing and drawing. For example, after checking in with his parents, we would take turns writing or drawing what happened before his mother or father gave him a warning, when he was being led to time-out, his time in the time-out room, and his activities there. Previously, he became overactivated and spoke with glee about the different destructive acts he did in time-out. However, as I wrote down each act, and praised his drawing abilities as he drew the destruction of each object, all the while being very serious, his affect became more and more contained. We would then calculate the dollar value of each broken item and tally that up. All of these sheets of paper would then be taped to the walls of the room in their appropriate sequence, and we would sit and admire the week he had revealed to me.

Not once did I try to directly discuss the self-defeating and inappropriate nature of his behavior. But my goal was for him to have, in a nonshameful, nonparental manner, a full appreciation of the entire time span leading up to and through time-out to his final exit from it. I was convinced that to do so could help make it meaningful and fully known, thus inhibiting future outbursts. In fact, the frequency of misbehavior did drop off markedly even before his parents started to fully invest in the therapy process.

SUGGESTED TREATMENT APPROACHES FOR THREE AGE GROUPS

The children that you see, whether in individual, group, or family therapy, will vary widely in a number of dimensions. This includes their level of cognitive development, the probability of prior sexual abuse, the role of the parent, the type of individual therapy provided, and the child's capacity to self-report. Some children will be better able to accurately monitor their thoughts and behaviors during the week, and with these children, the monitoring works best when done as part of the parent-child work you also do. The following is a summary of these various topics across three age groups.

Age: Preschool to age 7
Cognitive level: Preoperational.

Sexual abuse probability: High for both genders for sexual abuse or significant exposure to adult sexuality.

Parental role: Teach skills; increase general monitoring and maintain sexual rules; alter parental perceptions of the child; enhance safety; increase support for child.

Parent treatment: PCIT; confront attributions; educate about child sexuality; educate about how their own history can interfere with or aid their child's improvement; help them move from precontemplation to contemplation; establish sexual rules.

Individual therapy: Interactive; directive nurturing for the child; validate the parents by sharing their view of the child's need for therapy; reduce focus on either the child's sexual abuse or sexually intrusive behavior; assess boundary problems in session.

Individual therapy type: Visual analogue via cartooning of the effect of events on thoughts and feelings; role-play alternate responses; promote emotion identification skills.

Self-report: These children cannot accurately answer questions about feelings, so try to remove questions from the session and increase use of description and reflection.

Monitoring: Only by parent, which may be not possible for some parents.

Age: 8–10 years

Cognitive level: Beginning to move into concrete operations, with greater use of symbolic thought and a reduction in egocentricity; more logical.

Sexual abuse probability: Lower than younger group but still higher than is ever substantiated, especially exposure to adolescent and adult sexuality.

Parental role: Repair relationship with child so that parents can be the child's primary source of support and affection; monitor the child; increase safety in the home.

Parent treatment: PCIT; alter attributions about child; understand how their own history affects parenting problems.

Individual therapy: Supportive but directive stance; parent may provide much of the session's content, for example, things that happened during the week can be a focus with the child during session; review sexual rules; selective use of 21 Questions in a conversational format.

Individual therapy type: Saying no to future sexually intrusive behavior; self-control strategies; use of cartooning; role-play.

Self-report: Just developing, but child is able to help identify emotions and begin to reorganize how thoughts, feelings, and behaviors are related; the use of items from PTSD self-report measures can help form the basis for therapy.

Monitoring: Children are minor partners to parents, who are the primary monitors of targeted behaviors.

Age: 11–12 years

Cognitive level: Can more fully expect logic and the ability to take the other person's perspective; however, they still may not think that universal phenomena (e.g., death, shame, and guilt), apply to them.

Sexual abuse probability: The lowest of all the groups but present and undetected for many; externalizing problems are common; social immaturity and impulsivity are often contributors as well.

Parental role: Essential, but the combination of hopeless or defeated parent and entrenched patterns requires skillful confrontation and support; increase monitoring; improve safety; promote sexual rules.

Parent treatment: PCIT; reframe attributions about child; selectively use prescriptive statements.

Individual therapy: Use 21 Questions; increase use of cognitive behavioral strategies; explore fantasies; selectively assess for sexual preoccupation via drawings, projective pictures, and so on.

Individual therapy type: Supportive but also more directive in skill-building and staying on task; use of emotion-reorganization activities; cartooning still helpful; role-play.

Self-report: Most accurate; facilitated by structured interviews and self-report measures

Monitoring: More likely than previous two groups, but only in rare cases will children consistently do this on their own; requires considerable parental structuring, which utilizes skills some parents do not have.

PRESCHOOLERS

Preschool through age 6, and up to 7 for psychologically disturbed children, is a developmental period characterized by cognitive abilities that reflect a relative lack of if-then thinking (Cohen, 2002). These children routinely fail at perspective taking. They are quite egocentric and generally assume that others see the world as they do. Consequently, they are not in a position to either be able to think about what they have done or link their behavior with some prior event.

What this suggests is that you should eliminate all "why" questions when interacting with this age group. To ask a "why" question, which the child will not be able to answer, will only frustrate both of you.

The absence of perspective taking also negates the use of another favorite tool of adolescent and adult offender therapists: empathy-building exercises (Longo & Prescott, 2005). It is tempting to ask children of this age, "How do you think that made the other child feel?" and believe that their awareness will alter their future behavior. If they give you any answer, most likely it came from an adult in their life and not from themselves.

It is important to remember that these children live in the here and now, and operate according to the principle "out of sight, out of mind." Consequently, their ability to generalize what you did with them in therapy and apply it to subsequent behavior in the home setting is extremely poor unless it is supplemented by a parent's involvement or visual cues geared toward aiding the child.

I believe that both male and female children in this age group have a very high probability of either direct sexual abuse or significant exposure to sexual adults or sexual activity. With very young preschoolers, your degree of certainty about abuse is reduced. You are often working with a child whose sexual abuse status will never be known (Hewitt, 1999; Silovsky & Niec, 2002). But preschoolers who are sexually intrusive often behave in this manner because there is an immediate stressor in their minds or in their environment that drives this behavior. They have a limited capacity to inhibit, and they are much more immediate in their expression of what they have just seen or experienced. This awareness should be used to guide how you help the family plan for safety.

Individual therapy with these very young children is best done when accompanied by play and interaction aimed at nurturing the child. Your individual therapy should also have a reduced focus on their sexual abuse or their sexually intrusive behavior. For example, with older children I will use the 21 Questions format to guide some of my therapeutic interaction with them (see Chapter 8, Form F). However, I do almost none of this type of questioning with this younger age group. What I will do, however, is draw out and cartoon for the child how I believe sexual abuse or seeing sexual activity leads to sexual thoughts and then subsequent sexual behavior. I will also draw or relate therapeutic stories that involve a child of the same age in similar circumstances, having types of responses similar to those of the child in my office.

I use cartoon drawings often. If I want to explain a point or create an interaction, I will mark off several (three to five) cartoon panels on a sheet of writing paper and draw out a behavioral sequence, complete with bubble dialogue. These drawings provide a visual analogue that both enhances and supplements language-based therapy. Depending on the children, I may invite them to suggest dialogue and drawings, and even let them draw figures or entire sequences. Once again, the goal is to create an opportunity to focus on the target behaviors and help children see how thoughts, feelings, and behaviors are connected.

The parental role with this preschool-aged group will vary depending upon the degree to which you can elicit parental involvement. The younger the child, the more likely the biological parents are compromised and the child is in foster care (Farmer & Pollock, 1998). Foster parents vary in their willingness to expand their role in the child's life. They may not wish to get more involved at any level. However, individual therapy will not be successful unless it is accompanied by: (1) improvement in the level of overall safety in the home, and (2) enhanced monitoring of the child's positive and negative behavior, accompanied by improved reinforcement of prosocial behavior.

Your time with the parents should be focused on these two important tasks, along with a third goal: to identify and subsequently alter the parents' perceptions of the child so that the child can be seen more positively. This is also a time in which you teach the parents an array of skills, even if it is simply how to avoid being caught up in controlling interactions with the child. I have had some success with foster parents who learned the child-directed skills from PCIT (Hembree-Kigin & McNeill, 1995).

Do not expect children through the age of 7, and sometimes even older, to accurately and consistently answer questions about thoughts and feelings. However, as you reflect on their experiences and, over the course of therapy, introduce them to the idea of labeling their emotions, these children can develop greater self-awareness. For these children to self-monitor, it is essential that a parent is doing the reminding and recording.

The S. Family

I worked with S.S., a 6-year-old boy who regularly played video games with a 14-year-old boy. The older boy typically played these games while wearing underwear, and then transitioned to playing while nude. S.S. was also expected to play with no clothes on. The 14-year-old teen engaged him in extensive oral sexual contact, and S.S. continued to return to his home due to the promise of the video games.

S.S. lived with a single parent who had a significant sexual and physical abuse history. Also in the home were an older brother and younger sister. The abuse came to light when S.S. suggested oral sex to his brother. His mother's initial response was to minimize the possibility of abuse. She also criticized S.S. for having these ideas. Eventually the school principal told her that her son was talking about oral sex on the school bus and in class.

The majority of my therapy was spent teaching the mother and the boy's father (who saw him on many weekends) CDI techniques (Hembree-Kigin & McNeill, 1995) and problem solving with the mother about special time with her son. Other joint sessions with the mother and son or the father and son included discussions among all of us about the inappropriate nature of the 14-year-old's behavior. I also guided conversations about how sexual activities sometimes get stuck in our minds. We conversed and drew out in cartoon form the different ways people can remove these thoughts so that they do not have to act on them.

Both parents found this type of conversation difficult, the mother because of her abuse, and the father because of his lack of comfort in talking about emotions. Consequently, I did the majority of the talking. But their supportive presence and their verbalizations, along with mine, enabled the best opportunity we could create for resolution.

Establishing sexual rules was very helpful to them since they could see S.S. make progress. Since both of them were committed to their son and concerned for his welfare, sexual comments to his brother or children on the bus were quickly eliminated, and both parents reported having an improved relationship with him. He was also less reactive to their feedback, and his sleep improved.

EARLY ELEMENTARY SCHOOL AGE

Children in the early elementary age (ages 7 to 9) are moving into a more sophisticated way of thinking, which has long been labeled *concrete operations* (Cohen, 2002). Cohen reviews research that suggests that rather than the three cognitive transformations that occur from ages 3 to 12, there very well may be as many as four developmental shifts. As a result, I have tried to help the reader think about small age groups and more shifts in thinking.

When children enter this age range, there is an increased use of symbolic thought and a reduction of self-centered or egocentric perspective. Consequently, children can start to take another's perspective, although given the immaturity exhibited by most of them, they still struggle to think accurately about how their behavior affects others. Generalizations from one setting to the next are still not very likely without a significant level of parental input. An example of this comes from the early literature on social skills training, which often found reduced generalizability without parental involvement (Frankel & Wetmore, 1996).

These children are also beginning to think in a much more sequential manner. Consequently, they can be more readily engaged in a discussion on how thoughts lead to feelings and then behavior, and vice versa. However, because social cognitive development has a bilateral relationship to the child's progress with learning and school, highly disturbed children in this age group often will not be able to take a victim's perspective (Webster-Stratton & Reid, 2003).

In this age group, the probability of sexual abuse or exposure to adult sexuality is not as elevated as it is in younger groups. Externalizing boys can certainly come up with provocative behavior without sexual abuse. Data suggest that abuse continues to be much higher in girls with sexual behavior problems (Gray et al., 1997; Johnson, 1989).

Sexual abuse exists on a continuum, and when I say these children have been sexually abused, I think much of what they have experienced is in the milder, less serious range of the continuum. I have listened to too many teenage boys tell me that in addition to the behaviors they were charged with, they did others that were never discovered (e.g., stroking the inner thigh of a 3-year-old, grabbing crotches of preschoolers, always lifting their half sister up by cupping their hand under her crotch, masturbating by using a napping child, licking the genitalia of a 6-month-old, kissing nipples of a 2-year-old). None of these behaviors had ever been reported by the child.

The role of parents is paramount in the provision of safety and improved monitoring of the child. Parents are critical to both establishing and maintaining sexual rules so that they become ingrained in the child. Their role is to significantly increase their level of support and thus repair the relationship they have with their child. Older children will be less malleable, and greater assistance will be needed in teaching parents how to provide support for them without getting caught up in the many entanglements that may have prevented such support in the past.

To enhance parents' role, parent-based treatment continues to have PCIT as its centerpiece (Hembree-Kigin & McNeil, 1995). In addition, a sensitive assessment of parents' sexual abuse history can help them link their own abuse history to the attributions they make about their child. They will then be in a position to alter their responses to the child. Parents can also benefit from discussions about family sexuality and how it may influence their child's behavior.

The use of prescriptive statements by parents is also an important adjunct to your work, since they can also help the child feel understood. Examples of prescriptive statements are listed in the Assessment and Treatment Manual (Chapter 8, Form L), but are elaborated on here. Sensitive and attuned parents can help their child develop a reflective capacity, which is an essential component of social cognition and personal understanding (Fonagy et al., 1995; Fonagy & Target, 1997). This can be achieved through reflection, one of the PRIDE skills from PCIT (Hembree-Kigin & McNeil, 1995), where parents encourage their child to think about his or her actions and feelings as well as those of other people. Children who do so will become more sensitive, modulated, and empathic.

I was working with an expert foster mother and spoke to her about continuing my in-office activities during the week at her house. My hope was that at random times, when her foster daughter was not occupied by anything else and the two of them were alone, the foster mother would state such things as, "I feel sad when I think about your mom living with (the abuser)" and "Sleeping can be hard when you have nightmares about scary things." I wrote six phrases of this type and instructed her to use two to three per day, at random times when she was alone with the girl. The foster mother noted that her foster daughter initially acted as if she had not heard them, but after a few days began sharing details of her life with the foster mother for the first time. Later, when we were completing the PTSD Workbook (see Chapter 8, pp. 263–299), she identified the foster home as her safe place and her foster mother as someone she could talk to.

Since then, I have used these prescriptive statements with dozens of parents and foster parents. I try this strategy only after the parents have shown both a commitment to therapy and demonstrated sensitivity to their child. I have seen the improvements in my office as well, with some children becoming more open about their past.

The type of individual therapy that you can use with younger elementary-aged children builds on their increasing cognitive complexity and their greater use of representational thinking. For example, drawing cartoons of different behavioral sequences can be more useful at this age than with younger children. The children can also be engaged more fully in conversation. They will also benefit from learning to expand their vocabulary for emotions and feelings, and will become more precise from one session to the next. Self-control strategies that are taught to children at this age, like pleasant images at bedtime, need to include the parent, and there is a greater likelihood that when a caregiver reminds the child of this skill, the child will know what is being talked about and with prompts can begin to use it.

Early elementary-aged children who are emotionally healthy and live in families where conversations about feelings occur with some regularity are in a better position than younger children to self-report their emotions and behaviors. Data indicate that children are often better than parents at self-reporting internalizing symptoms such as anxiety and depression (Achenbach, 1991a). For example, some of these children will validly report elements of PTSD. I often structure several individual sessions around a questionnaire, such as the Trauma Symptom Checklist for Children (TSCC; Briere, 1996), the Child Inventory of Traumatic Events Scale–Revised (Chaffin & Shultz, 2001; Wolfe, Gentile, Michienzi, Sas, & Wolfe, 1991), or an attributional measure such as Spaccarelli's (1995) Negative Appraisals About Abuse. Each of these can be used as part of therapy. I also find it helpful to facilitate self-report by drawing, such as the flashbacks (see PTSD Workbook in Chapter 8). Usually the drawing takes the form of a figure lying on a bed, a moon outside a window, and a thought drawn on a bubble coming up from the head that reflects some intrusive thought that the child has either alluded to or reported to you.

This is the first age period where I start to use 21 Questions (see Chapter 8, Form F) to elicit information about children's sexual abuse and any sexual behavior they have exhibited toward other children. It is very important for many children with sexual behavior problems to talk about these events. However, it is also a difficult task and denial is common. I created this list so that children could know from the onset what I wanted to talk about. By having the list in front of them, children can also keep track of their progress and remain motivated to complete as many applicable questions as possible. By articulating these hidden and shameful thoughts and behaviors, they will provide an opportunity for increased support from you and begin to develop a more integrated awareness of themselves.

Children in this age range are still very much caught up in the here and now. At times they can answer questions if you ask, "How you are feeling now?" However, self-monitoring will remain frustrating if your hope is to get them to keep track of their feelings during the week. While some children find this useful, it will require a significant amount of parental support and input. This may further burden a parent.

The N. Family

N.N. was a 9-year-old boy who was referred for treatment after two younger children, one a stepsister and the other a neighbor boy, disclosed that N.N. had pulled their pants down and asked to see their genitals. The neighbor boy had just started school, and he also reported that N.N. had touched his genitals. N.N. lived with his mother and her fiancé and saw his father weekly. His parents' postdivorce period was characterized by significant tension that increased after N.N.'s father remarried. N.N. insisted that his stepmother disliked him, and his concerns were validated during subsequent weeks of working with him. Visitation with his father continued, but the stepmother would not allow it to occur at their house due to concerns about her daughter's safety.

I initially spent time with his mother, who was surprised at his behavior, did not believe he had been sexually abused, and described him as insecure, anxious, and impulsive. N.N.'s parents completed rating scales, but they did not reveal significant disturbance in any area (although his mother did say that he reported an increase in being picked on at school).

I was struck by N.N.'s relative openness with me and soon realized that this was related in part to his anxiety and immaturity. He also had no history of defiance or aggression. He reluctantly admitted to what he had done and provided some detail after supportive prompting. I wondered out loud why he had done this. He first stated that he did not know, and answered my questions about possible sexual abuse or exposure to adult sexuality in the negative. I brought his mother back, and she encouraged him to be honest and open. After she left, he told me he was curious and he wanted to see how big the boy's penis was and make sure he didn't look like a girl. Eventually, after several more sessions, he revealed that at summer camp he had been ridiculed about the size of his genitals. He had also recently verbalized concern about the size of his penis. Admitting to this appeared to be more shameful to him than his actions with the two children.

N.N.'s father joined N.N. and myself in one session and was able to reaffirm his love and support for his son. N.N. also wrote an apology note to both of the children involved. N.N.'s mother was committed to him but admitted that since the divorce, she had not been as attentive. She was open to learning PCIT and responded well to coaching. N.N. enjoyed this extra attention; in individual sessions, his anxiety decreased and he cooperated fully.

Difficulties arose when I encouraged a return to normal visitation with his father. Several meetings were needed to convince his stepmother that he was safe. I made my argument based on the relative absence of risk factors, his cooperation with therapy, and the absence of distress in the stepsister. I was also struck that his worries and concerns arose in part because he was now cognitively mature enough to contrast himself with other children, but his insecurity and the taunting he received had elevated his agitation to the point that he acted impulsively to figure it out. Many sessions were spent helping him to learn how to lower his anxiety (through, for example, imagery, distraction, and self-talk) and think about himself more positively.

This case illustrates the application of my treatment philosophy with a boy who had a rather atypical onset of sexual behavior. In this case, his anxiety was driven largely by the taunting he had received from peers. His relationship with his mother and father improved, and he felt supported enough to stay focused on the relatively directive path I took to address the anxiety and shame he was experiencing.

Older Elementary School Age

This group of children (usually 10–12 years) is more consistently in the concrete operations stage of development (Cohen, 2002). Their perspective-taking skills about other children and themselves are enhanced. They also have some appreciation of universality. Consequently, they can talk more generically about the impact of sexual abuse on other children. However, given the persisting egocentricity of the most disturbed, they may lack the capacity to understand that their experiences are similar to other children's. Nevertheless, some older children in this group can start to learn if-then thinking, which enhances perspective taking and leads to the development of empathy.

For example, you can create an exercise with the child called, "If I do X, then this will happen." I typically start off with some relatively benign and easy to understand actions, such as, "If I don't do my homework, then I will not pass my class." You can move from there to other interpersonal interactions that are suggested by either you or the child. I make a point of highlighting some to share with the parents when they come in. In this way, parents appreciate that their child is actually thinking about the impact of his or her behavior on the parents.

In terms of sexual abuse probability, I remain reasonably convinced that the majority of boys and an even larger percentage of girls in this age group with intrusive sexual behavior have been sexualized in some way, often via legally defined abuse or a mild form of sexual abuse. However, the actual details may never be forthcoming from the majority of these children. In addition, family sexuality is always an operative force and how that shapes behavior depends on each child-family combination. For example, oppositional behavior and emerging conduct disorder carry with them an increased likelihood of some sexual behaviors and can be a primary driving force for intrusive behavior (American Psychiatric Association, 1994).

The parental role for this group of children parallels that of the school-age group. It includes the provision of safety and enhanced monitoring of the child. Children of this age begin to spend much more time unsupervised and thus more vulnerable to exploitation. Parents need to hear that their child has an increasingly separate world from them and may have access to pornography or peer interactions of which the parents are unaware or choose to ignore. They may be aggressive with peers or peers may be aggressive to them. All of these new issues with older children contribute to the need for increased monitoring.

The parents will need to appreciate their child's need for more support, although that may require some persuasion. This group of children is particularly challenging since they know their parents well, and interaction patterns are more difficult to change. Teaching parents how to be neutral in response to badgering and other behaviors that in the past have pushed their buttons will be quite a challenge.

PCIT (Hembree-Kigin & McNeil, 1995) and its various elements continue to be my treatment of choice. However, it will become harder to find scenarios that lend themselves to special time, both at home and in your office, once you are practicing CDI. I have found that collaborative art projects, collages, and using CDI as part of feelings identification exercises can work well. Parents' negative attributions about their child can be corrected in the context of the PCIT exercises. However, your sessions alone with parents will be the best place to help them understand why it is essential to think and act more positively with their child.

My individual therapy with these children concentrates on support, repeated psychoeducational efforts so that they appreciate that events lead to outcomes, and also skill building (e.g., self-control and anger control). I use the sexual behavior rules as a framework to talk about why they need to change. Individual therapy is also where you can guide a discussion about what makes it easy or hard to follow the rules and explore the degree to which children sexualize interactions.

The turtle technique (see Chapter 8, Form M) lends itself to the exercises you will do with these children. As a physical activity, you can get on the floor and demonstrate how to "become a turtle and draw in your head" when children get scared or start thinking of doing something they should not do. You model this to the child several times. Then the child gets on the floor and imitates you once or twice and eventually shows you how and when it is done. The shared activity builds rapport and also provides a nice break from conversation. I like to have a menu of certain scenarios to "be a turtle" that are specific to the child (you and the child can take turns reading from this list). Parents are typically pleased when they come in at the end of session and see that their child has actually learned something in the time with you. This is another time when the parent can learn to cue the child in a positive way (e.g., "Maybe it's time to be a turtle!"), so that this technique can be used in the future.

The H. Family

I saw an 11-year-old boy, H.H., who lived with his cognitively limited single mother and a female companion who had two children of her own, one older and another a preschooler. He originally came to see me as a sexual abuse victim, but his mother had interfered with his openness to me. Even so, screening data from a respite care parent, his mother, and the caseworker were very concerning. For example, 14 of Hall et al.'s (1998) risk factors were endorsed, he had significant elevations on all three CSBI scales, and generic behavior ratings revealed problems with peers, reduced empathy, and conduct.

I started to wonder about his sexual interests after receiving this information from other adults who knew H.H. well. Prior to this, he had felt to me like a somewhat simple, pitiable, and lonely boy who enjoyed spending time with me and was generally compliant in return.

So I started our fourth individual session by asking H.H. if kids in his class were "going out," and if so, whom did he want to go out with. He smiled and spoke with more interest than he had ever shown. So I asked about "sexy" kids on the school bus, sexy teachers, and then on a whim, who was the sexiest person, first at respite care and then his house. I was writing all these names on a list and this seemed to help him talk more openly. He had answers for all of these questions, and seemed to enjoy the extra attention I afforded by writing down names and sexiness characteristics. He identified a preschool boy and girl at the two homes he lived in and was quite energized when talking about each. He dismissed my curiosity about liking a boy and a girl, and told me he had heard people could be "bi" and he thought he was one of those people. The respite care parent confirmed my suspicions about his interest in playing with her preschooler, and she had interfered with at least one possibly concerning interaction.

As I worked with the adults in H.H.'s life, the focus of the therapy changed and sexual rules and monitoring were increased in both homes. I also began talking to him about why people insisted that he play with some children only when adults were around. His mother was more motivated than before and learned enough skills that therapy was ended. However, this is the type of child whose risk level may increase in adolescence, and he should be followed again at that time.

This is also the first age when the child can start to think about future risk situations. I like to use an interactive drawing "How to Get Sexual Behavior Problems Off Your Territory" as an exercise. As part of this activity, the child can list strategies that the two of you have been working on. Both of you may arrive at a metaphor for your combined efforts that can tie some sessions together. For example, one 11-year-old foster child, who was extremely preoccupied with sexuality and made sexual comments, drew a castle with a moat (and laser guns as well). This provided me and his foster parents a chance to reference his efforts by talking about "things or ideas coming over the castle walls."

The K. Family

K.K. was an 11-year-old girl who fondled a younger female cousin on one occasion. This prompted the referral for assessment and treatment. K.K.'s family was intact, and she denied ever having been sexually abused. Her parents also reported no concerns about maltreatment. Only after several months of work was she able to talk about continued thoughts of sexually touching a neighbor child who was younger than she. She did not volunteer this information outright, and it came out only when I did a network mapping of everyone in her neighborhood.

K.K. was a lonely child who spent a considerable amount of time riding her bike. So I brought in maps and we enlarged the streets onto another sheet of paper. She opened up as we expanded the map and added details of different buildings, stores, and parks she rode past. I praised her skills, map knowledge, and energy, and wrote up a growing list of her positive characteristics, which I would pull up on my computer at each session.

We then created a list of everyone in K.K.'s neighborhood, and together we drew where they lived on the block. We then systematically talked about each child, what she did with them, and different thoughts she had about them. I also had K.K. rate on a four-point scale whether or not she had ever had any thoughts about sexually touching that child. She was a fairly inhibited girl, and so her revelation about the neighbor child took me by surprise. I believe she disclosed in part because she was truly preoccupied. Once this information was on the table, we could start talking about alternate behaviors, using the activity, "How to Get Sexual Thoughts Off My Property."

Together, we were able to come up with several activities she could do that would distract her. These included video games, reading, and instant messaging her friend at school. We also talked about the need to talk more with same-age friends and role-played some examples of things she could talk about.

I was left with the dilemma of how to share this information with K.K.'s mother, who continued to have a fairly negative view of the girl. I accomplished this by including the mother in part of the next session. She reported some improvements with CDI. I then praised K.K.'s "determination to get better" and shared my concerns about her.

K.K. taught me a great deal about how to facilitate greater openness in children and not discount the possibility of continued sexual thoughts even if a child superficially appears compliant and a parent seems less rejecting and more positive.

Children at this age, with support, can be even more valid in their self-report of thoughts and emotions than their younger peers. Therapy with these children requires building a basic foundation for conversation, and I think that self-report measures completed collaboratively can be very useful in doing this.

Completing the 21 Questions (see Chapter 8, Form F) is much more critical for this group of children than for the two younger groups. The older sexually intrusive children are, the more concerned I am about the possibility that they have a developing pattern of sexually intrusive behavior. I want to know as much as possible about what has happened and how open they can be. If you use the questions collaboratively (share them with children) and proceed through them in a less structured and more conversational manner, children are usually more forthcoming and the entire process more therapeutic. In addition, I view this review of their sexuality as an opportunity for exposure, in the same manner that cognitive behavioral therapy uses exposure to alleviate PTSD symptoms. Exposure gives you a vehicle to reduce anxiety, alter cognitions, and provide support. The more information you can obtain from a reliable caregiver about the sexual incidents, the more you will be able to facilitate the child's movement from initial denial or defensiveness to some measure of disclosure, occurring in a supportive context.

This older group is the one I get concerned about regarding their level of sexual preoccupation. Because they are older, their actions are less likely the result of impulsivity and more likely a function of their thought process or immature social relations. I become even more concerned when there is no reason to believe they were only recently molested or exposed to adult sexuality. We do not have any definitive strategies for assessing sexual preoccupation, although some strategies are described in Chapter 4.

However, self-monitoring remains variably useful, even with older elementary children who have sexual behavior problems. I have seen it work with children who are simply anxious or depressed but rarely with children who have sexually intrusive behavior. Self-monitoring will help, and sometimes achieve the desired outcome, only with an enormous amount of parental support. However, when it works, do not ask for more than one to two symptoms or thoughts to be monitored more than one to two times per day. Work only with parents who easily demonstrate support and who have better skills for interacting with their child than the majority of parents in this category. This will often be a foster or adoptive parent who has received specialized training.

FANTASY

I raise this issue since the patient's fantasy forms the basis of some of the therapy in adult offender programs. The thought is that fantasy is a clue to one's thinking and also may lead to subsequent illegal sexual behavior.

Fantasies develop early in a child's life and are seen as normal behavior. As children get older, they can privately process and reprocess their thoughts, imagine new ones, and develop fantasies. For example, very young children will often act as if they are a favorite TV character. They will often spend time each day engrossed in activities related to what they have seen or imagined. However, they are also easily distracted, and overt events typically drive their thinking more than their private world does.

It has been suggested that it is not until 11 to 13 years of age or so that sexual fantasy has its onset. This finding is based on retrospective reports of adults (Daleiden, Kaufman, Hilliker, & O'Neil, 1998). Children whose mental world now includes frequent thoughts of past abuses and thoughts of touching other children are very concerning.

These are typically children whose abuse has lasted longer and been much more severe. However, there are always exceptions. I have seen children whose abuse was less severe, but they tended to be ruminative and obsessive and could not let go of the trauma as easily as other, less focused children. Enabling preteens to talk about sexual fantasies requires extra effort and laying groundwork for discussion. I have been able to talk minimally to only a few older elementary-aged children about their sexual fantasies, and in most of these cases, therapy was prematurely terminated due to family chaos and pathology. In the several cases where these conversations were more extended, the children were in alternate care, and managing their overt behavior required most of the time they spent in therapy.

The Case of I.I.

I.I. was 10 years old when she was referred to me after her aunt observed her using her dolls to play out elaborate sexual themes. The aunt had custody and, at intake, reported, "Her play goes way beyond getting married to a prince." While on one level the play was fantasy based, I concluded by the end of therapy that it reflected more closely her intrusive thoughts about her prior victimization.

I.I. had earlier reported several incidents of sexual abuse while living with her mother. The abuse had involved a teenage male relative and had started out under the guise of "getting married." I began treatment by first meeting with the aunt for two sessions. I then alternated between working with the aunt and I.I. in CDI and individual therapy sessions. These latter sessions were focused on understanding the earlier abuse and its effect on her.

After our fourth individual session, I asked I.I. to bring in her dolls. My intention was to have her show me the sexual play she had exhibited with the dolls. She became ashamed and refused to cooperate. This certainly is a reminder of how much shame surrounds sexual abuse and interferes with the child's ability to talk. The same is true for fantasies, particularly those that are tied to the abuse.

One of the sexual rules we had created was to only play with her dolls in front of the aunt, but she was not compliant with this. This suggested that sexualized doll play still occupied some part of her thinking. After another session with I.I. and the aunt, I asked both of them to attend the following week and make sure the dolls came along. Both she and her aunt were present when I used them to role-play what she had reported about her previous abuse. She started off quite reserved as I was beginning to role-play. Then she stood up to watch me more closely and even corrected me on a few details. Her involvement led me to believe that she and I were finally in a better position to begin talking about her abuse.

This led to a discussion in that session, primarily between the aunt and me, of how the continued use of the dolls, in private, was like a reenactment of I.I.'s prior abuse. On a whiteboard in my office, I wrote down several reasons why continuing to play with the dolls in this way was not helpful. This then transitioned into cartooning while I.I. stood by and commented on the drawings. First, I drew the abuse, the various emotions she had as a result, the reactions of the people in her life, and her feelings about the role-play. It was after this session that the aunt reported a significant reduction in the sexualized doll play at home. This reduction of doll play and improved compliance with her aunt continued through the end of therapy and a 4-month follow-up.

SPECIAL TREATMENT ISSUES

In addition to the need to consider developmental issues, children with sexual behavior problems often present challenging treatment issues. While PCIT focuses on improving the parent-child relationship and decreasing externalizing disruptive behavior, individual therapy provides an excellent arena to both assess and treat the internalized distress that is reflected in these symptoms. These special issues include PTSD, dissociation, children who are cognitively compromised, children who experienced very early abuse of which they have no memory, and finally, children who will not talk about their abuse or their symptoms.

PTSD

By now, the reader should certainly know my bias about the important role that cumulative stress plays in the development of intrusive sexual behavior. The same is true for PTSD, which is manifested more often in vulnerable children who are predisposed by prior trauma, reduced familial support, and premorbid behavior problems (Wolfe et al., 1994). Consequently, PTSD and its various

elements, such as flashbacks, hyperarousal, and avoidance, are typically present in these young children and interfere with the ease with which they are
parented, and with their success at school and with peer relationships.

Not only is there strong empirical support for a cognitive behavioral
approach to children with PTSD (Cohen & Mannarino, 1997; Kolko, 1996;
Saunders et al., 2004), there are other reasons to utilize this approach in therapy. I have seen many situations where reexperiencing of prior abuse, in combination with a hyperaroused and impulsive child, have led to sexual acting
out in children of various ages. For example, one 9-year-old who got caught
up in rough-and-tumble play with two 11-year-old boys started to disrobe and
pose herself sexually. When her foster mother came to check on the noise, she
saw the 9-year-old masturbating and the older boys staring at the girl.

Medication is often suggested in these cases, but my child psychiatry colleagues are more restrained about the utility of stimulants, SSRI, and other
medications for PTSD, particularly those aspects that result in heightened
impulsivity and hyperarousal. When ADHD is absent, these colleagues have
observed either minimal response or sometimes adverse responses to stimulants. They attribute this to the fact that these children become more focused
on their distress, because their usual avoidant stance does not work as efficiently as it did prior to the stimulants. Once again, a structured approach that
appreciates the trauma, sorts through it sensitively with the child, offers alternative ways to think about the child's responses, including guilt and shame,
and is combined with learning some self-soothing techniques can be enormously helpful for these children.

The PTSD Workbook in Chapter 8 is designed to provide the structure
necessary to clinically address PTSD. The workbook enables children to better elaborate on a topic that they typically avoid. Therapists who use this
workbook need to be familiar with PTSD as well as such cognitive behavioral techniques as exposure, imagery and relaxation, and changing self-talk.
I wanted to create something that had utility across all ages from 4 to 13. In
addition, I do believe that a positive reframe of flashbacks is useful to children;
that is, you can learn from your flashbacks. Drawings are emphasized and a
collaborative process is encouraged. Another PTSD therapy resource is the
workbook developed by Cunningham and MacFarlane (2001).

A related problem is issues of traumatic grief. Many of the children I see
with sexual behavioral problems have lost parents due to court action, for
example, termination of parental rights related to failure to protect children, parent figures who are now out of their lives because they have been
in a perpetrating role, or parents who will not leave the offender. The trauma
symptoms that the child is already experiencing will interfere with the child's

ability to grieve normally and can result in complicated bereavement (Cohen & Mannarino, 2004).

Cohen and Mannarino make a number of critical points in their very useful article on treating childhood traumatic grief. For example, the child's tendency to avoid thinking about the trauma interferes with the ability to think more accurately about the lost parent and achieve reconciliation. They also suggest that optimal treatment when these children are dealing with traumatic grief should include both trauma- and grief-focused treatment elements. They review a protocol with five treatment elements including a focus on traumatic experiences, reminders of trauma and loss, bereavement and interplay of trauma and grief, posttrauma adversity, and developmental progression. It is important to note that the parent's emotional distress is related to the child's ability to resolve both the trauma and the traumatic grief. This argues for a significant parent component when that is possible.

Specific and focused interventions aimed at children with sexual behavior problems who have also experienced a loss would include psychoeducation about death, permission to mourn, identifying ambivalent feelings about the deceased or absent parent, and figuring out some way to preserve positive memories if possible. The relationship can be redefined as something that continues in the child's mind even if the adult is not present. The child can be assisted in learning how to derive support from other relationships and make some sense out of the traumatic loss. It is best to do this in the context of sessions that include a supportive adult, the parent, and the child.

DISSOCIATION

Liotti (1999) suggested that dissociation is the response of children to disorganized attachment. Typically, dissociation is viewed as a response to severe and chronic trauma, but he presented it as a naturally evolving and long-term outcome by the child in response to a parent who is contradictory and, at times, terrifying. In the face of this, the child becomes unable to organize an integrated self and thus presents various part-selves to the world. This is often operative with sexually intrusive children (and also their parents). One of the nonintegrated selves is a child who can superficially appear to be prosocial and act as if few things are wrong. This extends into school settings, which provide structure and stability. Schools also typically have fewer cues to trigger the child's inappropriate behavior, and school staff may be unaware of any sexual behavior problems. The children whose issues spill over into school are typically the most disturbed and sexually preoccupied.

Criteria for a dissociation-spectrum disorder diagnosis, as rated by both self-report and staff report, were met by one in seven males (14.3%) in a sample of adolescent sex offenders (Friedrich et al., 2001). This is surprisingly common relative to epidemiological data (American Psychiatric Association, 1994). These adolescents were contrasted with a sample of adolescent psychiatric inpatients, of whom only 4.2% met the criteria. As part of the study, cumulative adversity was also assessed, and the rates were staggering in the sex offender group. For example, rates of substantiated abuse were as follows: physical abuse (52.8%), neglect (45.7%), emotional abuse (50%), domestic violence (32.8%), and sexual abuse (52.8%). These rates were typically two to six times higher in the teen offenders than in the psychiatric inpatients.

There is no proven strategy for reducing the frequency of dissociation, but some tips can be derived from Steele and her colleagues (2003), whose securely attached adoptive mothers reduced the frequency of aggressive and destructive thoughts by 70% in their adoptive children. Therapists who provide safety, in combination with parents who do the same, will help reduce these acute symptoms. For children whose home lives have stabilized and whose parents provide greater safety and nurturance, episodes of staring blankly and sudden behavioral changes have been reported to drop in frequency.

Four Sisters

One example of dissociation at work involved four sisters. They came into foster care after their mother was sentenced to drug treatment. They did very well in this new setting, which was vastly different in many ways from their earlier home. It was only when the foster mother mentioned that their mother was coming to live with them that the oldest blurted out, "I don't want to play the Charlie game."

Over a several-week period, I was involved in their assessment and consulted social services about how best to manage them. These girls were some of the most extremely sexually focused children I have ever worked with. They were constantly seeking out ways to touch and kiss each other, and the foster mother believed they could not be controlled in her household. They provided information to me and to detectives, which was later confirmed by maternal confession, about repeated sexual abuse and the making of pornography. (I would never work with them as a male therapist because my presence was too evocative. However, the oldest was sexually intrusive on at least one occasion with a female therapist.)

The older girls were in school and were poor students. Teachers reported that they stared off into space and tracked poorly. ADHD was considered. They generally confined their sexual behavior to the foster home and each other. It was as if they had compartmentalized their lives to such an extent that they acted out only when reminded. True to the symptoms of dissociation, the girls had segregated different aspects of themselves; it was as if the sexual play existed only in the context of each other.

The sexual play was reduced only after all four girls were placed separately in different foster homes. These issues were quickly replaced by other behavior problems reflecting defiance, episodes of cruelty, and persisting problems with passivity and staring episodes. Seizures were ruled out in the two that were examined by neurologists. Regrettably, their longer-term outcomes have typically been poor.

COGNITIVE IMPAIRMENT

My CSBI research samples contain over one hundred 5- to 12-year-old children who were identified by their parents as having developmental disabilities. The sample was never as large or well defined as I needed in order to publish my analyses with the data set. However, I did run some analyses for this book. The primary findings for the entire group of nonabused children with disabilities were: (1) more problems with personal boundaries, and (2) typically more obvious and persistent self-stimulating behaviors than same-age children without a developmental delay. This is similar to data reported in another study of cognitively impaired youth who also had severe mental illness (McCurry et al., 1998).

The results have also been validated in my clinical practice, and several of the persistent self-stimulators that I have consulted on have been cognitively limited. Those with supportive caregivers have seemed to respond to the same masturbation protocol that has worked with nondelayed children, that is, increase support, use distraction, enforce sexual rules, and schedule masturbation to occur at an inconvenient time and place. The few with a more probable sexual abuse history and other limitations have been challenging to treat. I have also had to use reinforcement and consequence programs more often to reduce the frequency of the masturbatory behavior.

Y.Y. and Pornography

Y.Y. was an 11-year-old boy, with mild cognitive impairment, who was very persistent at accessing Internet pornography. He had been exposed to this in his biological home, where he had also been severely neglected. His foster parents prevented this with locks on the computers. They were slowly extinguishing his occasional sexual comments via withdrawal of attention, but the gains were very gradual. It was at school that his pornography usage prompted a bureaucratic reaction that initially resulted in suspension and threatened expulsion. Only after visiting with the principal and school counselor did I realize that given the layout of the school, Y.Y. could easily access computers all over the building. It required modifying his educational plan so that he had no access to those rooms before we saw a reduction in usage. But during his visits to my office, Y.Y. typically asked if I could leave the room and he could use the computer. I never believed that I helped reduce his motivation to use pornography. External controls are all that you can do for some children like him.

PREVERBAL ABUSE

Working with sexually intrusive children teaches you to be humble about what you will ever know for certain. I see many preverbal children who have sexually intrusive behavior but it is not likely that they were recently abused. However, their early lives were in homes characterized by sexual abuse of other children or overt adult sexuality. The child has no memory of these events and, thus, cannot talk about the abuse in therapy. How do you view the child? Sexually abused? Not abused? How do you introduce this topic into the therapy? Or do you?

I strongly urge against explicitly telling children of this age that they were sexually abused. Rather, I suggest using better known events in their life as an explanation; for example, losing a parent made them confused about what was okay to do. Telling them they were sexually abused has the potential to derail the relationship and destroy an important treatment opportunity.

It was a case of this type that led to one of my first uses of prescriptive statements (see Chapter 8, Form L).

The Case of O.O.

O.O. was a 9-year-old foster child. Her primary sexual problem was going without underwear, chasing and hitting boys at school and in the neighborhood, and occasionally exposing herself to males. However, what irritated her foster mother the most was that the 9-year-old constantly interfered with her care of her younger half sibling, who was also living in the foster home. O.O. insisted on changing diapers, putting the child to bed, and feeding the child.

It was clear that this girl had been a surrogate parent to several younger children, including the toddler now in foster care. An eyewitness had stated at the court hearing that resulted in placement that O.O. had been fondled on many occasions prior to her second birthday.

O.O. largely ignored the sexual rules we established during the first few weeks of therapy. What got her attention were the prescriptive statements that spoke more clearly to her known past. I instructed the foster mother to randomly and neutrally say such things as, "When kids have to take care of babies, they don't get a chance to play," and, "When kids have to cook meals since their parents won't, they sometimes cut or burn their hands." I created a total of five statements, and the foster mom usually said three to four per day.

After 1 week of using these statements, O.O. still was not cooperative with her sexual rules and claimed that she did not know why she continued to act provocatively. We brainstormed for portions of two sessions while working on cartooning her behavior and completing a list of strategies with the "Getting Sexual Behavior Off My Property" activity. Her provocative behavior did lessen, but still occurred several times per week. A behavioral plan to reinforce her wearing underwear was also created and resulted in some dropoff in frequency.

O.O. started talking about different memories during the second week of using the prescriptive statements. All of her memories were related to these statements. She expressed sadness about her past life to her foster mother and to me. Six weeks after she began using these statements, O.O. had her first week with no sexual rule violations. This behavioral improvement variably persisted, but with a clear overall decline in frequency. In addition, she was less controlling of the care of her half sister. Her foster mother started speaking more positively of her and sat through one PCIT coaching session. This only seemed to solidify the gains O.O. made. She continued reasonably positive adjustment at follow-up roughly 2 months later.

I do not believe the exact history of the child's experiences is essential to the therapy process. What is essential is the parent-child combination in front of you. These are often adoptive or long-term foster care relationships. I have seen situations where the relationship between this child and parent was already tentative and the onset of sexual behavior several years after placement was too much for the parent to manage. The parent then emotionally withdrew further and was not as available to nurture the child. Once the behavior could be controlled, the foster parent was better able to reengage with the child.

The Case of G.G.

G.G. was 4 years old when she moved into a preadoptive placement with a childless couple. The first 6 weeks constituted a honeymoon phase and their time together went wonderfully. She was described as compliant and the mother and daughter quickly formed what reportedly was a very strong and mutual connection. I have seen this type of placement have a much longer honeymoon period. I believe when that happens, it illustrates a high level of parenting skill, including a history of secure attachment in the adoptive parents (Steele et al., 2003).

Her early history was with a very neglectful teenage mother, and at the age of 2 she had been left with a terminally ill maternal grandmother. Living in the home with the grandmother was an uncle who had molested his sister, the mother of this child. G.G. never spoke of this man, although she became upset if his name was mentioned.

I completed an intake with the adoptive mother and father and, at their request, agreed to see G.G. in some play therapy sessions mixed in with assessment of her functioning. She played appropriately, although she was immature. She did not display persisting problems with boundaries.

However, G.G.'s honeymoon came to an end with the onset of bedwetting at week 4 of therapy. G.G. was then suspected of being mean to a family pet. A few weeks later, the adoptive mom reported to the adoption worker that G.G. was trying to take her husband away from her. She said that G.G. would follow her adoptive dad into the bathroom whenever he used it and would also try to watch him get dressed in the morning. She felt her daughter had much more interest in him than in her.

When I saw them again for Session 8, the mother was overtly critical of G.G. I tried to help her appreciate that G.G.'s behavior was not willful but reflected her early history. We started with CDI at Session 8 and also established sexual rules related to bathroom privacy. These rules were then included as part of our individual play therapy involving role-play with dolls. The bathroom behavior was quickly eliminated via the sexual rules. Despite the fact that the mother was quite socially skilled, she proved resistant to CDI and ignored my prompts at least a third of the time. I was very puzzled by this quick turnaround. She and her husband opted to have the placement terminated before the adoption was formalized. My impression is that even though sexual abuse of G.G. was never addressed, she was able to make improvements in behavior that may well have persisted if not for the adoption breakdown.

Children Who Will Not Talk

Many children will not talk about prior abuse or intrusive behavior. This is despite their ability to talk about many other, often closely related topics, including losses and scary events. Individual therapy can still be structured to be useful for this type of child.

When children are able to articulate what has happened to them, they take steps toward integrating this event into their awareness and self-perception (Aldrige & Wood, 1997; Toth et al., 1997). Integration is always a positive since it is more mature than fragmentation (Elliott, 1994). Articulation also adds to the probability that related behaviors can be inhibited. For example, when I meet children who are perseveratively acting on their own abuse (e.g., masturbating, making statements about having been hurt, or inserting objects into their own or another child's orifices) they are usually younger and extremely affected by what has happened to them. The challenge is how to articulate this so children can hear it and integrate it.

The Case of J.J.

J.J. was a 6-year-old who had been anally raped less than 2 years earlier by an older half sibling. Although he had spoken about the incident at the time, he had long since refused to talk about it. J.J. also refused to talk about the sexual acts he was now doing to himself and to animals. He was in an atypical foster-type placement, but was being parented by very conscientious people who were willing to keep close track of his behavior.

He now was inserting objects into the anuses of family pets. He persisted in spite of having been scratched fairly severely by one of the animals. In addition, he was routinely caught putting his finger or a pen into his own anus. His foster mother noted that his shorts were typically off in the morning and his finger smelled of feces. On one occasion, he asked his foster mother for help in retrieving a small plastic figure from his rectum. She refused but took him to the family doctor for help in doing so. J.J. was also self-injurious and would hit himself in the face, slap his crotch, and pick at sores and scabs. His placement was becoming more strained because his foster parents found his behavior increasingly difficult to tolerate. His foster mother said, "Now that he is comfortable with us, he is showing us his worst behavior."

I saw J.J.'s foster mother as part of the intake and she began to monitor the frequency of three of his behaviors, insertion into self or an animal's anus, and self-injurious behaviors of any type. She was willing to learn CDI, and after two sessions that were designed for me to evaluate and play with J.J., we had three sessions that primarily focused on CDI. I also taught both foster parents how to respond more neutrally to J.J.'s provocative behavior, the place for withdrawal of attention, and also catching J.J. being good. Both parents became better at predicting when he was upset and close to self-injury. As a result, we created several competing responses such as touching his toes to interrupt it and using the turtle technique (see Chapter 8, Form M). While they expressed relief to now have a few new parenting tools with this very difficult boy, these interventions had little effect on the insertion behavior, although the self-injurious behavior started to decrease.

During Session 8, which was another individual session, I began to talk about boys who had things stuck in their bottoms and how that made them want to put things into their own bottoms. I also drew several cartoon series in which the boy in the cartoon thought of what had happened to him (e.g., got something stuck in his ear), then got an idea to try it on himself, and then did so. I included ears and nostrils as orifices in the first two series. He and I also used several human and animal doll figures and looked at their anuses, and I wondered about what they would feel like if someone put something into them. J.J., at times, looked uncomfortable, and so we would each "become a turtle" to calm down. However, although he helped with the drawings, he did not talk about either his behavior or his abuse experience.

I brought in the foster mother and we reviewed the drawings with her. I suggested that J.J. was not sure we knew what had happened and that he needed to keep telling us "until we got the message." I then gave her a statement to say to J.J. whenever she saw any insertion behavior from him. We wrote it out on the computer with J.J.'s help and sent it home. The statement read, "Thank you for telling us again what Tyler did."

By Session 10, the insertion behavior, with both self and animals, had dropped off noticeably and was now absent for up to 2 days at a time. The foster mother created her own statement to use when she saw self-injurious behavior ("Thank you for telling us that you don't like yourself right now"). That behavior also dropped off even further. Not only were all three target behaviors nonexistent at the end of therapy (26 sessions), but they also remained at that level at 3-month follow-up. However, J.J.'s biological mother resumed contact with him shortly after he turned 8 and he was back in my office a few weeks later. He had once again started to hit and scratch his face with only minimal provocation, but the anal insertion behavior did not return.

My approach to children who refuse to verbalize their abuse or their sexual behavior problem has several components. It is important that their home environment is supportive. You also must take the lead to introduce difficult topics. I do not find nondirective play, while enjoyable for me and the children, to be very helpful at reducing the frequency of the target behavior. You must also spell out very clearly, and in multiple formats, for several weeks at a time, the connection between an event and their behavior. The child must be engaged in this process as well, and you have to continue to maintain a strong alliance. In addition, increasing the level of support to the child, and adding in opportunities for articulation with prescriptive statements between the sessions, seem to add to the utility of your intervention over and above the usual parenting strategies of withdrawal of attention, limit setting, and the use of rewards.

Prescriptive statements are crafted to be specific to the child and designed to come across as supportive and facilitative of the child understanding himself. If the child becomes persistently agitated or angry when these statements are made it could be a sign that the child perceives them as controlling or abusive. When that occurs, I instruct the parent to immediately stop and apologize.

CONCLUSION

I have three ongoing thoughts during individual therapy with a sexually intrusive child. The first is, how does my work facilitate the parent-child relationship? The second thought is that it is my job to keep children focused on the referral issues. They would avoid this topic if I did not take a directive stance. It is important to use a variety of verbal and nonverbal avenues so that they start to see their behavior objectively and take steps to change. Finally, I want children to feel maximally supported in a manner that is tolerable to them, given their history with disappointing relationships.

However, individual therapy works best if children are also working in parent-child therapy. They then feel supported as they correct their thinking about such topics as self-defeating behaviors, inaccurate cognitions, and relationship patterns. In addition, many of these children have PTSD, struggle with loss, and are depressed. Here is where individual therapy can have a unique contribution.

One of the phenomena I observe in children over the course of successful therapy is their increased ability to speak more accurately about who they are, why they are in therapy, and what they have accomplished. In other words, they become more coherent. This is the desired outcome, since experiences that cannot be known or spoken about are at the root of incoherence in the discourse between therapist and child (Slade, 1999). More important, children have hopefully learned a framework that enables them to think in a more coherent manner about their life experiences. I believe that a long-term result of having this coherency is greater consistency, reduced impulsivity, and sensitivity about the impact of their behavior on other people.

The therapy community will always debate about the treatment elements that are critical for this or another population. The healing power of enhanced parenting cannot be underestimated, and the therapeutic relationship only adds to successful child therapy.

PART II

ASSESSMENT AND
TREATMENT MANUAL

7

OVERVIEW AND SEQUENCE
OF SESSIONS

THIS MANUAL DESCRIBES a treatment protocol for 3- to 12-year-old children of either gender who exhibit sexualized behavior that warrants intervention. Such behavior is often due to sexual abuse, but it can stem as well from exposure to peer or adult sexuality, pornography, domestic violence, or other maltreatment. Sexualized behavior can also be one component of other behavioral difficulties in the child, such as oppositional-defiant disorder, conduct disorder, PTSD, and attachment problems. More likely than not, there are multiple contributors to persistent sexualized behavior.

Persistent sexual behavior problems are almost always a function of child and family variables, as well as any other trauma or exposure that the child has experienced. For example, some children are more impulsive and are more easily activated by what they see or experience. While learning theory can explain the emergence of the problems, they are maintained and exacerbated by a combination of some if not all of the following: a family sexual climate, parent-child conflict that reflects insecure attachment, unresolved sexual abuse, comorbid physical abuse, emotional neglect, and poor parental monitoring (Friedrich, 1988). The caregiver may not understand the connection between prior abuse, overstimulating behavior in the home, and the child's sexualized behavior. This will often lead the caregiver to blame the child for the behavior.

Consequently, the children that you see with persisting sexual behavior problems are typically, as a group, more disturbed than children with a primary history of sexual abuse or other maltreatment who are not acting out sexually. The frequency of impaired attachment is almost universal; victimization history in the parent is more likely than not, and when present, victimization of the child is likely to have been more severe and be accompanied by symptoms of PTSD (Friedrich, Davies, Fehrer, Trentham, & Wright, 2003).

As a result, developing a therapeutic relationship with the parent requires more effort than in other child therapy cases. These cases challenge you to be a therapeutic chameleon, someone who is true to his core but who is flexible in his approach to the parent (Friedrich, 1995). Parents and children who are prior victims can vary widely in their presentation, but some of them may fall into such categories as angry/ambivalent, avoidant/passive, and self-defeating/ rejecting. It is important that you observe how you behave differently for each of these types as you engage them. For example, you will want to start out as neutral/accepting to the first group, supportive/energizing to the second group, and one-down/neutral to the third group.

This protocol is used in combination with the child and parent or caregiver. The majority of parents who have completed this program have been single mothers, but it has also been used successfully with two-parent families and an occasional custodial father. Absent fathers cast a long shadow on these families, and any prior criminal or offending history in their lives is often well known by the child.

The provision of additional group therapy only enhances the effectiveness of therapy (MacFarlane & Cunningham, 1990; Mandell & Damon, 1989). Pair therapy involving two developmentally similar children is a strategy that uses the advantages of group therapy with only two children (Friedrich, 1995). While group therapy can provide an arena for skill building and acceptance, it is not a necessary condition. Some agencies do not see enough children for groups to work. These families also have a hard time making regular therapy appointments, and group continuity would suffer. In addition, the inclusion of only one really disturbed child with intrusive sexual behavior into a small group of two to three other children with sexual behavior problems could be disastrous and requires very skilled group leaders to be successful.

Therapy is provided in weekly 1-hour sessions, or less often if the family cannot manage this frequency. However, the first one to two sessions work best if they are 1.5 hours each. The number of sessions can range from as few as five to as many as 35 or more, depending on the complexity of the issues. Parents should be key participants in this protocol and are involved from the onset and in frequent parent-child sessions. This may be less possible when the caregiver is a foster parent who is already a very adequate parent or who does not feel any need to participate given their transient role in the child's life.

It is important to meet with the parents or caregivers before or after the child-only sessions to review their monitoring of the child's behavior and problem solve any pressing issues. With some children, multiple child-only sessions in a row will be needed to establish rapport, start to address prior victimization, and examine children's thoughts and feelings related to their sexually coercive behavior. This is typically reserved for older children who are better able to benefit from learning some self-control strategies, and who can engage in a cognitive therapy approach that is combined with activity.

Familiarity with the principles of parent-child interaction therapy (PCIT; Hembree-Kigin & McNeil, 1995) and also cognitive behavioral play therapy techniques (Bodiford-McNeil et al., 1996) will enhance the therapist's overall success when using this manual.

This protocol includes the following components:

1. Assessing the extent of the sexual behavior problem and the contingencies that are related to the behavior.

2. Increasing the number of positive interactions per day between the parent and the child, including both verbal (e.g., praise) and physical (e.g., touch).

3. Addressing and resolving the child's sexual abuse or other traumatic experience by first addressing PTSD symptoms.

4. Incorporating sexual rules into the family's culture.

5. Introducing the family and child to the importance of parental monitoring of the child's behavior.

6. Connecting the observed sexual behavior to precipitating events or contingencies in the child's life or family. This makes the behavior more understandable and also solvable.

7. Teaching parents how to deliver corrective phrases to the child that not only communicate that they understand and care for the child but that also serve to inhibit the child's sexualized and aggressive behaviors.

8. Instructing parents in how to set limits, particularly for the sexual behavior, but for other oppositional behaviors as well.

9. Improving the family's sexual climate so that nurturing behaviors can be exhibited and sexualized behaviors by adults and teenagers in the home are reduced and no longer overwhelming for the child.

10. Establishing goals with the parents and the child that focus on reducing the frequency of the behavior, increasing the amount of positive interactions between parents and child, and enhancing the child and parents' compliance around setting limits in a reasoned and nonaggressive fashion.

11. Altering parents' negative attributions about their child. These are usually both generic and also more specific to the child's sexual behavior.

PRETHERAPY CONTACT

I recommend that the therapist initially complete a brief telephone interview with the parents or caregiver. This call helps with rapport building and you can obtain information about the nature of the sexual behavior problem, how long it has been going on, and whether there is any involvement with either protective services or the court. You can also remind parents how important it is to come to the first appointment alone, and problemsolve with them if that is an issue.

This pretherapy contact is critical to facilitating a solid connection with the parents. Inform parents as well that they will receive several behavior rating scales that need to be brought in at the time of the first appointment. Double-check their address and mail out two forms: the Child Sexual Behavior Inventory (CSBI; Friedrich, 1997) and a behavior rating scale, such as the Child Behavior Checklist (CBCL Achenbach, 1991a), Behavior Assessment System for Children (BASC Reynolds & Kamphaus, 1998), or the brief, 25 item Strengths and Difficulties Questionnaire Goodman, 1997). It is best to proceed with this protocol only after the child has made a clear statement about the abuse. However, sometimes that is neither the issue nor possible for the child.

SESSIONS 1–2

Who attends: Parents. The child typically begins to attend with Session 3. These are often disadvantaged parents with limited access to child care, so you must have a contingency plan if they show up with one or more of their children even after being told to come alone.

AIMS OF SESSIONS

1. Begin to establish a therapeutic alliance with parents and instill hope that change can occur. To do so convincingly, you will need to learn about their theory as to why their child behaves the way he does. Do not rush to offer reassurances when parents are quite pessimistic. To do so would interfere with your developing relationship with them. Simply express concern for their difficult situation and agree that this can take time. Rapport building works best if you start by mirroring their presentation and wait to hear what they have to say.

    For example, you will hear from a number of these parents that their child is deeply disturbed in some basic way. Over the years, I have found that best initial response to these very rejecting comments and negative perceptions is to say one of the following: "That must make you so sad, to know that about one of your own children," or "I would be so sad if I were in your shoes." I do think that loss and sadness are so rife in these parents' lives that you will not miss the underlying emotion when you frame it in that way.

2. Determine the frequency, context, and potential contributors to the child's sexual behavior.

3. Interview the parents regarding the child's sexual abuse, physical abuse, and emotional abuse.

4. Find out about parents' prior maltreatment and determine if any steps have been taken to resolve this with personal therapy.

5. Determine the positives in the parent-child relationship, such as special time each day. Introduce them to the idea of catching their child being good, and model a few possibilities.

6. Explain how treatment works; for example, you and the parent are equal partners, they are the best observers, together you figure out what needs to change and take steps to do so.

7. Inform parents about what they can expect, including the need to monitor their child's behavior once or twice daily, increase positives between parent and child, learn limit setting, and decrease the sexual or aggressive triggers in the family.

8. Review the overall safety in the family using the Safety Checklist (see Chapter 8, Form B). If there are clear safety issues, determine if parents can take some consistent steps to establish greater safety.

9. Instruct parents about daily monitoring, demonstrate how to do this, and obtain their agreement to comply with this very important component of the treatment (Weekly Monitor Sheet is contained in Chapter 8, Form I). Begin the process of thinking about treatment goals since that activity will become a centerpiece of the therapy by the second session.

By the end of the first session, you will make a decision regarding the complexity of the family as well as the nature and extent of the child's sexual behavior problems. If this is a complex case, you will need a second entire session with the parents. It will also be very important for you to determine the need for additional sessions over and above the minimum of five to six. Additional tasks needed for complex cases are to enhance parental monitoring, improve the parents' problem-solving capabilities about their child's behavior, and make the parent-child relationship more positive, which includes having parents see their child more positively. These cases require that you provide follow-up telephone contact to make sure monitoring is occurring. During these calls, pay very close attention to issues of safety, other types of abuse that may be occurring in the home such as domestic violence, and psychiatric problems in child or parent.

Cases increase in complexity with each of the following factors:

1. Unresolved parental abuse.
2. A history of disruption in the parent-child relationship, such as foster care due to other maltreatment, psychiatric hospitalization of parent, children residing with relatives, father absent from home.
3. Psychiatric problems in the parent that are not well managed.
4. Substance abuse issues.
5. Conduct disorder or oppositional-defiant disorder diagnosis in the child.
6. The child's sexual behavior problems involve repeated coercive behaviors with one child or coercive behavior with more than one child.
7. Multigenerational parenting problems characterized by estrangement or entanglement with grandparents.
8. Previous or current involvement with social services related to abuse or neglect of the child in question.

SPECIFIC ACTIVITIES

1. Thank parents for filling out the questionnaires. Validate their efforts by showing them that you are now more knowledgeable about their child. Ask if they learned anything about their child while doing this, for example, "Some parents realize their kid has been through a lot and they could be showing some symptoms . . ."
2. Review the overall safety of the home (Safety Checklist, Form B). This can be done either as a structured part of the interview or in a less structured and more informal manner.
3. You may wish to interview parents about the emotional climate in the family with the Parent-Child Conflict Tactics Scale (Straus et al., 1998; see Chapter 8, Form E). Start by praising them for any of the more positive discipline strategies they describe and then move into the more negative ones that they have reported. You may want to bring these up

by saying, "I can see that he really gets to you since you reported here that you have threatened to kick him out of the house. Tell me more."

4. Determine the frequencies of the sexual behaviors by reviewing items on CBCL/CSBI as well as the four additional CSBI items (Chapter 8, Form B). It is also very important to inquire as to when these behaviors are most likely to occur and identify what triggers them. Younger children are more likely to act out their sexual thoughts or experiences when they are in a situation similar to where they were abused, for example, touching younger siblings in the bathtub (Hewitt, 1999).

   Because PTSD is an important treatment consideration, you may want to know about a study that identified CBCL (Achenbach, 1991a) items that validly screen for PTSD (Sim et al., 2005). If you use the CBCL as part of your screening battery, these items enable you to screen for PTSD as well. The items are listed in the Assessment and Treatment Manual (Chapter 8, Form G) along with average scores. There are other strategies to screen for PTSD via the parents, and several of these are outlined in Friedrich (2002).

5. If parents have been cooperative up to this point, appear willing to engage, and seem to have the energy for this task, then instruct them about monitoring specific behaviors. You may want to tell them that monitoring is a key function of parenting. If children know they are being watched, they will usually inhibit their behavior. Then go over the Weekly Monitor Sheet and brainstorm about how to involve the child in a positive way in completing the sheet, for example, the child helping the parent to chart those times the child has not exhibited the behavior. Make sure this is the only monitoring at this point, and be sure to tell parents that they will learn ways to change the behavior once you get a clearer picture of what is going on. Remind them again to catch their child being good and, in order to increase the odds that this will happen, have them identify a few times when that is likely.

6. Help parents to articulate their understanding of why the behavior is occurring. This may elicit statement reflecting how negatively parents view the child, such as, "He's twisted," "He's a pervert," "He's just like my ex," "She's a little shit." You may need to give resistant or lower functioning parents some multiple-choice options as to why the child may be exhibiting the behavior. "Let me give you a list. One, he's doing this because he was sexually abused. Two, he is doing this because he watches too many sexual things on TV. Three, he wants to make you crazy. Which one do you think is the most correct?"

7. Determine if parents can start to view the child more accurately and positively. You do this by first offering a small reframe of the child and observing if the parents can even entertain it. For example, if they have just said something very negative about their child, you could say, "He sounds like a lot to deal with. But I've found that parents who can be honest with me about the negative things their child does can usually be honest about some good things as well. You could probably tell me something about him that you like." Another response to a child who is very active and even angry is to say, "He sounds really intense. I like for kids to have a lot of energy like that, rather than to be passive. Now do you think we can channel this in a new direction?"

8. Contract to improve safety in at least one area (more if possible). Depending on the family and the complexity of the problem, introduce them to the Goal Attainment Scaling Sheet (Chapter 8, Form J) and write in Goal #1 (Safety in Our Home). See Aim No. 8, Session 3 for guidance.

KEY QUESTIONS TO ASK

1. Parents are always trying to figure out why their child does certain things. So what are your thoughts about why your child is acting this way?
2. Do you think your child's behavior gets worse in certain situations? When he or she is around certain people?
3. If sexual abuse is a contributing factor to the behavior, is anything that could remind your child of the sexual abuse still present in the home, school, or neighborhood? This could mean pictures of the perpetrator, phone calls from the perpetrator to another family member, mention of the perpetrator? When the child visits with the noncustodial parent?
4. One of our goals is to help your child feel less stirred up. Are there steps you could agree to take to help your child feel less stirred up or reactive in the house?
5. Is the perpetrator still interacting with your child?
6. When you see (hear about) your child behaving in a sexual way, how do you feel? What happens in your gut?
7. How do you typically respond when you see him or her do sexual things? Describe the last time this happened. What were the emotions on your face? What have you tried to do to change them? What would it take for all your efforts to be helpful?

8. Were you ever sexually abused? (You may first need to ask if they ever "had any unwanted sexual experience" prior to the age of 18. A sensitive discussion of this is likely to help them be more open about childhood abuse. A structured interview format is available in Friedrich, 2002, Appendix P. This enables you to ask questions about specific acts, which will likely be more accurate than if you simply ask about abuse.)

   a) If yes, do any feelings from your own abuse come up when your child is behaving sexually?

   b) Is this affecting your relationship with your child in any way; for example, do you find that you are spending less time with him or her?

9. Have you ever received any counseling for your abuse? Did it help? Were you able to talk about your abuse in your therapy? To tell the whole story? How long did you see someone? Do you remember their name?

10. Some parents are not very affectionate with their children. Others are. How do you feel about hugging or kissing your children? How often do you pat them on the back, comb their hair, and so on? What do you feel like doing when they want a hug? Do you think you touch or hug your child more than or less than other parents do with their children?

11. When you see your child behaving in other ways that you don't like, how do you respond? What have you tried to eliminate their behavior?

12. Think about all the people in your family and the child's other parent's family. That would include your sisters, brothers, fathers, mothers, sister-in-law, and so on. Which of these people is your child most like? Why is that? (The parental response can clue you in more precisely to negative biases about this child in particular.)

13. What are things you really like about your child? (You may try an alternate if you sense they are really negative, e.g., "What did you like about him before, but are having a hard time with now because of his behavior?")

14. How do you think your child will turn out? What kind of person will she or he be like in 10 years?

15. When will you be home next week so I can call and find out how things are going and help give you some ideas if they aren't going as well as we hope? I really want to help you realize that if we work together, we can help your child.

1. Parent-Child Conflict Tactics Scale (completed ahead but reviewed in the interview).
2. Preamble to the Safety Checklist.
3. Safety Checklist (completed during interview).
4. Child Sexual Behavior Inventory with four additional items (Table 1.2, p. 31).
5. Family Sexuality Index.
6. Weekly Monitor Sheet (given to parents to take home). Help parents to identify one to two behaviors that will be monitored; either you or the parent then writes these in on the monitoring sheet. These behaviors should occur with some frequency. Because sexually intrusive behaviors typically occur with very low frequency, more appropriate behaviors to monitor can include self-stimulating behavior, angry outbursts, sexualized talk, standing too close to others, and so on. They are instructed only to keep track of the behaviors on the sheet, and to try not to do anything differently than they have been doing. This establishes a baseline of behavior problems and helps them see improvement over time.

Call parents one time after both Session 1 and Session 2. This allows you to check on their monitoring, inquire how things are going, offer support, and so on. These two contacts are critical to establishing parents' sense that you are concerned about their situation and there is hope for change. Try to schedule the calls in the prior sessions so the parent is home when you call.

SESSION 3

Who attends: Parents and child.

What can be accomplished with a particular family may require more than one session, so pace yourself and the family.

1. Assess the quality of the parent-child relationship by observing how they interact in your office. Is the parent respectful and interested while the child is talking? What is their dominant mood when you go to retrieve them from the waiting room? Is the parent capable of providing support? Do the parent and child feel comfortable with each other?

Does the child's ability to talk to you reflect ambivalent support from the parent? Do they ever touch each other positively? (Some parents report that they frequently touch their child, but after watching their interaction, you realize that when it occurs, it is intrusive and not supportive. If that is the case, then the parent needs some additional skill building. One place to start is to ask if there is anyone in the parent's life who ever gives her a pat on the back that feels good. If so, you can use that as a place to start.)

2. Assess the child's impulse control and boundary problems and the parent's response to these behaviors. Can the parent set limits if the child is destructive? Respond consistently? Express positives to the child? Is the child calmer when the parent is not in the room? More stirred up?

3. Review the monitor sheets to determine when and where behaviors occur. Failure to have completed one or both sheets is a potential sign that the parent is not fully engaged in the treatment, and more investment in the therapist-parent relationship is needed.

4. Determine how the parent has responded to each of the behaviors recorded during monitoring. Involve the child in this discussion and use this discussion to see whether the two can agree on important topics. Observe the child for signs of embarrassment, shame, defensiveness, or indifference when these topics are being discussed.

5. This session may provide a chance to have the parent and child role-play one of the behaviors from the Weekly Monitor Sheet or one mentioned in the intake, such as tantrums (see No. 8 below). If done appropriately, this has the effect of "prescribing the symptom" and is a strategic therapy maneuver that functions to inhibit the behavior (Schaefer, Briesmeister, & Fitton, 1984). Rather than put the parent on the spot, you may take the lead and simply ask the child to "show me one of those tantrums that you do at home. There is a lot of space in my office and the carpet is kind of soft. Please show me one right there."

6. Introduce the concept of sexual safety rules and help the parent and child engage in a discussion of them. This often requires an initial discussion that focuses on how learning rules about life just does not happen until adults clearly spell them out. For example, I told one girl, in front of her mother, that "no one ever told you that you aren't supposed to put your tongue in someone's mouth when you kiss. They never told you the rules. That is why you did that with Tom, who got worried and told your mom, who then brought you here to my office." My stating it this way also helped her mother view her daughter a bit more positively

as a girl who needed to learn the rules, as opposed to someone who was destined for promiscuity. Other questions may include the following: Which sexual rules would apply to your child's situation? Where will they post the list of rules in the house? How can they review them in a positive way each day? Are there older siblings in the house who will use the sexual rules as a way to make fun of the child? Brainstorm ways to manage this possibility. If appropriate, create the expectation that compliance with sexual safety rules results in social rewards (the amount of time being read to, playing a game with the parent, etc.). (A history of a supportive parent-child relationship is a key to introducing the concept of positive reinforcement at this time. If there is strain or clear conflict in the parent-child relationship, it may be too early to suggest or introduce social rewards.) Sample sexual rules are in Form K.

7.   If the primary behavior of concern includes self-stimulating behaviors of the masturbatory type that occur frequently in younger children (e.g., six years old or less), and if the parent seems able to be consistent and positive with the child, then consider a strategy that creates a special time and place for the child to masturbate (Friedrich, 1990). However, as positivity increases via PCIT, masturbation is likely to decrease and withdrawal of attention can become very effective as an additional, mild intervention.

8.   Discuss openly with the parent and the child the link between the child's sexual behavior, sexual abuse, exposure to sexuality, other maltreatment, pornography, and so on. Enhance their understanding by drawing this out on a chalkboard or flip chart. You can send this version or a smaller copy home—it becomes a gift to the family.

9.   Develop a parental response to the child's sexualized behavior and role-play the response until the parent can respond neutrally (this may take some time). Do this first between the parent and therapist with the child as an observer.

   a) How can parents stay calm and matter-of-fact when they see children touch themselves?

   b) How can they deal with the child's defensive or angry reactions to the parents' charting of the child's behavior?

10. Develop a verbal response for the parent to the child's sexual behavior, for example, "Mom will write down (the behavior on the monitor sheet). That way we know if this is a little problem or a big problem." "Sometimes kids do this when they think about bad things that happened to them." "I wonder if you were thinking about (name of perpetrator)." Have the parent utilize this last response only if the child is

nondefensive, the parent can do so in a supportive way, and the connection with the perpetrator is undisputed.

11. Begin to establish goals related to the frequency of a behavior (Goal #3) and a consistent parental response (Goals #4, 5; fill out one or two columns on the Goal Attainment Scale; see Friedrich, 1995, pp. 91–94). The first goal that is established is typically related to increasing safety in the home (Goal #1). This may have already been worked out in Sessions 1 or 2. Another key goal pertains to monitoring the child's behavior, whether it is the sexual behavior in question or another relatively frequent externalizing behavior (e.g., tantrums, noncompliance). The third goal is often related to increasing the parent's supportive presence. Another early goal targets an accepted frequency of the behaviors in question. These goals will evolve over time as the parent and child move forward.

12. At the end of this session, based on your observations about what the primary issues are, you may opt to work directly to repair the parent-child relationship through the use of CDI. If so, then transition to Sessions 5 through 8, described later. Reasons for moving ahead with CDI at this point include the following:
    a) Sexual abuse is not the etiological factor for the behavior.
    b) Child's oppositionality is evident.
    c) Parent is amenable to "repair," "enhance," or "make parent-child time more fun" as a critical treatment element.
    d) Spending individual time with the child is not likely to be helpful at this stage but may be more so after the child is feeling more supported in the home.

SPECIFIC ACTIVITIES

1. Teach the parent to provide a consistent response (Nos. 4, 9 and 10 above).

2. Role-play the parent interacting with the child (Nos. 5, 9, and 10 above), or the therapist substituting for the child (as needed and based on what family will tolerate).

3. Guide a discussion about the link between sexual abuse, exposure, and the child's sexual behavior. If the parent cannot be counted on to provide consistent support toward the child, this discussion may best occur later with just the parent or alone with the child. Have a flip chart or whiteboard available to illustrate this connection graphically.

4. Create the sexual rules specific to this family. Instruct the family to

review them daily in the first week and less often once they are well learned. Before they leave, have parents suggest a time when they will be able to review the rules with the child.

5. Teach the child rules around the specific sexual acts, for example, "It sounds like no one ever taught you the rules about . . . That is one of the things you will learn while we work together." Remember, each time you "say out loud" the shameful behavior, you lessen the impact it has, reduce the probability of it being exhibited, and you begin to alter the less healthy connections that have been formed by the child or parent.

KEY QUESTIONS

These questions will vary with the age of the child.

1. Have the two of you ever talked about the (abuse, sexual behavior, seeing pornography, etc.)? (Asked first of the parent in front of the child.)
2. What do you remember your mom (dad) saying to you about _____ _____? (Directed at the child.)
3. Why do you think your child _____? (Directed at the parent.)
4. What is your mom's (dad's) idea about why you _____? (Directed at the child.)
5. I am asking your mom (dad) to keep track of _____. Do you think you will get upset when you see her writing this down on the sheet? (Problem solve if that is likely.)
6. Can you remember that her (his) doing this will help us all know how fast you are getting better at controlling _____?

MATERIALS

1. Weekly monitor sheet.
2. Copy of Goal Attainment Scale (one copy for you, one copy for the parent).
3. Copy of sexual rules for family to take home. This list should be tailored specifically for the family with the most pertinent rules drawn from possible rules in Chapter 8, Form K.

Call parent one time in between sessions; discuss monitoring, parental responses, how it went when they discussed the sexual rules; provide encouragement and support, and so on.

SESSION 4

Who attends: Child (parent involved at end of session to review what the child learned).

Aims of Session

1. Continue developing an alliance with child.
2. Nondirective play or face-to-face verbal session with child, depending on age and developmental level. Sometimes, a joint activity about a relevant issue (e.g., collage of scary pictures) mixed with conversation works best (see Bodiford-McNeil et al., 1996, for suggestions).
3. Interview older children about PTSD symptoms (use questions from the TSCC; Briere, 1996). An alternative is to use the PTSD Workbook as a strategy to both assess and work with the child. You should have some idea by now from the parent or caregiver about the child's PTSD symptoms and what traumatic event they are related to. Starting to address traumatic issues early on and in a sensitive manner is a point of departure from adolescent and adult treatment programs. These programs typically expect accountability about the teenager's offending behavior as the primary treatment accomplishment at this first stage of treatment.
4. Review compliance with sexual rules and have a discussion about them. (You will have obtained information about the child's week ahead of time from the parent.) Were there any violations? How does the child feel about this? How did the parents respond? Was their response any different than it was the previous times the child violated a rule? If so, heap on the praise.
5. Discuss rules about boundaries, hugging, and touching. Role-play safe distance, or teach child how to greet you with a handshake (the grown-up way) rather than a hug. Role-play this several times, show the parent or caregiver the child's skill (using praise), and agree that this "grown-up way" is how you will greet child next time.

Activities

1. Play session with younger child that builds on relevant topics.
2. Mutual interaction with older children that builds connection and introduces the topics of sexual behavior, self-control, sexual abuse, and sexually intrusive behaviors.

3. PTSD interview with TSCC items that pertain to PTSD.
4. Begin PTSD Workbook. (see p. 263–299)
5. Begin to teach child about safe distance, respect of boundaries.
6. Meet 10 to 15 minutes with parent to review monitoring, problem solve any issues that come up, and provide encouragement. Here is also where the child can demonstrate some new knowledge about boundaries (from No. 5 above).
7. Rate the younger child's behavior with you on the Therapist's Rating Scale (see Chapter 8, Form D). This allows you to gain a better understanding of the child's boundary problems, sexualization, sexual focus, and so forth.

KEY QUESTIONS

1. I wonder what would be on your mom's list of the five scariest things that ever happened to you?
2. I wonder what would be on your dad's list?
3. I wonder what would be on your list? (This is also the list where you can talk about the things that happened that got the child to your office.)
4. Guess what would be on my list of the five scariest things that ever happened to you?

HANDOUTS

1. Weekly monitor sheet to parent
2. PTSD Workbook
3. Therapist's Rating Scale (Chapter 8, Form D)

Call parent one time in between sessions; discuss monitoring and parental responses; provide support, and so on.

SESSION 5

Who attends: Parent, or parent with child if you have opted to move forward with CDI based on criteria suggested in Session 3 (Aims of Session, No. 12). The child typically participates when it is time to help parents practice their new skills.

AIMS OF SESSION

1. Review monitoring; praise parents for appropriate behavior (help them realize the value of the monitoring by commenting on progress and identifying connections to behavior that are becoming more clear; explain that in monitoring they are seeing their child show more self-control, have more opportunities to catch their child being good, etc.).

2. Review progress.

3. Review compliance with sexual rules.

4. Inquire further about parental attributions regarding their child and the child's future outcome.

5. Begin to teach the parent behavioral play therapy skills and basic concepts of PCIT (Hembree-Kigin & McNeil, 1995, Chapter 4). These are the PRIDE skills (see Chapter 5; i.e., praise, reflect, imitate, describe, and enthusiasm). I have found it useful to create some simple sheets to hand out to the parent and have pulled some together (see Chapter 8, Form O). Despite your experience as a therapist, you must thoroughly read the PCIT text and work out any rough spots via some preliminary role-play practice with a colleague or two. When parents feel supported and respected by you, and they notice the child responding to them, and the child is eagerly looking for the next positive from the parent, you can have a truly peak experience as a therapist. The potential for growth and improvement will be crackling in the room. I have enjoyed some of these coaching sessions more than any other therapy I have ever done.

ACTIVITIES

1. Parents routinely feel threatened at the onset of this process. Some get over it quickly and others require more time and support to see your efforts as helpful and not critical of them. They will often feel uncomfortable with you scrutinizing them. One way to alleviate their discomfort is to mention their distress, for example, "This is really tough being watched like this."

    Many of them will feel on some level that their child already gets enough positives and not enough negatives. When parents persistently act as if they are simply going through the motions, you are often seeing evidence not only of their pathology but also of their closeness to bolting from therapy.

One way I try to get around this resistance is to introduce parents to the concept of creating an emotional bank account with their child. The child has an "ATM account." The more parents put into the account, the more they can withdraw from the ATM. You want to teach them a way to put a lot of good feelings into the child so that the child can pay them back by not doing the negative behavior and doing more of a prosocial behavior. In that manner, parents will also be settling a bank account with the child. For example, every time parents ask a question (to which they know the answer) or criticize their child (two of the don'ts of PCIT), they are asking for a $40 cash advance. Children need to have deposits if they are to give out these cash advances. I have found this to be a gentle and effective way to convince the parent of the need for praise and provide an easily understandable rationale for the do's and don'ts list.

2. Review activities the child likes to do that involve the parent. Make sure that you can approximate one of those with the play materials in your office. With younger children, I might remove a few distracting toys ahead of time so that they are more likely to remain focused when they come in.

3. Determine if parents can let the child take charge of a joint activity. How would they respond to cheating? Can they be neutral? Describe a few situations where they could criticize but will choose not to.

4. Review each PRIDE skill and provide examples. Have the parent generate responses to some specific cues that you generate, based on the activity that you have planned to do. Explain the coaching process. Since I use in-room and not bug-in-the-ear coaching, a low-tech option that is supported by Brinkmeyer and Eyberg (2003), I demonstrate the table we will sit at, the selected activities the child will use, where the parent will sit, and how I will sit next to and slightly behind the parent. I make sure this is tolerable to the parent, given her history. In this way, my cues can be less distracting to the child. I will then say that this first time is aimed just for the three of us to get comfortable with the process, but since I know the parent can improve over the course of the coaching, I will keep track of each of the skills, emphasizing praise, describing, and the use of enthusiasm this first time. Usually I will show her the checklist I use to keep track so I can praise her efforts. Review the do's and don'ts list and provide examples. Emphasize that the child is to direct the interaction and the parent is to follow and not command, negate, or ask questions.

5. This is where a parent may resist again, complaining that she is always praising her children, that what the child needs is tough love, and so on. Agree with her, reflect back her concerns, and reiterate the advantages of the various types of praise (e.g., labeled, unlabeled), the fact that her good efforts can get lost in the noise of a busy family, and why special time makes the child more focused on these good efforts. The last step before the practice is to repeat the need for cooperation. The parent should start off doing exactly what you ask. If you say, "Smart fingers" to a 7-year-old playing with Legos, you want the parent to say, "Smart fingers!" shortly after you say it. The parent may worry the child will not think she knows what she is doing if she just repeats what you say. Reassure her and convince her that children quickly buy into the system and enjoy the extra attention. Explain as well that if the child resists, you will ask her to turn away from the child, or the two of you may talk or even start to play together with the toys. If the parent resists you at this early stage and does not imitate right away or alters what you said, take a time-out by saying, "I must be doing something wrong here. Am I pushing you too hard? Too fast?" You may need to allow time for the parent's resistance to decrease.

6. If it appears that the parent can participate in a positive way, invite the child back to the room and explain the process. The child will get to choose an activity, and the parent will be getting coaching from you on what to do. Provide some guidelines about (a) remaining in the seat, (b) no throwing of toys or objects, and (c) how long the activity will last. Role-play the parent behaving positively with the child and accepting feedback from you.

7. Once an activity has been chosen, offer a quick description, such as, "I see you have chosen . . ." followed by a quick praise: "You are good at that." Praise any level of parental follow-through and keep quietly offering short, clear, and frequent suggestions. You want her to be saying something four to five times per minute.

8. If the first extended coaching session has proceeded well, this is your chance to praise the parent and child, and in general build on the positive feelings that have been started. Choose positive activities for parent and child to engage in over the next week. For older children this may involve board games, though they are not as preferable since they invite a more passive response or may involve competitive play. Some suggestions of useful activities appear in the PCIT textbook.

9. Plan times during the next week for the parent to initiate play, conversation, activity, and to catch the child being good.
10. Add to Goal Attainment Scale another goal (Goal #5) about increased parental involvement with child (list activity).

KEY QUESTIONS

1. What's helping you make all these nice changes I am seeing?
2. What's helping your child make these changes?
3. How are you doing dealing with your own abuse? Anything get triggered this past week?
4. Are you seeing some new positive behavior in your child?
5. Have you seen some signs of your child practicing self-control?
6. When did you decide to become a better parent than your own parent? (Use this with parents who have obviously overcome a lot of adversity and are doing better than their history would suggest.)
7. Did you decide to be a better parent because of something your father or mother did to you? Not do to you?
8. How are you fulfilling the decision (to be a better parent)?

MATERIALS

1. Weekly monitor sheet.
2. Lists of PRIDE skills, examples of each, and examples of labeled and nonlabeled praise, do's and don'ts, activity list from Hembree-Kigin and McNeil (1995).
3. Update the Goal Attainment Scale.

Touch base via telephone call with parent between sessions; discuss monitoring, provide support, and so on.

SESSIONS 6–8

Who Attends: Parent and child. These sessions will help to solidify the parent's PRIDE skills from CDI and, if done successfully, will result in readily noticeable behavioral improvement and increased positive affect between parent and child. Successful completion of this process will vary from one dyad to the next, but if done successfully, many parents do not need the PDI portion of PCIT, since you will have been able to improve compliance and model some limit-setting skills in these sessions.

AIMS OF SESSIONS

1. Review how special time activities have gone since you last met with them. Discuss any problems that may have come up and determine how they can be resolved.
2. Continue to help the parent become more comfortable with the coaching process and look for opportunities to praise her; use some PRIDE skills with her.
3. Remind the parent that touch, including pats on the back, quick sideways hugs, playful jabs, and so on are part of praise and enthusiasm and these sessions will give the child a chance to get good touch from the most important person in his life, the parent.
4. Help parent increase the overall rate of using PRIDE skills. Discuss opportunities to imitate and reflect. Provide examples.
5. Review Goal Attainment Scale.
6. Review compliance with sexual rules.

ACTIVITIES

1. In-session coaching with parent and child.
2. Conjoint session can be used for other topics, such as how to use the techniques with other children in the home, problem solving about the necessity for special time, or other crises that come up regularly in these families.
3. You may wish to develop some conjoint imagery for closing the sessions, to send them off with feelings of quiet and connection.
4. Discuss and plan for any prescriptive statements.
5. You can model some limit setting in these sessions from the latter part of PCIT. For example, if you are talking to the parent and the child is getting restive, you may show how tokens get used or you may demonstrate how to give a command.
6. If you see the child the next week, and he has shown boundary problems with you, remind him that you will be looking for a handshake greeting.

KEY QUESTIONS

1. What seemed to work this week?
2. What can I keep doing that you have found helpful?
3. How have you noticed the PRIDE skills showing up during the week, even when you aren't doing special time?
4. What do you think your child's new ATM balance for feeling good is? Is he giving any of that back to you so that you can add to your bank account?
5. What was it like for you to touch him? Can you do this during the week? (Instruct parent that for now, use touch several times; for example, "Give the child a pat as he's sitting next to you and the two of you are watching TV, or as a way to catch him being good."

MATERIALS

1. Goal Attainment Scale
2. PCIT handouts
3. Weekly Monitor Sheet (if applicable)

Touch base via telephone call with parent between sessions; discuss monitoring, provide support, and so on.

SESSIONS 9–11

Who attends: Child. This is typically the start of several child sessions in a row. The decision to do this should reflect the clinical need to focus more exclusively on the child's victim or victimization issues.

AIMS OF SESSIONS

1. Despite gains in the parent-child relationship—which should improve the child's ability to engage with you on these sensitive and shameful topics—it is important to stay aware that you may appreciate, for the first time, the true extent of the child's sexual thinking and preoccupation. Roughly 1 in 6 of the 8- to 12-year-olds who have reached this point in therapy will report some continued preoccupation, disturbed thinking, possible fantasy, and so forth.
2. Complete review of PTSD symptoms and the PTSD Workbook.
3. Begin to assess the nature and extent of the child's intrusive sexual behav-

ior via the 21 Questions (Chapter 8, Form F). These are not that useful with developmentally delayed children or preschoolers. They are most useful for children with average capabilities who are at least 8 years old.

4.   Help the child learn more about how the behavior came about (Question 16 from 21 Questions), and what he can do to "say no to it," "get it off my property," "dump it in the garbage can," and so on. This can lead to a collective drawing activity with the child wherein the two of you draw the child proactively doing something along the lines of response prevention.

5.   Assess and begin to correct issues of shame, guilt, and other attributions. Selected questions, compiled from several measures, are in Chapter 8. They can be used to guide more discussion about shame and responsibility for abuse. A useful separate reference is *Treatment Strategies for Abused Children* (Karp & Butler, 1996).

6.   You can use kinetic family drawings to begin to address family dynamics via play or drawings (e.g., drawing a picture of your family when people are happy; a picture of your family when people are upset, etc.).

7.   As appropriate, use material from *Steps to Healthy Touching* (MacFarlane & Cunningham, 1990). This should be reserved for children, typically older than 8, whose behavior is intrusive and who could benefit from a cognitive approach. I use these strategies with children who seem to have a clear preoccupation with the sexual behavior in question. Keeping parents aware of this focus is necessary, particularly if they can be helpful to their child at this time, for example, developing some prescriptive statements that are related to the child's cognitions and keeping that awareness operative between sessions. For example, in the case of an 11-year-old boy who masturbated and was self-injurious to his penis, the prescriptive statement his foster mother used when she saw him exhibit either of these behaviors was to say, "Thank you for reminding us that you are thinking of bad memories. Soon you will think of something to push those thoughts away."

8.   Review compliance with sexual rules.

9.   This session also enables you to see how the child is doing with maintaining personal boundaries around you.

ACTIVITIES

1.   If child uses a handshake greeting, praise him.

2.   Check in with parent about monitoring and sexual rule compliance.

3. Use structured play activities. I regularly break up the sessions with a few minutes here and there of tossing a soft object, such as a "koosh" ball or nerf ball, back and forth with the child. The back-and-forth cooperative play that it can engender facilitates your therapeutic relationship on a nonverbal level. However, oppositional children may make it aggressive, and in these cases you will need to search for other ways to foster rapport.

4. Hypnosis or imagery on self-control, self-calming, and so on. This could be a place to introduce the turtle technique related to self-control (see Chapter 8, Form M, for instructions). This technique works best when it is both practiced in the session and demonstrated to the parent. The parent now has the therapist's permission to say to the child, "Looks like you need to be a turtle!" Or the parent may reserve some time at the end of the day for the child to get quiet and calm down using the imagery that was taught in the session.

5. For children who are old enough, usually age 9 or 10, enlist their support for self-monitoring their behavior.

6. Further drawing (similar to Session 4).

7. Finish up the PTSD Workbook (as appropriate; see pp. 263–299).

8. Show the list of 21 Questions to children and have them cross off each number when they have answered it. Remind them of the importance of being honest.

Key Questions

Some of these are taken from 21 Questions.

1. How often do you think you have (the behavior)?
2. How often does your mother (father) think you do this?
3. What do you think you were thinking? Feeling? Can you draw the feelings? Use the colors that work best.
4. Our thoughts and feelings are all connected. Let me draw a picture for you about how that works.
5. Can you keep track of (behaviors, thoughts) for me this next week? When I see you next time, I will ask you about (behaviors, thoughts). (Share this with the parent at the end of the session.)
6. Sometimes kids need to (touch themselves, grab at other children's sexual parts, etc.) for a long time after they have been sexually abused, or after seeing people have sex, and so on. How long do you think you need to do (the behavior)?

7. When you think about what happened to you, do you ever want to do (the behavior)?
8. How could you keep (the behavior) from sneaking up on you and taking over? (Role-play this with doll figures.)
9. Imagine that you, your toys, and your bedroom are your property. How could you keep the urge to (the behavior) from taking over your property? How could you keep it out of your house? Let's draw your ideas on this piece of paper.

MATERIALS

1. PTSD workbook
2. 21 Questions
3. Monitor sheet for child (only if the child is 9 or 10 years old and has a high chance of success)
4. Shame items to use in therapy discussions
5. Turtle technique or another self-control strategy
6. PCIT handouts
7. Drawing activity (Keeping _____ Off My Property; described on p. 171).

Call parent one time between sessions: discuss monitoring, parental response to the child; provide support, and so on.

SESSIONS 12–14

Who attends: Parents, child.

AIMS OF SESSIONS

1. Review monitoring sheet of parent (and of child, if applicable).
2. Increase the positive interaction between parent and child using CDI in the session.
3. Add or modify this goal about positive interaction to the Goal Attainment Scale Sheet (Friedrich, 1995, pp. 91–94).
4. Review compliance with sexual rules. If there has been no change in behavioral frequency, develop a point system tied to compliance with these rules. However, take this step only if parent has complied thus far

with monitoring, increasing positives, and so on, and can behave in a positive and consistent manner with the child.

5. Spend time with the child talking more about the prior abuse or exposure.

    a) Explore feelings, thoughts, and PTSD symptoms with older children.

    b) Complete 21 Questions.

    c) Continue to explore issues of self-blame with Children's Impact of Traumatic Events Scale–Revised (CITES-R) items and Shame and Related Issues Questions (Chapter 8, Form N)

6. Ensure that the child has permission to talk about abuse with therapist.

ACTIVITIES

1. Conjoint family session. If there has been some resistance by the child in talking about the abuse and intrusive behavior, the parent can give permission here for the child to do so.

2. Role-play positive family interaction (e.g., child chooses joint activity, parent delivers positives to child, therapist provides coaching as needed).

3. Determine if a point system is needed to enhance compliance with sexual rules.

4. Brief therapy with child each session. Use the format described in Bodiford-McNeil and colleagues (1996) to divide the session into child's work and child's play. The working portion of the session may focus on boundaries, review of sexual rules, and drawing the connection between abuse, feelings, and behavior.

5. Make sure parent is continuing special time with child between sessions. If things are going well, a target frequency would be at least three to five times per week. Problems with this can come up if there are other siblings, a single parent who is overwhelmed, and so on. Give parent a new copy of the praise list if it has been misplaced by this time.

KEY QUESTIONS

1. What kinds of things do the two of you do together that make you feel good about being a family? (parent/child)

2. What do you do with your mom/dad that makes you feel happy? (child)

3. Could you let (child) know that it is okay to talk about the bad things that happened? (parent)

MATERIALS

1. Weekly monitor sheet
2. Revised Goal Attainment Scale sheet
4. Laminated copy of sexual behavior rules to replace prior one
5. Point system sheet (as needed)
6. CITES-R
7. Shame questions

Call parent one time between sessions: discuss monitoring, parental response to child, provide support, and so on.

SESSION 15

Who attends: Parents, child.

AIMS OF SESSION

1. Review monitoring by all parties.
2. Review positive interactions (e.g., special time) that have occurred during the week.
3. If the problematic sexual behavior is continuing and the parent has shown improvement in overall involvement with the child, help the parent discuss the child's sexual behavior in an objective manner.
4. If positive interactions have increased and seem to have had a desirable effect, begin to work on limit setting and giving commands as part of PDI (Chapter 8, Form P).
5. If progress is slow, take another look at safety concerns in the home. Reinterviewing the parent with key items from the Safety Checklist does this. (The sexual and aggressive items will be the most likely contributions.) To get past their defensiveness, you may need to explain that sometimes parents only become aware of things that they can change after a few visits.
6. Review compliance with sexual rules. Both child and parent may benefit from a small prize for compliance.

ACTIVITIES

1. Role-play the parent interacting with the child in a positive fashion.
2. Teach and practice communication tools that focus on positive behaviors and also the sexualized behavior. For example, "When you do _____ _____, I feel _____."
3. Begin to teach limit setting from Hembree-Kigin and McNeil (1995, pp. 58–62) but only if parent has demonstrated consistent use of special time as required in PCIT the prior 2 weeks.

KEY QUESTIONS

1. How are you doing about keeping the home a place for (child) to feel calm and safe?
2. Can you begin to see some positive effects from all your efforts?

MATERIALS

1. Weekly monitor sheet
2. Limit-setting guidelines from Hembree-Kigin and McNeil (1995)

Touch base with parent via phone call; discuss monitoring, provide support, and so on.

SESSION 16

Who attends: Parents, child. The focus of the remaining treatment sessions is on the persisting issues that remain, which may include sexuality, anger, and self-control. Hopefully, parental support of the child, monitoring, and appropriate limit setting are now in place. If not, then continued focus on these will be needed, and the anger focus should start only if significant progress is being made or the child is in foster care. Children receive these interventions if the CBCL Aggressive *T* score is 65 or above, there are reports of angry outbursts, or there are concerns about future sexual offending. These individual interventions, without concomitant family changes, will be insufficient to modify the behavior of conduct-disordered children. Specific suggestions for managing the angry feelings and behavior of these more resistant children are provided by Bloomquist (1996) and Kolko (1996).

AIMS OF SESSION

1. Introduce child to the concept of self-control.
2. Help child understand the connection between anger and other feelings and his or her thoughts.
3. Choose one to two areas where child has problems with anger and self-control (use information from parent as well).
4. Practice self-control in session via role-play and instruction in self-talk. Self-control activities can include practice in going slow, for example, driving a toy car as slowly as possible across a desk top, walking as slowly as possible to your office, across your office, to the waiting room.
5. Choose a self-control goal and share it with parent. Be specific about where this should occur, what the child is to do, what the parent is to do, and so on.

ACTIVITIES

1. Model self-talk with puppets while receiving taunts.
2. Jointly write down self-talk phrases to practice during the week.
3. Begin anger worksheets from Bloomquist (1996).
4. Teach Turtle Technique (Chapter 8, Form M).
5. Introduce the child to cartooning by creating the framework for a six- to eight-cell cartoon, then drawing in the child coming to your office, with any thoughts or statements written in. You can then transition to cartooning angry outbursts, PTSD flashbacks, and so on. This activity can be quite helpful with developing perspective taking and if-then thinking in the child.

KEY QUESTIONS

1. How could I make you mad? What would your mom or dad have to do to make you mad?
2. Do you want to get mad so often?
3. How could we make the mean words of other kids bounce off you? (Drawing task)

1. All materials are obtained from separate resources.

SESSION 17

Repeat Session 8 until goals are achieved.

SESSION 18

Repeat Session 9 until goals are achieved.

FINAL SESSION

Who attends: Parents, child.

AIMS OF SESSION

1. Review positive activities that have been consistent in the relationship.
2. What are their plans for continuing special time?
3. Review future issues about limit setting by the parent.
4. Review safety features in the home.
5. Review monitoring.
6. Have parent repeat the CSBI (with four additional items).
7. Review final Goal Attainment Scale results.

THREE-MONTH FOLLOW-UP

Contact parent by phone to inquire how child is doing with the referral behavior. Ask about current status of the final goals on the Goal Attainment Scale. Send out a generic behavior rating scale and a copy of the CSBI (Friedrich, 1997) with a return envelope.

SUGGESTIONS WHEN MASTURBATION
IS THE PRIMARY PRESENTING PROBLEM

Roughly one in six of the children I have treated presented with masturbation as their most salient and frequent symptom. Others have masturbation as one of several behavior problems. Often the children who are primary masturbations fall into one of two categories. The first are typically distressed preschoolers or immature grade schoolers. They are a bit immature and have discovered that touching genitals or actual masturbation can be pleasurable. There are often other issues in the home that cause the child to use masturbation as a way to cope (e.g., divorce, domestic violence). When sexual issues are present, like pornography or overt sexuality in the home, then you may think about the behavior as more serious.

The other group—which displays masturbation as one of several behavior problems—is often younger than 9 and the majority of them are female. Over half were in foster care and I believe that many of them never would have come to my attention if they were not. I say this because masturbatory behavior seems to emerge as often as not in the context of neglect and overwhelming affect. I believe these children use masturbation as a way to distract themselves at times and to self-soothe at other times. I have also seen this same self-soothing phenomenon at work with some children who have daytime enuresis. They often have experienced neglect and overwhelming affect, and the self-wetting is a brief self-soothing process. These children have been deeply neglected, and they often loathe eliminating this behavior since it is one of the few things they can do that makes them feel good or derives some attention, albeit negative. Consequently, it is important to make sure that their lives are filling up with other good things.

It is important to note when the masturbatory behavior started to develop. To determine this, you will need to rely on information provided by parents (who are often poor observers) or caregivers (who often have only spent a brief period of time with the child). However, when you can determine the time the behavior developed, it can help you identify what is triggering it. For example, in the case of two children I evaluated but did not treat, the masturbatory behavior was nonexistent when the children moved into foster care but then resumed when they started to have visits or some form of contact with their biological family members—in one case the mother, and in the other case the mother and stepfather. More important, the masturbatory behavior stopped after this contact was ended. These children stand out in my mind since both of them denied flashbacks of their family, were quite protective of family members, and denied sexual abuse. However, their masturbatory behavior (and the frequency of nightmares recorded by the foster parent) certainly suggested that their family was a source of stress.

The general strategy for dealing with masturbatory behavior is similar to what I described in an earlier book (Friedrich, 1991) but has been modified as follows.

1. Determine what constitutes masturbatory behavior—arrive at a definition with the caregiver.
2. Establish frequency or baseline.
3. Help the parent see the behavior in a different light, such as a way the child copes with stress.
4. The parent must demonstrate some improvement in CDI sessions and be using special time.
5. Teach the parent how to behave neutrally to the child's provocations and masturbatory behavior; this often requires role-play.
6. Create a time and place for the child to masturbate; discuss this with both the parent and the child. At the same time, reiterate what is meant by masturbation. Typically the special time will be in the child's room, for a brief period that is not the most convenient time for the child.
7. Role-play the parent enforcing this rule with the child.
8. Develop and use prescriptive statements about anxiety and masturbation that can be used at other times during the day.
9. Monitor frequency at home on a baseline so that the child can see the progress.
10. Create a school-based response if necessary
11. Set a goal on the Goal Attainment Scale form.

If the child is receiving some special time with the parent, and there are no other stressors that are interfering with his adjustment, you should see a marked reduction and even cessation in frequency within 6 weeks. Some parents cannot do this without becoming negativistic and if that is the case, then stop this strategy for the time being.

CONCLUSION

In summary, each session after the first will be based on reviewing the monitoring sheets and taking stock of the positive changes in overall safety for the child. Be on the alert for negative statements about the child and praise the parents when they talk about their child more positively. It will also be critical that you enquire about the number of positives that the parent and child engage in each week. Continue to expand and review the list of positive activities. Utilizing role-plays specific to the parent-child relationship in the session will be essential to treatment success. Reinforcing parents' efforts to work on their own abuse issues or referring them for therapy will be another critical component. In addition, it is important that each week you carefully orient the family for the upcoming week (e.g., remind them to review the sexual rules) and distribute relevant handouts. Stock up on appropriate prizes and reinforcers for both the child and the parent.

Key issues with children are to address prior maltreatment and link that to their behavior. Older children can also benefit from a review of their sexually intrusive behavior through the use of 21 Questions. Children who are particularly intrusive need to learn competing responses, take responsibility for their actions, and understand what gets them into trouble in terms of their sexual behavior. Children will also need to learn the rules about sexual behaviors.

Termination is appropriate if child is symptom free, parents have consistently increased positives, and monitoring quality has been enhanced.

MATERIALS UTILIZED FOR ASSESSMENT

This is a single page unless otherwise indicated.

1. Summary sheets (two pages)
2. Preamble to the Safety Checklist (one page)
3. Safety Checklist (six pages)
4. Four Additional Sexual Behaviors (administer these along with CSBI)
5. Family Sexuality Index
6. Therapist's Rating Scale
7. Parent-Child Conflict Tactics Scale (three pages)
8. 21 Questions
9. CBCL PTSD Items

MATERIALS UTILIZED FOR TREATMENT

This is a single page unless otherwise indicated.

1. Monitoring sheet for child: How Did I Do Today?
2. Weekly Monitor Sheet for parent
3. Goal Attainment Scale sheet (one page)
4. Sexual rules (choose as many as are appropriate)

5. Corrective phrases for parents
6. Turtle technique instructions
7. Keeping _____ Off My Property
8. Guidelines from PCIT (14 pages)
9. PTSD Workbook (13 pages)
10. Shame questions

8

ASSESSMENT AND TREATMENT FORMS

THIS CHAPTER CONTAINS copies of the assessment forms that have been described in earlier chapters. The forms include Summary Sheets, (Form A) which have the major elements covered in the child and family's treatment program; an overall rating of the parents' and child's monitoring performance; the treatment elements used; and a checklist of factors about the child, the parent-child relationship, and the caregiver's characteristics. It is recommended that completed copies of the following measures be attached to the form: the initial Child Behavior Checklist, Child Sexual Behavior Inventory, monitoring sheets, the final Goal Attainment Scale, Safety Checklist, Parent-Child Conflict Tactics Scale, Child Behavior Checklist from the final session, and 21 Questions. The Summary Sheets (Form A) and the attached instruments will serve as a condensed report of the child and caregiver's treatment program.

The chapter also contains an introduction to the Safety Checklist for the provider to use to introduce the measure to the parents. The list contains items assessing cosleeping, cobathing, family nudity and sexuality, the availability of pornography, whether the child has seen sexual intercourse, family and community violence, and triggers for post-traumatic stress disorder. The Safety Checklist (Form B) has a total of 15 positive safety points and 58 negative safety points.

Other assessment forms in the chapter are:

- Four additional sexual behavior problems to rate in addition to the items included in the Child Sexual Behavior Inventory (Form B)
- The Family Sexuality Index, a 17-item instrument with higher positive scores indicating problematic sexual behavior in the child's home or the caregiver's history (Form C)

- The Therapist's Rating Scale a checklist to assess the child's behavior regarding boundaries and other sexual behavior in the initial session (Form D)
- The Parent-Child Conflict Tactics Scale, a measure assessing the parent's history of physical discipline with the child, and supplemental questions for parents, a measure that asks additional questions about the parent's behavior with the child, covering recent physical discipline, neglect, sexual maltreatment, the parent's experience with sexual abuse as a child, and the child's history of sexual abuse (both Form E)
- 21 Questions, a list of questions for the child that asks more specific questions about the child's problematic sexual behavior (Form F)
- Items from the Child Behavior Checklist that evaluate PTSD, Dissociation, and PTSD/Dissociation. The items will be helpful to the reader in assessing these particular disorders in children (Form G)

Treatment forms included in this chapter are:

- How Did I Do Today?, a form for the child to complete to assess their problematic behavior (Form H)
- Weekly Monitor Sheet, a day-by-day sheet for the parent to record the instances of problematic behaviors in the morning and evening (Form I)
- Goal Attainment Scaling Sheet, a form to record progress over the course of treatment (Form J)
- Sexual Rules for _____(child's name)_____, a list of rules for the child to learn and practice (Form K)
- Prescriptive Parent Statements, a list of statements parents can use at home with their child (Form L)
- Turtle Technique, a technique used with children to teach them self-control (Form M)
- Shame and Related Issues Questions, a list of questions that can be used in therapy sessions with older children (Form N)
- Overview of Parent-Child Interactive Therapy (PCIT), a set of techniques used to improve the parent-child relationship (Form O)
- Commands (PDI), a set of commands for parents to use as part of PCIT (Form P)

FORM A

SUMMARY SHEETS

Name _____

Age _____

Gender _____

Race _____

Court social services involvement _____yes _____no

Other maltreatment child has experienced (D = documented, S = suspected)

_____ Physical abuse

_____ Sexual abuse

_____ Emotional abuse

_____ Emotional neglect

_____ Physical neglect

# of sessions attended _____	# of parent-only sessions _____
# of sessions canceled _____	# of child-only sessions _____
# of sessions no-shows _____	# of parent-child sessions _____

Did parent monitor (Y/N) _____ How well (1–10 best) _____
(10 = completed monitor sheets every session; 1 = never completed any despite prompting)

Did child (>8 years old) monitor (Y/N) _____
How well (1–10 best) _____

Rate overall compliance with treatment (1–10 best) _____
(10 = no canceled sessions; all monitoring completed; positives increased with child; child made significant progress)

Rate overall involvement with treatment (1–10 best) _____
(10 = open, honest, rapport easily established)

Treatment elements used (check all that apply)

_____ Increased positive involvement by parent with child
_____ Established sexual rules
_____ Altered discipline patterns
_____ Taught limit setting
_____ Instituted behavioral consequences for sexual rule violations
_____ Used role-play with parent or child
_____ Used parent labeling of behaviors
_____ Increased safety in home
_____ Prescriptive statements

Attach copies of following forms:

_____ CBCL
_____ Parent-Child Conflict Tactics Scale
_____ CSBI
_____ CSBI obtained (at final session)
_____ Monitoring sheets
_____ Final Goal Attainment Scale Sheet
_____ 21 Questions
_____ Safety Checklist

Check all that apply to this child's case.

Sexual abuse experience of the child:

_____ Sexual arousal of the child during the abuse
_____ Sadistic abuse of the child
_____ Active involvement of the child in the sexual activity
_____ Child acted in "offender" role during child-to-child sex acts (see Table 1.1)
_____ Child blames self or is ambivalent about whom to blame for the sexual abuse

Child:

_____ Lack of warmth or empathy
_____ Restricted range of affective expression
_____ Hopelessness or depression
_____ Poor internalization of right and wrong
_____ Blames others or denies responsibility

_____ General boundary problems (nonsexual)
_____ Sexualized gestures or frequent or compulsive masturbation
_____ Domestic violence in the home
_____ Death of a parent or significant adult
_____ Use of illegal drugs in the home

Child's history:

_____ Frequent moves
_____ Physical abuse
_____ Emotional abuse
_____ Permanent loss of father (males)

Parent-child relationship:

_____ Intrusive or enmeshed mother-child relationship
_____ Sexualized interaction style within family
_____ Role reversal, inappropriate parent-child roles

Caregiver characteristics:

_____ Mother shows PTSD symptoms
_____ Mother competes with child/high level of neediness
_____ Mother has history of childhood physical neglect
_____ Father observed family violence in own parents during his childhood
_____ Mother experienced childhood separation or loss of own parents
_____ Maternal boundary problems with child
_____ Mother has history of sexual abuse

FORM B

SAFETY CHECKLIST

Preamble to the Safety Checklist

"I am now going to ask you some very personal questions. They can make you feel uncomfortable or even squirm. They can even make you want to deny to me that you have any problems in this area. But I'll be very frank with you and tell you that your child cannot have the problems he or she has [in the case of a child with sexual behavior problems] if everything is perfect in your house. So if we go through and you tell me nothing is wrong, then I will know that you are not being honest and I will have to write that in my report. Not being honest is a bigger strike against you than being honest, because if you are straight with me then we have a place to start to help you and your family. Here's an example. If I ask you about [insert a behavior that you are reasonably certain goes on in the family, e.g., yelling], and you say that never happens, I know you aren't being completely honest.

"Here's another example. You already told me that you were sexually abused. One of the questions in this interview has to do with any sexually abused people living in your house. You will want to say yes to that one. That way you will be honest. Is this clear?"

By using this preface with even resistant families, and feeling free to be gently confrontational if you are on sure ground, the validity of the interview is vastly improved.

Copyright © 1996, Mayo Foundation. Not to be reproduced without permission of the author.

Name of Child _____

Age _____   Sex _____

Who is living in the home and what are their ages?

_____

_____

_____

_____

Who visits the home?

_____

_____

_____

_____

Have any of these visitors ever been accused of sexual abuse of a child?

_____ Y   _____ N

Check all that apply about the child in question. Please rate the frequencies as precisely as possible, for example, how many times per week.

Cosleeping

I am going to begin by asking you questions about the sleeping arrangements in your home. These pertain to the child we named above. First, who is usually home when your child is sleeping?

_____

_____

1. _____ Sleeps every night in own bed in private bedroom. ___ Y ___ N

2. _____ Sleeps in same bed as sibling. ___ Y ___ N
   How often _____ Age of sib _____
   Sexual abuse history of sib _____

3. _____ Sleeps in same room as sib, but not in same bed. ___ Y ___ N
How often _____ Age of sib _____
Sexual abuse Hx of sib _____

4. _____ Sleeps in parent's bed. ___ Y ___ N
How often _____

5. _____ Parents have had sex while child is in bed. ___ Y ___ N
How often _____

6. _____ Parents never behave sexually while child is in bed. ___ Y ___ N

7. _____ Sleeps in parents' bedroom but not in their bed. ___ Y ___ N
Where _____

8. _____ Child's bedroom is next door to the parents' bedroom.
___ Y ___ N

9. _____ Parents' bedroom door is left open. ___ Y ___ N

10. _____ Parents have a lock on their bedroom door. ___ Y ___ N

11. _____ Child has a lock on bedroom door. ___ Y ___ N

12. _____ Absolutely no cosleeping occurs. ___ Y ___ N

COBATHING

I am now going to ask you about who your child bathes or showers with. Where is the bathtub or shower located in your house? _____

13. _____ I can hear what is going on in the bathroom from where
I usually am. ___ Y ___ N

14. _____ Bathes or showers together with mother. ___ Y ___ N
How often _____

15. _____ Bathes or showers together with father. ___ Y ___ N
How often _____

16. _____ Bathes or showers together with sibling. ___ Y ___ N
How often _____

17. _____ Absolutely no cobathing occurs. ___ Y ___ N

FAMILY NUDITY

Now let's discuss your family's attitudes about nudity. Every family is going to be different. Some are more relaxed. Others are more strict. There is no right answer.

18. _____ Father is nude in the home. ___ Y ___ N
How often _____

19. _____ Mother is nude in the home. ___ Y ___ N
How often _____

20. _____ Siblings are nude in the home. ___ Y ___ N
How often _____

21. _____ Father wears only underwear around the house. ___ Y ___ N
How often _____

22. _____ Mother wears only underwear around the house. ___ Y ___ N
How often _____

23. _____ Teenage sibling wears only underwear around the house. ___ Y ___ N
How often _____

24. _____ Parents sleep in the nude. ___ Y ___ N
How often _____

25. _____ Absolutely no nudity occurs in the home. ___ Y ___ N

FAMILY SEXUALITY

Families vary as well in how affectionate they are in front of each other.

26. _____ Parents grab each other's breasts, butt, or crotch (even when clothed). ___ Y ___ N

27. _____ Parents French kiss in front of child. ___ Y ___ N

28. _____ Teenage siblings grab each other's breasts, butt, or crotch (even when clothed). ___ Y ___ N

29. _____ Teenage siblings French kiss. ___ Y ___ N

30. _____ Parents talk about sex acts in front of the child. ___ Y ___ N

31. _____ Teenage siblings talk about sex acts in front of the child. ___ Y ___ N

32. _____ Child sees pets or other animals mating. ___ Y ___ N

33. _____ Absolutely no opportunities to witness sexual behavior. ___ Y ___ N

PORNOGRAPHY AND WITNESSING SEXUAL INTERCOURSE

Here are some more questions about sexual materials and behavior in the house.

34. _____ Magazine pornography is in the home. ___ Y ___ N
Where kept _____ Accessible _____
What magazines _____

_____

35. _____ Video pornography is in the house. ___ Y ___ N
Where kept _____ Accessible _____ What are the
titles _____

36. _____ Child has unlimited access to TV, including sexually explicit shows. ___ Y ___ N

37. _____ Child has access to Internet, including pornographic Web sites. ___ Y ___ N

38. _____ Child has seen intercourse. ___ Y ___ N
Live _____ Video/movie _____ How often _____

39. _____ Child has absolutely no opportunities to see pornography or witness intercourse. ___ Y ___ N

FAMILY VIOLENCE

Some families are more open about violent behaviors in the home. Others are not as open. Where does your family fall in terms of:

40. _____ Child is hit or slapped. ___ Y ___ N
If so, by whom? _____

41. _____ Child is punched or beaten. ___ Y ___ N
If so, by whom? _____

42. _____ Parents hit each other. ___ Y ___ N
Does the child see this? ___ Y ___ N

43. _____ Child hits parents. ___ Y ___ N

44. _____ Child is yelled or screamed at. ___ Y ___ N

45. _____ Parents yell or scream at each other. ___ Y ___ N

46. _____ Siblings punch each other. ___ Y ___ N

47. _____ Siblings hit or slap each other. ___ Y ___ N

48. _____ Parent is intoxicated. ___ Y ___ N

49. _____ Guns are displayed in the home. ___ Y ___ N

50. _____ Guns are waved around in a threatening manner. ___ Y ___ N

51. _____ Guns are discharged in the house. ___ Y ___ N

52. _____ Violent or horror videos are available. ___ Y ___ N

53. _____ Drug dealing occurs in the house. ___ Y ___ N

54. _____ Absolutely no family violence of the physical or verbal types.
___ Y ___ N

COMMUNITY VIOLENCE

Some families live in dangerous settings, crowded buildings, and so on.

55. _____ Drive-by shootings occur in the neighborhood. ___ Y ___ N

56. _____ Drug dealing occurs in the neighborhood. ___ Y ___ N

57. _____ Child is beaten up by peers. ___ Y ___ N

58. _____ Child has no age-appropriate peers. ___ Y ___ N

59. _____ House is unsafe or unclean and you wish you lived elsewhere.
___ Y ___ N

60. _____ Absolutely no community violence. ___ Y ___ N

PTSD TRIGGERS

Sometimes we forget that there are things that trigger our child's behavior.
Sometimes these are reminders of bad things from the past.

61. _____ Reminders of the perpetrator are in the house. ___ Y ___ N

62. _____ Pictures of the perpetrator are in the house. ___ Y ___ N

63. _____ There are other sexually abused children in the house.
___ Y ___ N

64. _____ There is a sexually abused child at my child's day care.
___ Y ___ N

65. _____ Sexually abused adults live in the house. ___ Y ___ N

66. _____ Sexually abused child, adolescent, or adult is involved in babysitting the child. ___ Y ___ N

67. _____ Sexual perpetrators visit or live in the house or in the neighborhood. ___ Y ___ N

68. _____ Child has visual contact with the perpetrator. ___ Y ___ N

69. _____ Absolutely no triggers of past events are around our house. ___ Y ___ N

MONITORING

It's important for me to get an idea of how easy it is for you to keep track of your child and whether anything from your own past gets in the way of you keeping him or her safe.

70. _____ Number of hours per day the child is not being visually or auditorily monitored by the parents or another adult. _____

71. _____ Parents would have a hard time objectively seeing sexual behavior (due to depression, cognitive limitations, sexual abuse history, psychiatric problems, rejection of the child, neglectful pattern of parenting). ___ Y ___ N

72. _____ Parents would have a hard time objectively seeing rule violations. ___ Y ___ N

73. _____ Parents would have a hard time being consistent. ___ Y ___ N

74. _____ Absolutely no problems monitoring their child's behavior. ___ Y ___ N

Positive safety points (sum up Items 1, 6, 8, 10–13, 17, 25, 33, 39, 54, 60, 69, 74)

Total _____

Negative safety points (sum up Items 2–5, 7, 9, 14–16, 18–24, 26–32, 34–38, 40–53, 55–59, 61–68, 70–73)

Total _____

PROBLEM AREAS

Check all that apply.

_____ Cosleeping

_____ Cobathing

_____ Family nudity

_____ Family sexuality

_____ Pornography

_____ Family violence

_____ Community violence

_____ PTSD triggers

_____ Monitoring

ADDITIONAL SEXUAL BEHAVIOR PROBLEMS

Rate these along with the items included in the CSBI. Rate in terms of frequency over the past 6 months, with 0 = never, 1 = less than once a month, 2 = one to three times a month, and 3 = at least once a week.

1.	Touches other children's private parts after being told not to.	0	1	2 3
2.	Plans how to sexually touch other children.	0	1	2 3
3.	Forces other children to do sexual acts.	0	1	2 3
4.	Puts finger or object in another child's vagina or rectum.	0	1	2 3

FORM C

FAMILY SEXUALITY INDEX

Please answer yes (Y), possibly (P), or no (N) to each question.

Y P N   1. My child has seen naked adults on TV or in a movie.

Y P N   2. My child has seen adults or teenagers having sex in the home.

Y P N   3. My child has showered or bathed with an adult in the past 6 months.

Y P N   4. We have magazines at home with naked pictures in them.

Y P N   5. My child has seen me or another adult naked in the past 6 months.

Y P N   6. I became pregnant before I was married.

Y P N   7. Sexual stuff grosses me out.

Y P N   8. My child has seen adults having sex on TV or in a movie.

Y P N   9. We have a computer at home and adults use it to look at pornography.

Y P N 10. My child has showered or bathed with another child in the past 6 months.

Y P N 11. I was sexually touched as a child.

Y P N 12. Adults or teens in the house walk around partially dressed or undressed.

Y P N 13. My spouse or boyfriend and I are very open about our sexual feelings for each other in front of the child.

Y P N 14. An adult in our family has sexually abused someone.

Y P N 15. We respect bathroom privacy in our family.

Y P N 16. Being sexual is really hard for me.

FORM D

THERAPIST'S RATING SCALE

Rate the presence or absence of the following behaviors in the initial interview.

Boundary Variables	Yes	No
1. Child physically touches you.	____	____
2. Child is physically destructive of objects in office.	____	____
3. Child moves about office without permission.	____	____
4. Child hits, kicks, bites, or shoves you.	____	____
5. Child touches objects in office without asking.	____	____

Sexual Variables		
1. Child kisses or hugs you.	____	____
2. Child sits with underwear exposed.	____	____
3. Child touches own sexual parts.	____	____
4. Child lifts clothing or removes clothing in office.	____	____
5. Child spontaneously talks about sexual acts or sexual body parts.	____	____

FORM E

PARENT-CHILD CONFLICT TACTICS SCALES

Children often do things that are wrong, disobey, or make their parents angry. We would like to know what you have done when your [age of referent child]-year-old child did something wrong or made you upset or angry.

I am going to read a list of things you might have done in the past year, and I would like you to tell me whether you have: done it once in the past year, done it twice in the past year, 3 to 5 times, 6 to 10 times, 11 to 20 times, or more than 20 times in the past year. If you haven't done it in the past year but have done it before that, I would like to know this, too.

1 = Once in the past year
2 = Twice in the past year
3 = 3–5 times in the past year
4 = 6–10 times in the past year
5 = 11–20 times in the past year
6 = More than 20 times in the past year
7 = Not in the past year, but it happened before
0 = This has never happened

_____ A. Explained why something was wrong
_____ B. Put him or her in time-out (or sent to his or her room)
_____ C. Shook him or her
_____ D. Hit him or her on the bottom with something like a belt, hairbrush, a stick, or some other hard object
_____ E. Gave him or her something else to do instead of what he or she was doing wrong
_____ F. Shouted, yelled, or screamed at him or her
_____ G. Hit him or her with a fist or kicked him or her hard
_____ H. Spanked him or her on the bottom with your bare hand
_____ I. Grabbed him or her around the neck and choked him or her
_____ J. Swore or cursed at him or her
_____ K. Beat him or her up, that is, hit him or her over and over as hard as you could
_____ L. Said you would send him or her away or kick him or her out of the house
_____ M. Burned or scalded him or her on purpose
_____ N. Threatened to spank or hit him or her but did not actually do it

_____ O. Hit him or her on some other part of the body besides the bottom with something like a belt, hairbrush, a stick, or some other hard object

_____ P. Slapped him or her on the hand, arm, or leg

_____ Q. Took away privileges or grounded him or her

_____ R. Pinched him or her

_____ S. Threatened him or her with a knife or gun

_____ T. Threw or knocked him or her down

_____ U. Called him or her dumb or lazy or some other name like that

_____ V. Slapped him or her on the face or head or ears

SUPPLEMENTAL QUESTIONS FOR PARENTS

Weekly Discipline
Recommended when corporal punishment is a focus.

Sometimes it's hard to remember what happened over an entire year, so we'd like to ask a few of these questions again, just about the last week. For each of these questions, tell me how many times they happened *in the last week*.

1 = Once in the last week
2 = Twice in the last week
3 = 3–5 times in the last week
4 = 6–10 times in the last week
5 = 11–20 times in the last week
6 = More than 20 times in the last week
0 = This has not happened in the last week

_____ WA. Put him or her in time-out (or sent to his or her room)

_____ WB. Shouted, yelled, or screamed at him or her

_____ WC. Spanked him or her on the bottom with your bare hand

_____ WD. Slapped him or her on the hand, arm, or leg

Neglect
Sometimes things can get in the way of caring for your child the way you would like to: for example, money problems, personal problems, or having a lot to do. Please tell me how many times in the last year this has happened to you in trying to care for your child.

1 = Once in the past year
2 = Twice in the past year
3 = 3–5 times in the past year
4 = 6–10 times in the past year
5 = 11–20 times in the past year
6 = More than 20 times in the past year
7 = Not in the past year, but it happened before
0 = This has never happened

Please tell me how many times you:

_____ NA. Had to leave your child home alone, even when you thought some adult should be with him or her
_____ NB. Were so caught up with your own problems that you were not able to show or tell your child that you loved him or her
_____ NC. Were not able to make sure your child got the food he or she needed
_____ ND. Were not able to make sure your child got to a doctor or hospital when he or she needed it
_____ NE. Were so drunk or high that you had a problem taking care of your child

Sexual Maltreatment

The questions on sexual maltreatment (questions SC and SD) are preceded by questions on sexual maltreatment experienced by the parent (questions SA and SB). This was done on the assumption that it is somewhat less threatening to be asked about or reveal one's own victimization than it is to be questioned about sexual maltreatment of one's children.

Now I would like to ask you something about your own experiences as a child that may be very sensitive. As you know, sometimes, in spite of efforts to protect them, children get sexually maltreated, molested, or touched in sexual ways that are wrong. To find out more about how often they occur, we would like to ask you about your own experiences when you were a child.

SA. Before the age of 18, were you personally ever touched in a sexual way by an adult or older child, when you did not want to be touched that way, or were you ever forced to touch an adult or older child in a sexual

way—including anyone who was a member of your family, or anyone outside your family? (If "Yes," ask:) Did it happen more than once?
0 = No, it did not happen
1 = Yes, it happened just once
2 = Yes, it happened more than once

SB. Before the age of 18, were you ever forced to have sex by an adult or older child—including anyone who was a member of your family, or anyone outside your family? (If "Yes," ask:) Did it happen more than once?
0 = No, it did not happen
1 = Yes, it happened just once
2 = Yes, it happened more than once

SC. What about the experience of your own child? As far as you know, *in the past year*, has your child been touched in a sexual way by an adult or older child when your child did not want to be touched that way, or has he or she been forced to touch an adult or an older child in a sexual way—including anyone who was a member of your family, or anyone outside your family? (If "Yes," ask:) Has it happened more than once? (If "No," ask:) Has it ever happened?
0 = No, it did not happen
1 = No, has not happened in the past year, but has happened
2 = Yes, it happened just once
3 = Yes, it happened more than once

SD. In the last year, has your child been forced to have sex by an adult or an older child—including anyone who was a member of your family, or anyone outside your family? (If "Yes," ask:) Has it happened more than once? (If "No," ask:) Has it ever happened?
0 = No, it did not happen
1 = No, has not happened in the past year, but has happened
2 = Yes, it happened just once
3 = Yes, it happened more than once

FORM F
21 QUESTIONS

1. Who was the first kid you touched in a sexual way?

2. Where were you when this happened? Where else did it happen?

3. Help me figure out the first time it happened, like what grade you were in. Help me figure out the last time it happened.

4. How many times could this have happened all together?

5. Now tell me what kind of sexual things you did? Let's make a list.

6. What other sexual things did you do?

7. I need to know if any clothes were off. For you? For the other kid? How often was there touching inside the clothes?

8. Please show me on this picture everywhere you touched.

9. Did you say you would hurt them if they ever told? Did you scare them in any way, such as raise your voice, make a fist, and look angry at them?

10. Who else have you touched?

11. What feelings did you have inside when you were doing this?

12. What do you think the other kid was feeling?

13. What naked pictures have you seen? Where? Magazines? Computer?

14. What people in your family have you seen naked?

15. Who has touched you in a sexual way?

16. Where did you get the idea to touch this kid?

17. How long had you thought about touching someone before you touched the first one?

18. Who gets yelled at in your family? Who gets hit in your family?

19. Who in your family has hit you?

20. How many times do you get pictures in your head about what you did to this child? How many times do you think about it? How many times do you get pictures in your head about what happened to you?

21. Have you told me the truth for each question? Which answers do you need to change?

FORM G

CBCL PTSD ITEMS

CBCL items comprising expert-derived scales for PTSD, dissociation, and PTSD/dissociation

PTSD

9 Can't get his or her mind off certain thoughts; obsessions
29 Fears certain animals, situations, or places other than school
45 Nervous, high strung, or tense
47 Nightmares
50 Too fearful or anxious
76 Sleeps less than most kids
100 Trouble sleeping

DISSOCIATION

13 Confused or seems to be in a fog
17 Daydreams or gets lost in his or her thoughts
80 Stares blankly

PTSD/DISSOCIATION

8 Can't concentrate, can't pay attention for long
9 Can't get his or her mind off certain thoughts; obsessions
13 Confused or seems to be in a fog
17 Daydreams or gets lost in his or her thoughts
29 Fears certain animals, situations, or places other than school
40 Hears sounds or voices that aren't there
45 Nervous, high strung, or tense
47 Nightmares
50 Too fearful or anxious
66 Repeats certain acts over and over; compulsions
76 Sleeps less than most kids
80 Stares blankly
84 Strange behavior
87 Sudden changes in mood or feelings
92 Talks or walks in sleep
100 Trouble sleeping

Source. Achenbach (1991a), Sim et al. (2005).

FORM H

HOW DID I DO TODAY?

My name is _____

Please check how you did controlling the behaviors that you are working on
with _____.

Day 1 _____
Not too good _____ So-so _____ Very good _____
How many times did I have a problem? (circle one)
1　2　3　4　5　6　7

Day 2 _____
Not too good _____ So-so _____ Very good _____
How many times did I have a problem? (circle one)
1　2　3　4　5　6　7

Day 3 _____
Not too good _____ So-so _____ Very good _____
How many times did I have a problem? (circle one)
1　2　3　4　5　6　7

Day 4 _____
Not too good _____ So-so _____ Very good _____
How many times did I have a problem? (circle one)
1　2　3　4　5　6　7

Day 5 _____
Not too good _____ So-so _____ Very good _____
How many times did I have a problem? (circle one)
1　2　3　4　5　6　7

FORM I

WEEKLY MONITOR SHEET

Please rate how often you see your child do the behaviors we are watching.

Behavior 1 _____

Behavior 2 _____

	DAY 1 Date: ___	DAY 2 Date: ___	DAY 3 Date: ___	DAY 4 Date: ___	DAY 5 Date: ___	DAY 6 Date: ___	DAY 7 Date: ___
A.M.	Behavior 1 ___	Behavior 1 ___	Behavior 1 ___	Behavior 1 ___	Behavior 1 ___	Behavior 1 ___	Behavior 1 ___
	How often: ___	How often: ___	How often: ___	How often: ___	How often: ___	How often: ___	How often: ___
	Behavior 2 ___	Behavior 2 ___	Behavior 2 ___	Behavior 2 ___	Behavior 2 ___	Behavior 2 ___	Behavior 2 ___
	How often: ___	How often: ___	How often: ___	How often: ___	How often: ___	How often: ___	How often: ___
P.M.	Behavior 1 ___	Behavior 1 ___	Behavior 1 ___	Behavior 1 ___	Behavior 1 ___	Behavior 1 ___	Behavior 1 ___
	How often: ___	How often: ___	How often: ___	How often: ___	How often: ___	How often: ___	How often: ___
	Behavior 2 ___	Behavior 2 ___	Behavior 2 ___	Behavior 2 ___	Behavior 2 ___	Behavior 2 ___	Behavior 2 ___
	How often: ___	How often: ___	How often: ___	How often: ___	How often: ___	How often: ___	How often: ___

FORM J

GOAL ATTAINMENT SCALING SHEET

GUIDELINES FOR USING THE GOAL ATTAINMENT SCALE

1. Keep the goals simple and objective.
2. Change them over course of treatment.
3. Make the first goals relatively easy to achieve.
4. To calculate change over time, the first level (Where Are We Now?) is given a value of –1, the second level a value of 0, and the third a value of +1. If you have five goals and the family starts off at –5, then if they reach all five goals, they would earn a total score of +10; that is, from –1 to 0 on five goals = +5; from 0 to +1 on the five goals = +5, for a total of +10. These change scores are often more useful than changes on the CBCL or the CSBI.

GOALS FOR THE _____ FAMILY

	SAFETY IN OUR HOME		FEELING MORE CONNECTED	
	Goal #1	Goal #2	Goal #4	Goal #5
WHERE ARE WE NOW?				
GOOD SUCCESS				
GREAT SUCCESS				

FORM K

SEXUAL RULES

Sexual Rules for _____

1. I do not touch other people's private parts.
2. I only touch my private parts when I am alone in my room.
3. I do not say sexual words to my friends or family.
4. I practice safe distance when I am with my friends and family.
5. If I am thinking about doing something sexual, I can distract myself by doing something else.
6. I wear clothes when I am outside of the bathroom.
7. I let my parents know if anyone does sexual things to me.

FORM L

PRESCRIPTIVE PARENT STATEMENTS

1. Sometimes children touch their private parts/stand too close when they remember what happened to them.
2. Sometimes children touch their private parts/stand too close when they are worried/scared.
3. Sometimes children touch their private parts when they are feeling lonely.
4. You have really been working hard watching your boundaries/keeping your personal space.
5. You have been doing great all morning [afternoon] following the sexual rules.
6. When I see you _____ [sexual behavior], I know it is time for you to spend a few minutes in your room/on the chair/at the table in the kitchen.

FORM M

TURTLE TECHNIQUE

This is a self-control strategy best done with a prop (e.g., puppet of a turtle with a retractable head). However, this prop is not necessary. Use only with children who have problems with self-control and are developmentally capable of learning this strategy.

Introduce the notion of how turtles protect themselves by withdrawing into their shell. They do this when it's getting dangerous and they need to stop and figure out a way past the danger.

The sexual behavior problem is a danger, something that can get the child into trouble. To survive like a turtle, they need to:

1. Recognize danger
2. Withdraw into their house to think about their options
3. Create a plan
4. Stick their head out and follow this plan

Each of these steps can be discussed, acted out, and written down in detail. The child can demonstrate the ability to carry out each stage via role-play. Contract with child to practice. Share this briefly with parent.

FORM N

SHAME AND RELATED ISSUES QUESTIONS

(TO BE USED IN THERAPY SESSIONS WITH OLDER CHILDREN)

SHAME QUESTIONNAIRE (FRIEDRICH, 2002)

1. I feel ashamed about the sexual abuse.

1	2	3	4	5
Never	A Little	Sometimes	Lots of Times	Always

2. When I think about my abuse, I want to go away and hide.

1	2	3	4	5
Never	A Little	Sometimes	Lots of Times	Always

3. Being abused makes me feel dirty.

1	2	3	4	5
Never	A Little	Sometimes	Lots of Times	Always

4. Because of my abuse, I feel different than other children at school.

1	2	3	4	5
Never	A Little	Sometimes	Lots of Times	Always

SELECTED ITEMS FROM SPACARELLI (1995)

In relation to what happened with that person, did it ever make you think or feel that:

	Not at All	A Little	Some-what	A Lot
B1 You did something bad or wrong	1	2	3	4
B2 You were not as good as other kids	1	2	3	4
B3 You made someone do bad things	1	2	3	4
B4 It was your fault	1	2	3	4
B5 It was your fault for trusting too much	1	2	3	4
B6 You are a bad person	1	2	3	4
B7 You are not as good as other kids	1	2	3	4
B8 You make people do bad things	1	2	3	4

| B9 You trust people too much | 1 | 2 | 3 | 4 |

In relation to what happened with that person, did it ever make you think or feel that:

	Not at All	A Little	Some-what	A Lot
C1 Your sexual feelings were out of control	1	2	3	4
C2 You were too sexy	1	2	3	4
C3 You have too many sexual feelings or thoughts	1	2	3	4
C4 You lose control of your sexual feelings	1	2	3	4
C5 You are too sexy now	1	2	3	4
C6 You're not as interested in sex as you should be	1	2	3	4
C7 You won't like sex enough when you get older	1	2	3	4
C8 You will always have sex problems	1	2	3	4

In relation to what happened with that person, did it ever make you think or feel that:

	Not at All	A Little	Some-what	A Lot
D1 Someone you care about thought you did something bad	1	2	3	4
D2 Someone you care about was disappointed in you	1	2	3	4
D3 Someone you care about might say bad things about you	1	2	3	4
D4 Someone you care about might be disappointed with you	1	2	3	4
D5 You might get yelled at or punished	1	2	3	4

FORM O

OVERVIEW OF PARENT-CHILD
INTERACTION THERAPY (PCIT)

1. Designed to get the two of you back to feeling good about your relationship with each other again.
2. Five-minute daily play sessions following the Do's and Don'ts.
3. Parents learn effective commands and praise child for prompt compliance.
4. Catch your child being good during the day and use a PRIDE skill.
5. Selective use of two kinds of commands: highly directive and polite suggestion.
6. Decide on house rules and plan when to use highly directive commands.
7. Time-out:
   a. Teaching child to stay in time-out.
   b. Immediate time-out for aggressive behavior.
   c. Time-out for noncompliance after a choice statement.

Do Use the PRIDE Skills

RULE	REASON	EXAMPLES
Do **Praise** appropriate	Lets child know what you like	Terrific counting!
	Increases self-esteem	I like the way you're playing so quietly. You have wonderful ideas for this game.
	Causes the behavior to increase	
	Adds to warmth of the relationship	I'm proud of you for being polite.
	Makes both parent and child feel good	You did a nice job on that building. Your design is pretty. Thank you for showing the colors to me.
	Teaches child about good touch	Pat child on back.
	Builds connection	Touch child gently.

RULE	REASON	EXAMPLES
Do **Reflect** appropriate talk.	Shows child you're really listening, and not controlling the conversation	Child: I made a star. Parent: Yes, you made a star.
	Demonstrates acceptance	Child: The camel got bumps on top. Parent: It has two humps on its back.
	Improves child's speech and increases verbal communication	Child: I like to play with this castle. Parent: This is a fun castle to play with.
Do **Imitate** appropriate play.	Lets child lead	Child: I'm putting baby to bed. Parent: I'll put sister to bed too.
	Approves child's choice of play, shows child you are involved, shows child how to play with others (forms basis of taking turns)	Child: I'm making a sun in the sky. Parent: I'm going to put a sun in my picture, too.
Do **Describe** appropriate behavior.	Shows child you're interested, teaches concepts, models speech, allows child to lead, holds child's attention, organizes child's thoughts about play	That's a red block. You're making a tower. You drew a smiling face. The cowboy looks happy.
Do use **Enthusiasm**.	Keeps the child interested, helps to distract the child when ignoring	Voice is playful with lots of inflection.

Do's and Don'ts

Do's	Examples
Describe appropriate behavior	"You're really working on that rim shot." "Now you're adding some trees to your picture." "A blue windshield for *this* spacecraft . . ." "You're choking up on the bat . . . I bet you want to bunt!"
Reflect appropriate talk	Child: "Made it!" Parent: "You nailed it!"
	Child: "The leaves are going to be red and orange." Parent: "The autumn leaves are on the trees."
	Child: "These guys go in here." Parent: "They will ride in there."
	Child: "I'm going to hit a homer." Parent: "You are really going to slug this one."
Imitate appropriate play	Important not to upstage child by outperforming him or her. Parent: "I'm going to work on my rim shot, too." "I should put some trees in my picture." "Let's see if I can make one like yours . . ." "I want to get my feet set like you do . . ."
Praise appropriate behavior	Be sure to say what it is that you like. Plan ahead so you are ready to praise behavior that you would like to see more of. "Good shot!" "Way to go!" "Thank you for sharing the markers. It's nice of you." "I really like the grown-up voice you are using. Thanks for asking so nicely!"

"You're really putting a lot of careful thought into your design!"
"Wow! All your hard work is really paying off!"
Think about touch as a form of praise.

Ignore inappropriate behavior and talk unless it is dangerous or destructive	Do not look at child. Do not speak to child. Do not frown, smile, or react in any way. Turn away from the child and describe your own play in an animated tone. As soon as child is behaving appropriately, say in a neutral tone, for example, "I'm glad you decided to talk nicely to me. Now I can play with you again." If the child does not quickly become more appropriate, say, "I guess we can't play any more today. I'd better get back to _____." Time-out may be warranted if the child is aggressive or destructive.

<u>Don'ts</u>	<u>Examples</u>
Give commands	Give indirect commands like, "Why don't you choke up a little on the bat?" (This is not a time to teach.) Give direct commands like, "Don't bite your nails." "Stand like this."
Ask questions	"What are you working on?" "*That's* a space station?" "Are you getting ready for my fastball?"

Criticize

"You'll get better with practice."
"Don't you think it would look better if you put in the horizon?"
"I wish you'd think to do that more often."
"You blew that one. Too bad you didn't listen to me."

Remember that these don'ts take money out of your child's emotional ATM.

FORM P

COMMANDS (PDI)

Highly directive (use *only* when prepared to enforce):

(Please) Pick up the blocks.
(Please) Throw that away.
(Please) Empty the dishwasher.
(Please) Turn off the TV.

Polite suggestion (use for "less direct commands" and whenever you cannot enforce the command):

It would be a big help if you'd fold the towels.
I'd like it if you'd take out the trash.

Command forms to avoid:

You need to . . .
Would you please . . . ?
Why don't you . . . ?
Time for bed, okay?

Give an explanation before the command:

It's time for school. (Please) get your shoes on.

Praise prompt compliance specifically and enthusiastically:

Thanks! I really like it when you do what I ask right away.

EXAMPLES OF LABELED PRAISE

Ways to Praise It . . .	Praisable Behaviors
You did a great job of . . .	Sitting still
I like the way you're . . .	Talking in your inside voice
That's an excellent way to . . .	Staying at the table
That's a good idea to . . .	Working quietly
I'm proud of you for . . .	Raising your hand quietly
I think it's wonderful that you . . .	Waited quietly in line
You are smart to . . .	Do what I asked you
You're terrific for . . .	Accepting help from teacher/ another student
I like it when you're . . .	Working carefully
Thank you for . . .	Sharing
Good girl for . . .	Trying hard
Nice job of . . .	Doing it all by yourself
You should be proud of yourself for . . .	Listening carefully Using good manners Playing nicely

SPECIAL PLAYTIME RECORD SHEET

Did you practice special playtime for five minutes?

DATE	YES	NO	NOTE ANY PROBLEMS THAT CAME UP
Monday			
Tuesday			
Wednesday			
Thursday			
Friday			
Saturday			
Sunday			

MY OWN PTSD WORKBOOK

This workbook will help you to understand how we are affected by bad and scary things that happen to us.

P.T.S.D. & YOU
What happens is called *PTSD*.

It is really important that you have a helper/therapist as you work on this workbook.

Who is your helper?

_____

Helper's name

And who are you?

_____

You may want to take 2–3 sessions working on the things in this booklet. So let's keep track of the date. What day is today?

_____

The letters P-T-S-D really stand for *post traumatic stress disorder*. These are words that doctors came up with to describe something lots of kids get when something scary or bad happens to them or to someone close to them.

PTSD affects the way some people think. It also makes us have strong feelings. We may even act or behave very differently after something really awful has happened. A lot of kids with PTSD have a hard time falling asleep. An easier way to think about PTSD and the feelings that go with it is:

PTSD =
*P*owerful and *T*ough *S*tuff to *D*eal *with!*

When something really bad or scary happens to somebody, it is called a *trauma*. Some examples of traumas are getting hurt badly and going to the hospital, being physically or sexually abused, losing someone that you love because of divorce, losing someone because they moved away or died, seeing a parent hit or yell at another parent, or seeing a pet or somebody that you love get hurt.

Traumas are stuff that gets you really, really upset. More upset than ever before! You can feel really shaken.

I want to help you with this. But to just start talking might be too much. So we will try drawing. On this page, draw a picture to tell a story. This can be any picture, or any story. It does not have to be scary.

Some children really worry about what their mom or dad thinks about them when they talk about the powerful things that have happened to them. Does that sound like you?

You might even worry about what I will think about you when you talk about _____. Does that sound like you?
(your trauma)

My first thought is that _____ is tough and
(your name)
brave when you talk about scary things.

So let's look over your drawing. What is it and was your mind already starting to feel a story about something scary?

_____

_____

_____

_____

_____

_____

We do need to talk or draw a picture of a *trauma* that you have had or seen. Drawing helps to start you thinking about your trauma in a new way.

Sometimes kids get nightmares after they have had a trauma. Sometimes they feel like nightmares during the day. They might just pop into your head. Do you have nightmares? Do you have nightmares during the day? If you do, draw one of your scariest nightmares:

How are you feeling after this drawing? Let's write down the
feelings you have.

_____   _____

_____   _____

_____   _____

_____   _____

_____   _____

_____   _____

_____   _____

Let's take a short break. You've drawn two pictures. Each one may have made you feel stirred up. Use the space below to either draw a happy picture or to write down some of the things you like about yourself.

Even though nightmares can be very scary, there are things you can do to feel better about them. How scary does your nightmare feel? _____

One thing you can do is make up a good ending for your nightmare or draw your nightmare in a way that makes it less scary. Let's see what we can change on your drawing so that you can draw a better ending to your nightmare. What are your ideas? Let's write them down!

_____

_____

_____

_____

_____

_____

_____

_____

Now draw or retell your nightmare with a good ending.

Keep drawing. The more you draw, the more your mind lets us know what is bothering you.

People who have traumas can react in certain ways. Sometimes they worry a lot or get really nervous or jumpy inside. At times they have nightmares or *flashbacks*. A *flashback* is a strong memory or picture in your mind. It can appear when you do not expect it. You can even get a smell or a physical feeling about a trauma in the past that makes you feel like it's happening right now.

Let's make a list of the pictures, the smells, the sounds, and the feelings you get when you have these sudden memories.

Pictures

Smells

_____

_____

_____

_____

_____

_____

Sounds
(people saying words?)

Feelings

_____

_____

_____

_____

_____

_____

Sometimes people who have had traumas get scared of anything that makes their heart start to race. This could include loud noises. Sometimes they feel numb or "spaced out." These feelings are your body's way of letting you know that during the trauma, your emotions were going all over, up-and-down, and out-of-control. Let's draw that.

Now let's draw how emotions usually go.

See the difference?

Sometimes after a trauma you may feel very jumpy inside. Your heart can pound when you think of what happened. This is when you can take some deep breaths and think of a safe place. Have your helper teach you how to take deep breaths so that you can calm your whole body down. Then draw a picture of a safe place.

Write down all the things that make this a safe place (your helper can help you with this).

1.

2.

3.

4.

5.

6.

7.

8.

9.

10.

Now let's imagine every part of the safe place. Let's start by getting very, very relaxed. Your helper will guide you through this.

Maybe we could take a break here and between now and your next session, how about keeping track of when you have flash-backs and how bad they are and what you do to calm yourself down. Let's talk to _____ and see if they can help you.   (parent or caregiver)

	MONDAY	TUESDAY	WEDNESDAY	THURSDAY	FRIDAY	SATURDAY	SUNDAY
HOW MANY Flashbacks TODAY?							
HOW BAD WAS THE WORST? (1–10)							
WHAT DID YOU DO TO CALM DOWN?							

When some people who have had traumas get flashbacks, they feel that the trauma is happening all over again. Has that ever happened to you? Flashbacks can be caused by things that remind you of the first time the trauma happened. A loud noise might make someone who was in an earthquake react as if the earthquake is happening all over again.

You might feel scared when you meet a person for the first time. The reason is because he or she reminds you of someone else who hurt or abused you. Has that ever happened?

_____ Yes
_____ No

How often? _____

Who is that person? _____

Do you think you feel as frightened when you see them as you used to? _____

Flashbacks are scary, but you can get help in dealing with them. One way is to talk to someone about what happened to you.

Imagine telling an adult who cares about you, "I am having a flashback about _____

_____

_____

and I'm feeling _____

_____.

Can you help me deal with it?"

Another way to deal with flashbacks is to talk to yourself. You can tell yourself, "What happened to me is over and this is just a flashback." Let's imagine you doing just that. Now let's try it out. This is called "self-talk."

How does that feel?

It can take practice sometimes before it helps even more. Practice helps make all your skills, like breathing, finding a safe place, and self-talk, stronger.

On this page write the scariest things about your trauma or draw the answers to these questions. If you want to draw the answers, a page for drawing follows this one.

The worst part about my trauma was

_____

_____

_____

_____

When it was happening, I felt

_____

_____

_____

_____

Right after it was over, I felt

_____

_____

_____

_____

Sometimes I still feel

_____

_____

_____

_____

Sometimes it can help to calm us down if we think of someone who could have prevented the trauma. This could be a person who rescued you. Do you think that could help? If so, who is that person? Let's draw their picture.

_____

(friend, relative, teacher, police officer, etc.)

probably could have rescued me by

_____

_____

_____

_____

Draw a picture of that person helping you.

PTSD is also a memory of a trauma. Sometimes the memory lasts a long time and it keeps coming back. But each time it comes back, we can learn something about ourself, like how brave we were, or how it's not our fault. What is something you have learned from your flashbacks?

With your therapist, make a plan of ways to control your flash-back and write it on this page. Write down the things you can say to yourself that can help you make the flashback go away. This is called "self-talk." Here are some examples of self-talk: "It feels like it's happening all over again but it is just a flashback" or "I've had these before. I can get over another one."

My plan is:

My self-talk will be:_____

_____

_____

_____

_____

_____

_____

_____

Now list the people in your life who understand what happened to you, or, on the back of this page draw pictures of them helping you.

People who understand: _____

_____

_____

_____

_____

_____

_____

_____

Sometimes after a trauma people feel "spacey." This is another part of PTSD. They have trouble concentrating and may feel "numb"—like your hand or foot feels after it's fallen asleep or like your mouth feels after you get a shot from the dentist. But this type of numb is about your happy, sad, and mad *feelings*. Sometimes people stop feeling happy, sad, or mad and they start feeling, well . . . nothing. Maybe they feel frozen. Is that how you ever feel?

When you feel numb, it is really important to sort out all these feelings. Talking with your therapist or someone important to you about the trauma will start to thaw the "ice cube" of numbness. The more you talk about what happened to you and about your feelings, the less numb you'll feel. It's like being unfrozen by the warm sun.

For example, you may realize that underneath you are also very sad. Maybe the trauma took someone away from you. Maybe you had to move to a different place.

Do you think you also feel sad?

If so, let's draw what is making you sad.

You've done a lot of work already. Let's double-check to make sure we have covered everything. Let's fill out 7 things.

1. One of my traumas is

_____

_____

_____

2. Another trauma is

_____

_____

_____

3. My flashbacks come at

_____

_____

_____

and they are like

_____

_____

_____

4. When I am feeling all jumpy or stirred up about my trauma I can do _____

_____

_____

5. When a flashback comes, I can say

_____

_____

_____

6. The safe place I can go to in my head is

_____

_____

_____

7. One thing I have learned is

_____

_____

_____

Now that you are done with this workbook, you have made a big step in controlling your feelings about your trauma. You have been brave and I congratulate you.

_____

Your Name

_____

Your Helper's Name

_____

Date

REFERENCES

Abidin, R. R. (1995). *Parenting Stress Inventory* (3rd ed.). Odessa, FL: Psychological Assessment Resources.

Achenbach, T. M. (1991a). *Manual for the Child Behavior Checklist/4-18 and 1991 Profile*. Burlington, VT: University of Vermont Department of Psychiatry.

Achenbach, T. M. (1991b). *Manual for the Teacher's Report Form and 1991 Profile*. Burlington, VT: University of Vermont Department of Psychiatry.

Ainsworth, M. D. S., Blehar, M. C., Waters, E., & Wall, S. (1978). *Patterns of attachment: A psychological study of the strange situation*. Hillsdale, NJ: Erlbaum.

Aldridge, M., & Wood, J. (1997). Talking about feelings: Young children's ability to express emotions. *Child Abuse and Neglect, 21*, 1221–1233.

Alexander, M. A. (1999). Sex offender treatment efficacy revisited. *Sex Abuse: A Journal of Research and Treatment, 11*, 101–116.

Alexander, P. C. (1992). Application of attachment theory to the study of sexual abuse. *Journal of Consulting and Clinical Psychology, 60*, 185–195.

American Psychiatric Association. (1994). *Diagnostic and statistical manual of mental Disorders* (4th ed.). Washington, DC: Author.

ATSA Professional Issues Committee. (2005). *Practice standards and guidelines for the Association for Treatment of Sexual Abusers*. Beaverton, OR: Author.

Bandura, A. (1986). *Social foundation of thought and action: A social cognitive theory*. Englewood Cliffs, NJ: Prentice-Hall.

Barbaree, H. E., Marshall, W. L., & Hudson, S. M. (1999). *The juvenile sexual offender*. New York: Guilford.

Beck, A. T. (1996). *Beck Depression Inventory–II*. San Antonio, TX: Psychological Corporation.

Beeghly, M., & Cicchetti, D. (1994). Child maltreatment, attachment, and the self-system: Emergence of an internal state lexicon in toddlers at high social risk. *Development and Psychopathology, 6*, 5–30.

Biglan, A., Mrazek, D. J., Carnine, D., & Flay, B. R. (2003). The integration of research and practice in the prevention of youth problem behaviors. *American Psychologist, 58*, 433–440.

Bloomquist, M. A. (1996). *Skills training for children with behavior disorders*. New York: Guilford.

Bodiford-McNeil, C., Hembree-Kigin, T. L., & Eyberg, S. M. (1996). *Short-term play therapy for disruptive children*. King of Prussia, PA: Center for Applied Psychology.

Bolton, F. G., Morris, L. A., & MacEachron, A. E. (1989). *Males at risk*. Newbury Park, CA: Sage.

Bonner, B., Walker, C. E., & Berliner, L. (2000). *Final report. Children with sexual behavior problems: Assessment and treatment*. Grant No. 90-CA-1469. Washington, DC: National Clearinghouse on Child Abuse and Neglect.

Bowlby, J. (1969). *Attachment and loss: Vol. 1. Attachment*. New York: Basic Books.

Brestan, E. V., & Eyberg, S. M. (1998). Effective psychosocial treatments of conduct-disordered children and adolescents: 29 years, 82 studies, and 5,272 kids. *Journal of Clinical Child Psychology, 27*, 180–189.

Bretherton, I., Fritz, J., Zahn-Waxler, C., & Ridgeway, D. (1986). Learning to talk about emotions: A functionalist perspective. *Child Development, 57*, 529–548.

Briere, J. (1995). *Manual for the Trauma Symptom Inventory*. Odessa, FL: Psychological Assessment Resources.

Briere, J. (1996). *Manual for the Trauma Symptom Checklist for Children*. Odessa, FL: Psychological Assessment Resources.

Brilleslijper-Kater, S. N., Friedrich, W. N., & Corwin, D. L. (2004). Sexual knowledge and emotional reaction as indications of sexual abuse in young children: Theory and research challenges. *Child Abuse and Neglect, 28*, 1007–1017.

Brinkmeyer, M. Y., & Eyberg, S. M. (2003). Parent-child interaction therapy for oppositional children. In A. E. Kazdin & J. R. Weisz (Eds.), *Evidence based psychotherapies for children and adolescents* (pp. 204–223). New York: Guilford.

Burkett, L. P. (1991). Parenting behaviors of women who were sexually abused as children in their family of origin. *Family Process, 30*, 421–434.

Burton, D. L. (2000). Were adolescent sexual offenders children with sexual behavior problems? *Sexual Abuse: A Journal of Research and Treatment, 12*, 37–48.

Burton, D. L., Miller, D. L., & Shill, C. T. (2002). A social learning theory comparison of the sexual victimization of adolescent sexual offenders and non-sexually offending male delinquents. *Child Abuse and Neglect, 26*, 893–907.

Carlson, E. A., Jacobvitz, D., & Sroufe, L. A. (1995). A developmental investigation of inattentiveness and hyperactivity. *Child Development, 66*, 37–54.

Carnes, C. N., Wilson, C., & Nelson-Gardell, D. (1994). Extended forensic evaluation when sexual abuse is suspected: A model and preliminary data. *Child Maltreatment, 4*, 242–254.

Cassidy, J., & Shaver, P. R. (1999). *Handbook of attachment*. New York: Guilford.

Chaffin, M., & Bonner, B. (1998). "Don't shoot, we're your children": Have we gone too far in our response to adolescent sexual abusers and children with sexual behavior problems? *Child Maltreatment, 3*, 314–316.

Chaffin, M., & Friedrich, W. (2004). Evidence-based practice in child abuse and neglect. *Children and Youth Services Review, 26*, 1097–1113.

Chaffin, M., Letourneau, E., & Silovsky, J. (2002). Adults, adolescents and children who sexually abuse children: A developmental perspective. In J. Myers & L. Berliner (Eds.), *The APSAC handbook on child maltreatment* (pp. 205–232). Newbury Park, CA: Sage.

Chaffin, M., & Shultz, S. K. (2001). Psychometric evaluation of the children's impact of events scale–revised. *Child Abuse and Neglect, 25*, 401–411.

Chaffin, M., Silovsky, J. F., Funderburk, B., Valle, L. A., Brestan, E. V., Balachova, T., et al. (2004). Parent-child interaction therapy with physically abusive parents: Efficacy for reducing future abuse reports. *Journal of Consulting and Clinical Psychology, 72*, 500–510.

Cicchetti, D., & Rogosch, F. A. (1997). The role of self-organization in the promotion of resilience in maltreated children. *Development and Psychopathology, 9*, 797–815.

Cicchetti, D., & Toth, S. L. (1995). A developmental psychopathology perspective on child abuse and neglect. *Journal of the American Academy of Child and Adolescent Psychiatry, 34*, 541–565.

Coddington, R. D. (1999). *Coddington Life Events Scales*. North Tonawanda, NY: Multi-Health Systems.

Cohen, D. (2002). *How the child's mind develops*. New York: Taylor and Francis.

Cohen, J. A., & Mannarino, A. P. (1997). A treatment study for sexually abused preschool children: Outcome during a one-year follow-up. *Journal of the American Academy of Child and Adolescent Psychiatry, 36*, 1228–1235.

Cohen, J. A., & Mannarino, A. P. (1998). Factors that mediate treatment outcome of sexually abused preschool children: Six- and 12-month follow-up. *Journal of the American Academy of Child and Adolescent Psychiatry, 37,* 44–51.

Cohen, J. A., & Mannarino, A. P. (2004). Treatment of childhood traumatic grief. *Journal of Clinical Child and Adolescent Psychology, 33,* 819–831.

Cole, P. M., Martin, S. E., & Dennis, T. A. (2004). Emotion regulation as a scientific construct: Methodological challenges and directions for child development research. *Child Development, 75,* 317–333.

Crittenden, P. M. (1984). Sibling interaction: Evidence of a generational effect in maltreating infants. *Child Abuse and Neglect, 8,* 433–438.

Crittenden, P. M. (1995). Attachment and psychopathology. In S. Goldberg, R. Muir, & J. Kerr (Eds.), *Attachment theory: Social, developmental, and clinical perspectives* (pp. 367–406). Hillsdale, NJ: Analytic Press.

Crittenden, P. M. (1997). Toward an integrative theory of trauma: A dynamic-maturational approach. In D. Cicchetti & S. Toth (Eds.), *The Rochester Symposium on Developmental Psychopathology, Vol. 10. Risk, Trauma, and Mental Processes* (pp. 34–84). Rochester, NY: University of Rochester Press.

Crittenden, P. M. (2006). Why do inadequate parents do what they do? In O. Mayseless (Ed.), *Parenting representations: Theory, research, and clinical implications* (pp. 388–433). Cambridge: Cambridge University Press.

Crittenden, P. M., & DiLalla, D. L. (1988). Compulsive compliance: The development of an inhibitory coping strategy in infancy. *Journal of Abnormal Child Psychology, 16,* 585–599.

Crittenden, P. M., Clausen, A. H., & Kozlowska, K. (2007, June). Choosing a valid assessment of attachment for clinical use: A comparative study. *Australia New Zealand Journal of Family Therapy, 28* (2), 78–87.

Cunningham, C., & MacFarlane, K. (1991). *When children molest children.* Orwell, VT: Safer Society Press.

Cunningham, C., & MacFarlane, K. (2001). *Pretty tough stuff dude! A post traumatic stress disorder workbook for children.* Brandon, VT: Safer Society Press.

Daleiden, E. L., Kaufman, K. L., Hilliker, D. R., & O'Neil, J. N. (1998). The sexual histories and fantasies of youthful males: A comparison of sexual offending, nonsexual offending and nonoffending groups. *Sexual Abuse: A Journal of Research and Treatment, 10,* 195–209.

Deblinger, E., & Heflin, A. H. (1996). *Treating sexually abused children and their nonoffending parents.* Thousand Oaks, CA: Sage.

Deblinger, E., Lippman, J., & Steer, R. (1996). Sexually abused children presenting with posttraumatic stress symptoms: Initial treatment outcome findings. *Child Maltreatment, 1,* 310–321.

DeLillo, D., & Damashek, A. (2003). Parenting characteristics of women reporting a history of childhood sexual abuse. *Child Maltreatment, 8,* 319–333.

DeMulder, E. K., Denham, A., Schmidt, M., & Mitchell, V. J. (2000). Q-sort assessment of attachment security during the preschool years: Links from home to school. *Developmental Psychology, 36,* 274–282.

Denov, M. S. (2004). The long-term effects of child sexual abuse by female perpetrators: A qualitative study of male and female victims. *Journal of Interpersonal Violence, 19,* 1137–1156.

Dodge, K. (1990). Developmental psychopathology in children of depressed mothers. *Developmental Psychology, 26,* 3–6.

Downs, W. R. (1993). Developmental considerations for the effects of childhood sexual abuse. *Journal of Interpersonal Violence, 8,* 331–345.

Dozier, M., Stovall, K. C., & Albus, K. E. (1999). Attachment and psychopathology in adulthood. In J. Cassidy & P. R. Shaver (Eds.), *Handbook of attachment* (pp. 497–519). New York: Guilford.

Egeland, B., Jacobvitz, D., & Sroufe, L. A. (1988). Breaking the cycle of abuse: Relationship predictors. *Child Development, 59,* 1080–1088.

Elliott, A. N., & Carnes, C. N. (2001). Reactions of nonoffending parents to the sexual abuse of their child: A review of the literature. *Child Maltreatment, 6,* 314–331.

Elliott, D. M. (1994). Impaired object relations in professional women molested as children. *Psychotherapy, 31,* 79–86.

Elliott, D. M., Kim, S., & Mull, S. (1997, August). *Impact of pornography on sexually abused and unabused children.* Paper presented at the annual conference of the American Psychological Association, Chicago, IL.

Erickson, M. F., & Egeland, B. (1987). A developmental view of the psychological consequences of child maltreatment. *School Psychology Review, 16,* 156–168.

Evans, G. W. (2003). A multimethodological analysis of cumulative risk and allostatic load among rural children. *Developmental Psychology, 39,* 924–933.

Farmer, E., & Pollock, S. (1998). *Sexually abused and abusing children in substitute care.* New York: John Wiley.

Feiring, C., Taska, L., & Lewis, M. (1996). A process model for understanding adaptation to sexual abuse: The role of shame in defining stigmatization. *Child Abuse and Neglect, 20,* 767–782.

Fitzgerald, M. M., Shipman, K. L., Jackson, J. L., McMahon, R. J., & Hanley, H. M. (2005). Perceptions of parenting versus parent-child interactions among incest survivors. *Child Abuse and Neglect, 29,* 661–681.

Fonagy, P., Steele, M., Steele, H., Leigh, T., Kennedy, R., Mattoon, G., et al. (1995). Attachment, the reflective self, and borderline states: The predictive specificity of the Adult Attachment Interview and pathological emotional development. In S. Goldberg, R. Muir, & J. Kerr (Eds.), *Attachment theory: Social, developmental, and clinical perspectives* (pp. 233–278). Hillsdale, NJ: Analytic Press.

Fonagy, P., & Target, M. (1997). Attachment and reflective function: Their role in self organization. *Development and Psychopathology, 9,* 679–700.

Ford, J., Racusin, R., Ellis, C. G., Daviss, W. B., Reiser, J., Fleischer, A., et al. (2000). Child maltreatment, other trauma exposure, and posttraumatic symptomatology among children with oppositional defiant and attention deficit hyperactivity disorders. *Child Maltreatment, 5,* 205–217.

Fraiberg, S., Adelson, E., & Shapiro, V. (1975). Ghosts in the nursery. *Journal of the American Academy of Child Psychiatry, 14,* 387–421.

Frankel, F. & Wetmore, B. (1996). *Good friends are hard to find: Help your child find, make, and keep friends.* Los Angeles: Perspective.

Frick, P. J., & Hare, R. H. (2002). *Antisocial process screening device.* North Tonawanda, NY: Multi-Health Systems.

Friedrich, W. N. (1988). Behavioral problems in sexually abused children: An adaptational perspective. In G. Wyatt & G. Powell (Eds.), (pp. 171–191). *Lasting effects of child sexual abuse.* Thousand Oaks, CA: Sage.

Friedrich, W. N. (1990). *Psychotherapy of sexually abused children and their families.* New York: Norton.

Friedrich, W. N. (1991). Mothers of sexually abused children: An MMPI study. *Journal of Clinical Psychology, 47,* 778–783.

Friedrich, W. N. (1995). *Psychotherapy with sexually abused boys.* Thousand Oaks, CA: Sage.

Friedrich, W. N. (1997). *Child Sexual Behavior Inventory: Test manual*. Odessa, FL: Psychological Assessment Resources.

Friedrich, W. N. (2002). *Psychological assessment of sexually abused children and their families*. Thousand Oaks, CA: Sage.

Friedrich, W. N., Baker, A. J. L., Parker, R., Schneidermann, M., Gries, L., & Archer, M. (2005). Youth with problematic sexualized behaviors in the child welfare system: A one-year longitudinal study. *Sexual Abuse: A Journal of Research and Treatment, 17*, 391–406.

Friedrich, W. N., Davies, W. H., Fehrer, E., Trentham, B., & Wright, J. (2003). Sexual behavior problems in preteen children: Developmental, ecological and behavioral correlates. *Annals of the New York Academy of Science, 989*, 95–104.

Friedrich, W. N., Fisher, J., Broughton, D., Houston, M., & Shafran, C. R. (1998). Normative sexual behavior in children: A contemporary sample. *Pediatrics, 101*, 1–9.

Friedrich, W. N., Fisher, J., Dittner, C., Acton, R., Berliner, L., Butler, J., et al. (2001). Child Sexual Behavior Inventory: Normative, psychiatric and sexual abuse comparisons. *Child Maltreatment, 6*, 37–49.

Friedrich, W. N., Gerber, P. N., Koplin, B., Davis, M., Giese, J., Mykelbust, C., et al. (2001). Multimodal assessment of dissociation in adolescents: Inpatients and sex offenders. *Sexual Abuse: A Journal of Research and Treatment, 13*, 19–29.

Friedrich, W. N., Grambsch, P., Broughton, D., Kuiper, J., & Beilke, R. L. (1991). Normative sexual behavior in children. *Pediatrics, 88*, 456–464.

Friedrich, W. N., Grambsch, P., Damon, L., Hewitt, S., Koverola, C., Lang, R., et al. (1992). The Child Sexual Behavior Inventory: Normative and clinical contrasts. *Psychological Assessment: A Journal of Consulting and Clinical Psychology, 4*, 303–311.

Friedrich, W. N., Jaworski, T. M., & Berliner, L. (1994). A survey of therapists' attitudes regarding sexual abuse treatment. *APSAC Advisor, 7*(2), 17–18, 24.

Friedrich, W. N., & Luecke, W. J. (1988). Young school-age sexually aggressive children. *Professional Psychology, 19*, 155–164.

Friedrich, W. N., Lysne, M., Sim, L., & Shamos, S. (2004). Assessing sexual behavior in high-risk adolescents with the Adolescent Clinical Sexual Behavior Inventory (ACSBI). *Child Maltreatment, 9*, 239–250.

Friedrich, W. N., & Malat, H. (2005). *Assessing PTSD in adolescent inpatients via self-report and parent report*. Unpublished manuscript, Mayo Clinic Department of Psychiatry and Psychology, Rochester, MN.

Friedrich, W. N., & Reams, R. A. (1987). Course of psychological symptoms in sexually abused young children. *Psychotherapy, 24*, 160–170.

Friedrich, W. N., & Share, M. C. (1997). The Roberts Apperception Test for Children: An exploratory study of its use with sexually abused children. *Journal of Child Sexual Abuse, 6*, 83–91.

Friedrich, W. N., & Sim, L. (2003, July). *Sexual abuse victims as mothers: Relationship to coping resources, perceptions of the child, discipline practices, and behavior problems*. Paper presented at the Eighth International Family Violence Research Conference, Portsmouth, NH.

Friedrich, W. N., & Sim, L. (2005). Attachment styles and sexual abuse. In R. Freeman-Longo (Ed.), *Current perspectives on working with sexually aggressive youth and youth with sexual behavior problems* (pp. 373–386). Holyoke, MA: NEARI Press.

Friedrich, W. N., Talley, N. J., Panser, L., Zinsmeister, A., & Fett, S. (1997). Concordance of reports of childhood abuse by adults. *Child Maltreatment, 2*, 164–171.

Friedrich, W. N., Tiegs, C. A., & Damon, L. (2003, July). *Sexual aggression and sexual behavior: The CSBI-Extended*. Paper presented at the Eighth International Family Violence Research Conference, Portsmouth, NH.

Friedrich, W. N., Tyler, J. D., & Clark, J. A. (1985). Personality and psychophysiological variables in abusive, neglectful, and low income control mothers. *Journal of Nervous and Mental Disease, 173*, 449–460.

Friedrich, W. N., Urquiza, A. J., & Beilke, R. L. (1986). Behavior problems in sexually abused young children. *Journal of Pediatric Psychology, 11*, 47–57.

Garbarino, J. (1999). *Lost boys.* New York: Free Press.

Garno, J. L., Goldberg, J. F., Ramirez, P. M., & Ritzler, B. A. (2005). Impact of childhood abuse on the clinical course of bipolar disorder. *British Journal of Psychiatry, 186*, 121–125.

George, C., Kaplan, N., & Main, M. (1985). *Adult attachment interview.* Unpublished manuscript, University of California, Berkeley.

George, C., & Main, M. (1979). Social interactions of young abused children: Approach, avoidance, and aggression. *Child Development, 50*, 306–318.

Gil, E., & Johnson, T. C. (1993). *Sexualized children.* Rockville, MD: Launch Press.

Gilgun, J. F. (1990). Factors mediating the effects of childhood maltreatment. In M. Hunter (Ed.), *The sexually abused male: Prevalence, impact, and treatment* (pp. 177–190). Lexington, MA: Lexington Books.

Gilgun, J. F. (1991). Resilience and the intergenerational transmission of child sexual abuse. In M. Q. Patton (Ed.), *Family sexual abuse: Frontline research and evaluation* (pp. 93–105). Newbury Park, CA: Sage.

Goodman, R. (1997). The Strengths and Difficulties Questionnaire: A research note. *Journal of Child Psychology, Psychiatry, and Allied Disciplines, 38*, 581–586.

Goodman, R., & Scott, S. (1999). Comparing the Strengths and Difficulties scale with the Child Behavior Checklist: Is small beautiful? *Journal of Abnormal Child Psychology, 27*, 17–24.

Gray, A., Busconi, A., Houchens, P., & Pithers, W. D. (1997). Children with sexual behavior problems and their caregivers: Demographics, functioning, and clinical patterns. *Sexual Abuse: A Journal of Research and Treatment, 9*, 267–290.

Gray, A., Pithers, W. D., Busconi, A., & Houchens, P. (1999). Developmental and etiological characteristics of children with sexual behavior problems: Treatment implications. *Child Abuse and Neglect, 23*, 601–621.

Greenberg, M. T., Speltz, M. L., & DeKlyen, M. (1993). The role of attachment in the early development of disruptive behavior problems. *Development and Psychopathology, 5*, 191–213.

Hall, D. K., & Mathews, F. (1996). *The development of sexual behavior problems in children and youth.* Toronto: Central Toronto Youth Services.

Hall, D. K., Mathews, F., & Pearce, J. (1998). Factors associated with sexual behavior problems in young sexually abused children. *Child Abuse and Neglect, 22*, 1045–1063.

Hall, D. K., Mathews, F., & Pearce, J. (2002). Sexual behavior problems in sexually abused children: A preliminary typology. *Child Abuse and Neglect, 26*, 289–312.

Hall, G. C. (1995). Sexual offender recidivism revisited: A meta-analysis of recent treatment studies. *Journal of Consulting and Clinical Psychology, 63*, 802–809.

Hare, R. D. (1991). *The Hare Psychopathy Checklist–Revised: Manual.* Toronto: Multi-Health Systems.

Harned, M. S. (2004). Does it matter what you call it? The relationship between labeling unwanted sexual experiences and distress. *Journal of Consulting and Clinical Psychology, 72*, 1090–1099.

Haugaard, J. J., & Tilly, C. (1988). Characteristics predicting children's responses to sexual encounters with other children. *Child Abuse and Neglect, 12*, 209–218.

Hazan, C., & Shaver, P. R. (1987). Romantic love conceptualized as an attachment process. *Journal of Personality and Social Psychology, 52*, 511–524.

Hembree-Kigin, T. L., & McNeil, C. B. (1995). *Parent-child interaction therapy*. New York: Plenum.

Hesse, E. (1999). The Adult Attachment Interview. In J. Cassidy & P. R. Shaver (Eds.), *Handbook of attachment* (pp. 395–433). New York: Guilford.

Hewitt, S. (1999). *Assessing allegations of sexual abuse in preschool children*. Thousand Oaks, CA: Sage.

Hussey, D. L., Strom, G., & Singer, M. I. (1992). Male victims of sexual abuse. An analysis of adolescent inpatients. *Child and Adolescent Social Work Journal, 9*, 491–503.

Jacobsen, T., & Miller, L. J. (1999). Attachment quality in young children of mentally ill mothers. In J. Solomon & C. George (Eds.), *Attachment disorganization* (pp. 347–378). New York: Guilford.

Jacobvitz, D. B., & Hazen, N. L. (1999). Developmental pathways from infant disorganization to childhood peer relationships. In J. Solomon & C. George (Eds.), *Attachment disorganization* (pp. 127–159). New York: Guilford.

James, B. (1994). *Handbook for treatment of attachment-trauma problems in children*. New York: Free Press.

Janov, A. (1970). *The primal scream*. New York: Putnam.

Johnson, T. (1988). Child perpetrators—children who molest other children: Preliminary findings. *Child Abuse and Neglect, 12*, 219–229.

Johnson, T. (1989). Female child perpetrators: Children who molest other children. *Child Abuse and Neglect, 13*, 571–585.

Karp, C. L., & Butler, T. L. (1996). *Activity book for treatment strategies for abused children*. Thousand Oaks, CA: Sage.

Kazdin, A. E. (2003). Problem-solving skills training and parent management training for conduct disorder. In A. E. Kazdin & J. R. Weisz (Eds.), *Evidence-based psychotherapies for children and adolescents* (pp. 241–262). New York: Guilford.

Kazdin, A. E., & Weisz, J. R. (2003). *Evidence-based psychotherapies with children*. New York: Guilford.

Keller, T. E., Spieker, S. L., & Gilchrist, L. (2005). Patterns of risk and trajectories of preschool problem behaviors: A personal-oriented analysis of attachment in context. *Development and Psychopathology, 17*, 349–384.

Kendall-Tackett, K. A., Williams, L. M., & Finkelhor, D. (1993). Impact of sexual abuse on children: A review and synthesis of recent empirical studies. *Psychological Bulletin, 113*, 164–180.

Kim-Cohen, J., Moffitt, T. E., Taylor, A., Pawlby, S. J., & Caspi, A. (2005). Maternal depression and children's antisocial behavior: Nature and nurture effects. *Archives of General Psychiatry, 62*, 173–181.

King, P. (2000, June 25). A "rebirth" brings death. *Newsweek*, p. 65.

Kobayashi, J., Sales, B. D., Becker, J. V., Figueredo, A. J., & Kaplan, M. S. (1995). Perceived parental deviance, parent-child bonding, child abuse, and child sexual aggression. *Sexual Abuse: A Journal of Research and Treatment, 7*, 25–44.

Kolko, D. J. (1996). Individual cognitive behavioral treatment and family therapy for physically abused children and their offending parents: A comparison of clinical outcomes. *Child Maltreatment, 1*, 322–342.

Kovacs, M. (1991). *Child Depression Inventory*. North Tonawanda, NY: Multi-Health Systems.

Lamb, S., & Coakley, M. (1993). "Normal" childhood sexual play in games: Differentiating play from abuse. *Child Abuse and Neglect, 17,* 515–526.

Larsson, I., Svedin, C. G., & Friedrich, W. N. (2000). Differences and similarities in sexual behavior among preschoolers in Sweden and USA. *Nordic Journal of Psychology, 54,* 251–257.

Leifer, M., Kilbane, T., & Grossman, G. (2001). A three-generational study comparing the families of supportive and unsupportive mothers of sexually abused children. *Child Maltreatment, 6,* 353–364.

Leifer, M., Kilbane, T., & Kalick, S. (2004). Vulnerability or resilience to intergenerational sexual abuse: The role of maternal factors. *Child Maltreatment, 9,* 78–91.

Letourneau, E. J., Schoenwald, S. K., & Sheidow, A. (2004). Children and adolescents with sexual behavior problems. *Child Maltreatment, 9,* 49–61.

Lichtenstein, J. P., Belsky, J. & Crnic, K. (1998). Earned security, daily stress, and parenting: A comparison of five alternative models. *Development and Psychopathology, 10,* 21–38.

Liotti, G. (1999). Disorganized attachment and dissociation. In J. Solomon & C. George (Eds.), *Attachment disorganization* (pp. 291–317). New York: Guilford.

Loeber, R., & Stouthamer-Loeber, M. (1998). Development of juvenile aggression and violence: Some common misconceptions and controversies. *American Psychologist, 53,* 242–259.

Longo, R. E., & Prescott, D. S. (2005). Introduction. In R. Longo & D. S. Prescott (Eds.), *Current perspectives on working with sexually aggressive youth and youth with sexual behavior problems* (pp. 31–44). Holyoke, MA: NEARI Press.

Lyons-Ruth, K. (2003). Dissociation and the parent-infant dialogue: A longitudinal perspective from attachment research. *Journal of the American Psychoanalytic Association, 51,* 883–911.

Lyons-Ruth, K., & Jacobvitz, D. (1999). Attachment disorganization. In J. Cassidy & P. R. Shaver (Eds.), *Handbook of attachment* (pp. 520–554). New York: Guilford.

MacFarlane, K., & Cunningham, C. (1990). *Steps to healthy touching.* Charlotte, NC: KIDS RIGHTS.

Main, M. (1995). Recent studies in attachment. In S. Goldberg, R. Muir, & J. Kerr (Eds.), *Attachment theory: Social, developmental, and clinical perspectives* (pp. 407–474). Hillsdale, NJ: Analytic Press.

Main, M., & Cassidy, J. (1988). Categories of response to reunion with the parent at age 6: Predictable from infant attachment classifications and stable over a 1-month period. *Developmental Psychology, 24,* 1–12.

Main, M., & Hesse, E. (1990). Parents' unresolved traumatic experiences are related to infant disorganized attachment status: Is frightened and/or frightening parental behavior the linking mechanism? In M. T. Greenberg, D. Cicchetti, & E. M. Cummings (Eds.), *Attachment in the preschool years* (pp. 161–182). Chicago: University of Chicago Press.

Main, M., & Solomon, J. (1990). Procedures for identifying infants as disorganized/disoriented during the Ainsworth Strange Situation. In M. T. Greenberg, D. Cicchetti, & E. M. Cummings (Eds.), *Attachment in the preschool years* (pp. 121–160). Chicago: University of Chicago Press.

Mandell, J. G., & Damon, L. (1989). *Group treatment for sexually abused children.* New York: Guilford.

March, J. S. (1997). *Multidimensional Anxiety Schedule for Children.* North Tonawanda, NY: Multi-Health Systems.

Marshall, W. (1993). The role of attachment, intimacy, and loneliness in the aetiology and maintenance of sexual offending. *Sex and Marital Therapy, 8,* 109–121.

Mathews, R., Hunter, J. A., & Vuz, J. (1997). Juvenile female sexual offenders: Clinical characteristics and treatment issues. *Sexual Abuse: A Journal of Research and Treatment, 9*, 187–199.

McArthur, D. S., & Roberts, G. E. (1982). *Roberts Apperception Test for Children.* Los Angeles: Western Psychological Services.

McCurry, C., McClellan, J., Adams, J., Norrei, M., Storck, M., Eisner, A., et al. (1998). Sexual behavior associated with low verbal IQ in youth who have severe mental illness. *Mental Retardation, 36*, 23–30.

Merrill, L. E., Guimond, J. M., Thomsen, C. J., & Milner, J. S. (2003). Child sexual abuse and number of sexual partners in young women: The role of abuse severity, coping style, and sexual functioning. *Journal of Consulting and Clinical Psychology, 71*, 987–996.

Meyer-Bahlburg, H. F. L., & Steel, J. L. (2003). Using parents as a source of information about the child. In J. Bancroft (Ed.), *Sexual development in childhood* (pp. 34–53). Bloomington: Indiana University Press.

Miller, W. R., & Rollnick, S. (1991). *Motivational interviewing.* New York: Guilford.

Moffitt, T. E. (1993). Adolescent-limited and life-course persistent antisocial behavior: A developmental taxonomy. *Psychological Review, 100*, 674–701.

National Center on Sexual Behavior of Youth. (2003, July). Children with sexual behavior problems: Common misconceptions and current findings. *NCSBY Fact Sheet*, 1–11.

New, M. J. C., Stevenson, J., & Skuse, D. (1999). Characteristics of mothers of boys who sexually abuse. *Child Maltreatment, 4*, 21–31.

Nichols, K., Gergely, G., & Fonagy, P. (2001). Experimental protocols for investigating relationships among mother-infant interaction, affect regulation, physiological markers of stress responsiveness, and attachment. *Bulletin of the Menninger Clinic, 5*, 371–379.

Noll, J. G., Trickett, P. K., & Putnam, F. W. (2003). A prospective investigation of the impact of childhood sexual abuse on the development of sexuality. *Journal of Consulting and Clinical Psychology, 71*, 575–586.

O'Brien, M. J. (1991). Taking sibling incest seriously. In M. Q. Patton (Ed.), *Family sexual abuse* (pp. 75–92). Newbury Park, CA: Sage.

O'Connor, T. G., & Rutter, M. (2000). Attachment disorder behavior following early severe deprivation: Extension and longitudinal follow-up. English and Romanian Adoptees Study Team. *Journal of the American Academy of Child and Adolescent Psychiatry, 39*, 703–712.

Paredes, M., Leifer, M., & Kilbane, T. (2001). Maternal variables related to sexually abused children's functioning. *Child Abuse and Neglect, 25*, 1159–1176.

Patterson, G. R. (1980). Mothers: The unacknowledged victims. *Monographs of the Society for Research in Child Development, 45*(5, Serial No. 186).

Patterson, G., Reid, J. B., & Dishion, T. J. (1992). *Antisocial boys.* Eugene, OR: Castalia.

Pithers, W. D., Gray, A., Busconi, A., & Houchens, P. (1998). Children with sexual behavior problems: Identification of five distinct child types and related treatment considerations. *Child Maltreatment, 3*, 384–406.

Prentky, R., Harris, B., Frizzell, K., & Righthand, S. (2000). An actuarial procedure for assessing risk in juvenile sex offenders. *Sexual Abuse: A Journal of Research and Treatment, 12*, 71–93.

Rademakers, J., Laan, M. J. C., & Straver, C. J. (2003). Body awareness and physical intimacy: An exploratory study. In J. Bancroft (Ed.), *Sexual development in childhood* (pp. 121–125). Bloomington: Indiana University Press.

Rasmussen, L. A. (1999). Factors related to recidivism among juvenile sexual offenders. *Sexual Abuse: A Journal of Research and Treatment, 11*(1), 69–85.

Reynolds, C. R., & Kamphaus, R. W. (1998). *Behavior assessment system for children.* Circle Pines, MN: American Guidance Service.

Ringer, F. & Crittenden, P. (2007). Eating disorders and attachment: The effects of hidden processes on eating disorders. *European Eating Disorders Review, 15,* 119–130.

Rutter, M., & Quinton, D. (1984). Parental psychiatric disorder: Effects on children. *Psychological Medicine, 14,* 853–880.

Saunders, B. E., Berliner, L., & Hanson, R. F. (Eds.). (2004). *Child physical and sexual abuse: Guidelines for treatment (revised report: April 26, 2004).* Charleston, SC: National Crime Victims Research and Treatment Center.

Schaefer, C. E., Briesmeister, J. M., & Fitton, M. E. (1984). *Family therapy techniques for problem behaviors of children and teenagers.* San Francisco: Jossey-Bass.

Schore, A. N. (1996). The experience-dependent maturation of a regulatory system in the orbital prefontal cortex and the origin of developmental psychopathology. *Development and Psychopathology, 8,* 59–87.

Schuetze, P., & Eiden, R. D. (2005). The relationship between sexual abuse during childhood and parenting outcomes: Modeling direct and indirect pathways. *Child Abuse and Neglect, 29,* 645–659.

Siegel, D. J. (1999). *The developing mind.* New York: Guilford.

Silovsky, J. F., & Niec, L. (2002). Characteristics of young children with sexual behavior problems: A pilot study. *Child Maltreatment, 7,* 187–197.

Silovsky, J. F., Niec, L., Hecht, D., & Bard, D. (in press). *Treatment for preschool children with sexual behavior problems: A pilot study. Clinical Journal of Child & Adolescent Psychology.*

Sim, L., Friedrich, W. N., Davies, W. H., Trentham, B., Lengua, L., & Pithers, W. (2005). The Child Behavior Checklist as an indicator of posttraumatic stress disorder and dissociation in normative, psychiatric, and sexually abused children. *Journal of Traumatic Stress, 18,* 697–705.

Slade, A. (1999). Individual psychotherapy: An attachment perspective. In J. Cassidy & P. R. Shaver (Eds.), *Handbook of attachment* (pp. 575–594). New York: Guilford.

Smith, H., & Israel, E. (1987). Sibling incest: A study of the dynamics of 25 cases. *Child Abuse and Neglect, 11,* 101–108.

Spaccarelli, S. (1995). Measuring abuse stress and negative cognitive appraisals in child sexual abuse: Validity data on two new scales. *Journal of Abnormal Child Psychology, 23,* 703–727.

Sroufe, L. A. (1989). Pathways to adaptation and maladaptation: Psychopathology as developmental deviation. In D. Cicchetti (Ed.), *The emergence of discipline: Rochester symposium on developmental psychopathology* (Vol. 1, pp. 13–40). Hillsdale, NJ: Erlbaum.

Sroufe, L. A. (1996). *Emotional development: The organization of emotional life in the early years.* New York: Cambridge University Press.

Sroufe, L. A., Jacobvitz, D., Mangelsdorf, S., DeAngelo, E., & Ward, M. J. (1985). Generational boundary dissolution between mothers and their preschool children: A relationship systems approach. *Child Development, 56,* 317–325.

Sroufe, L. A. & Ward, M. J. (1980). Seductive behavior of mothers of toddlers: Occurrence, correlates, and family origins. *Child Development, 51,* 1222–1229.

Steele, M., Hodges, J., Kaniuk, J., Hillman, S., & Henderson, K. (2003). Attachment representations and adoption: Associations between maternal states of mind and emotion narratives in previously maltreated children. *Journal of Child Psychotherapy, 29,* 187–205.

Stone, W. L., & Lemanek, L. K. (1990). Developmental issues in children's self-reports. In A. M. LaGreca (Ed.), *Through the eyes of the child: Obtaining self-reports from children and adolescents* (pp. 18–56). Boston: Allyn and Bacon.

Stoolmiller, M., Duncan, T., Bank, L., & Patterson, G. R. (1993). Some problems and solutions in the study of change: Significant patterns in client resistance. *Journal of Consulting and Clinical Psychology, 61*, 920–928.

Straus, M. A., Hamby, S. L., Finkelhor, D., Moore, D. W., & Runyan, D. (1998). Identification of child maltreatment with the Parent-Child Conflict Tactics Scales: Development and psychometric data for a national sample of American parents. *Child Abuse and Neglect, 22*, 249–270.

Swanston, H. Y., Tebbutt, J. S., O'Toole, B. I., & Oates, R. K. (1997). Sexually abused children five years after presentation: A case-control study. *Pediatrics, 100*, 600.

Terr, L. C. (1981). Forbidden games: Post-traumatic child's play. *American Journal of Orthopsychiatry, 20*, 740–759.

Timmer, S. G., Urquiza, A. J., Zebell, N. M., & McGrath, J. M. (2005). Parent-child interaction therapy: Application to maltreating parent-child dyads. *Child Abuse and Neglect, 29*, 825–842.

Toth, S. L., Cicchetti, D., Macfie, J., & Emde, R. N. (1997). Representation of self and other in the narratives of neglected, physically abused, and sexually abused preschoolers. *Development and Psychopathology, 9*, 781–796.

Troy, M., & Sroufe, L. A. (1987). Victimization among preschoolers: Role of attachment relationship history. *Journal of the American Academy of Child and Adolescent Psychiatry, 26*, 166–172.

Vaughn, B., Egeland, B., Sroufe, L. A., & Waters, E. (1979). Individual differences in infant-mother attachment at twelve and eighteen months: Stability and change in families under stress. *Child Development, 50*, 971–975.

Wahler, R. G. (1980). The multiply entrapped parents: Obstacles for change in parent-child problems. In J. P. Vincent (Ed.), *Advances in family intervention, assessment, and theory* (Vol. 1, pp. 29–52). Greenwich, CT: JAI.

Wainwright, J. L., Russell, S. T., & Patterson, C. J. (2004). Psychosocial adjustment's, school outcomes and romantic relationships of adolescents with same sex parents. *Child Development, 75*, 1886–1898.

Walker, C. E., & McCormick, D. (2004). Current practices in residential treatment for adolescent sex offenders: A survey. *Journal of Child Sex Abuse, 13*, 245–255.

Webster-Stratton, C., & Reid, M. J. (2003). The Incredible Years Parents, Teachers, and Children training series: A multifaceted treatment approach for young children with conduct problems. In A. E. Kazdin & J. R. Weisz (Eds.), *Evidence-based psychotherapies for children and adolescents* (pp. 224–239). New York: Guilford.

Widom, C. S., & Kuhns, J. B. (1996). Childhood victimization and subsequent risk for promiscuity, prostitution, and teenage pregnancy: A prospective study. *American Journal of Public Health, 86*, 1607–1612.

Wolfe, D. A., Sas, L., & Wekerle, C. (1994). Factors associated with the development of post-traumatic stress disorder among child victims of sexual abuse. *Child Abuse and Neglect, 18*, 37–50.

Wolfe, V. V., Gentile, C., Michienzi, T., Sas, L., & Wolfe, D. A. (1991). Children's impact of traumatic events scale: A measure of post-sexual abuse symptoms. *Behavioral Assessment, 13*, 359–383.

Wood, J. M. (1996). Weighing evidence in sexual abuse evaluations: An introduction to Bayes's theorem. *Child Maltreatment, 1*, 25–36.

Worling, J. R. (2001). Personality-based typology of adolescent male sexual offenders: Differences in recidivism rates, victim-selection characteristics, and personal victimization histories. *Sexual Abuse: A Journal of Research and Treatment, 13*, 149–166.

Worling, J. R., & Curwen, T. (2000). Adolescent sexual offender recidivism: Success of specialized treatment and implications for risk prediction. *Child Abuse and Neglect, 24,* 965–982.

Zeanah, C. H. (2000). Disturbances of attachment in young children adopted from institutions. *Journal of Developmental and Behavioral Pediatrics, 21,* 230–236.

Zeanah, C. H., Benoit, D., & Barton, M. L. (1996). *Working model of the child interview.* Unpublished manuscript, Tulane University Medical School.

Zeanah, C. H., Smyke, A. T., & Dumitrescu, A. (2002). Attachment disturbances in young children: II. Indiscriminate behavior and institutional care. *Journal of the American Academy of Child and Adolescent Psychiatry, 41,* 972–982.

Zeanah, C. H., & Zeanah, P. D. (1989). Integenerational transmission of maltreatment: Insights from attachment theory and research. *Psychiatry, 52,* 177–196.

Zimring, F. E. (2004). *An American travesty.* Chicago: University of Chicago Press.

INDEX

313